Praise for *In t*

'A creative masterclass for every moment.' MIKE MYERS

'Uber-practical ideas that bring magic to the mundane.'
CAROLINE GOYDER, AUTHOR OF *GRAVITAS*

'Provides practical insights for unlocking the creativity and innovation of your best self.' KELLY LEONARD, VP, THE SECOND CITY

'A powerful case for a more collaborative and more creative approach to work.' STEFAN STERN, COLUMNIST AND AUTHOR

'This insightful book combines the practice of improv with cutting edge behavioural science ideas to give you the tools to communicate, to feel more credible or to step up to lead.' HERMINIA IBARRA, CHARLES HANDY PROFESSOR OF ORGANIZATIONAL BEHAVIOUR, LONDON BUSINESS SCHOOL

'Sharpen your ability to collaborate, communicate and create at work with Neil Mullarkey's fascinating book. He has a super way with words.' SOPHIE DEVONSHIRE, CEO, THE MARKETING SOCIETY

'In a world that's more volatile and uncertain than ever, businesses need people who can communicate with confidence. This is what Neil Mullarkey does and he teaches it brilliantly.' MATT BRITTIN, PRESIDENT, GOOGLE EMEA

'A concise, powerful read that redefines collaboration and communication. Perfect for professionals eager to thrive in today's dynamic landscape' MICHELLE TAITE, GLOBAL CHIEF MARKETING OFFICER, INTUIT MAILCHIMP

'Innovative, smart, practical, original and, above all, a fun read.' NIGEL NICHOLSON, EMERITUS PROFESSOR OF ORGANIZATIONAL BEHAVIOUR, LONDON BUSINESS SCHOOL

'If you want to have a future in work then this is a book that demands to be kept within arm's reach' STEVE MARTIN, FACULTY DIRECTOR, COLUMBIA BUSINESS SCHOOL

'Neil Mullarkey has such incredibly diverse experiences and so many brilliant stories.' KATE AND HELEN RICHARDSON-WALSH, OLYMPIC HOCKEY GOLD MEDALISTS

'Neil Mullarkey has written a masterpiece.' MARK BOWDEN, AUTHOR AND COMMUNICATION COACH

'The Swiss Army knife of effective business communication.' VERONIKA ELSENER, CHIEF MARKETING OFFICER, VICTORINOX

'Technical ability is important but not enough. It's about relationships and communication. Neil Mullarkey takes you on a journey of stories with essential, practical tips.' LYNNE MAHER, ADJUNCT ASSOCIATE PROFESSOR, UNIVERSITY OF TASMANIA

'Amazingly eclectic, thought provoking and useful. There is something for everyone in Neil Mullarkey's great book, one that I will pick up time and time again.' ANDY CROSS, PROFESSOR OF PRACTICE, HULT EF

'Neil Mullarkey has written a stirring playbook for personal growth and leadership. The ease, clarity and depth with which he discusses these topics will rewire your thinking for good.' ASAD UR REHMAN, EXPERT MEDIA AND COMMUNICATION PROFESSIONAL

'Chockfull of practical tips, road tested with real leaders, and great fun to read.' DONALD SULL, SENIOR LECTURER, MIT SLOAN SCHOOL OF MANAGEMENT

'The warmth, wisdom and wonder of Neil Mullarkey radiate from every page of this entertaining, inspiring and rigorously researched book. If you want to be your best, buy this book!' SIMON LANCASTER, SPEECHWRITER AND AUTHOR OF *CONNECT!*

'This book is a menu of practical ideas that you can select as you wish to boost your esteem, presentation skills and creative powers.' BRENDAN BARNS, FOUNDER, LONDON BUSINESS FORUM

'Backed up by fascinating research, stories and case studies, Neil Mullarkey offers home truths and superb advice.' CAROLINE WEBB, LEADERSHIP COACH AND AUTHOR OF *HOW TO HAVE A GOOD DAY*

In the Moment

Build your confidence, communication and creativity at work

Neil Mullarkey

KoganPage

First published in Great Britain and the United States in 2023 by Kogan Page Limited

2nd Floor, 45 Gee Street	8 W 38th Street, Suite 902	4737/23 Ansari Road
London	New York, NY 10018	Daryaganj
EC1V 3RS	USA	New Delhi 110002
United Kingdom		India

www.koganpage.com

Kogan Page books are printed on paper from sustainable forests.

ISBNs
Hardback   978 1 3986 1078 1
Paperback 978 1 3986 1076 7
Ebook   978 1 3986 1077 4

British Library Cataloguing-in-Publication Data
A CIP record for this book is available from the British Library.

Library of Congress Control Number
2023934521

Typeset by Integra Software Services, Pondicherry
Print production managed by Jellyfish
Printed and bound by CPI Group (UK) Ltd, Croydon, CR0 4YY

To the Sparky–Mullarkeys
For all the moments we have shared

Contents

CONTENTS

Humour? You've either got it or you haven't?
No! 191
What is a sense of humour? 195
Creativity 200
Why do we laugh? 202
Instead of making hackles rise, why not make spirits
rise? 206
Summary 208

8 Serendipity 211

Embrace anomalies and outliers 214
Networking 217
Serendipity: Spotting where the energy is emerging 219
Let's get disorganized! 221
Is 'strategy' a straight line? 229
Are we taking the robots' jobs? 232

9 Storytelling 233

Why stories? 233
Story theory 237
What elements make a story? 241
Applying storytelling to business 251
Virtual presenting 267

10 Where next? 269

Notes 276

Index 297

About the author

Neil Mullarkey is a unique communication expert. He studied Economics and Social and Political Sciences at Cambridge University, where he was President of the Footlights sketch troupe. He still performs with the Comedy Store Players, Europe's top improv group, which he co-founded in 1985 with Mike Myers.

His credits include the films *Austin Powers – International Man of Mystery* and *Austin Powers – Goldmember*. On television, they include *Whose Line Is it Anyway*, *QI* and *The Pentaverate* on Netflix. He has featured in many BBC radio shows including *I'm Sorry I Haven't A Clue* as well appearing in and voicing TV and radio commercials. He has also performed in and written plenty of corporate videos.

Since 1999 he has travelled to 24 countries, bringing the skills of theatre and especially improv to public- and private-sector organizations large and small. Since 2020 he has run virtual workshops 'in' at least as many countries across the world.

This is his fourth book. The others are *Solitaire For Two* (Boxtree, 1995, a novelization of the film by Gary Sinyor); *Don't Be Needy Be Succeedy* (Profile, 1998, in the satirical guise of L Vaughan Spencer); and *Seven Steps to Improve Your People Skills* (London Business Forum, 2017).

Visit Neilmullarkey.com for more information.

(And, yes, Mullarkey is his real name.)

Acknowledgements

There are so many people I need to thank but I will start with those who were there early on as I began to swerve my career from showbiz to find my own 'Point B' (see the chapter on 'Serendipity'). The good people at Ashridge Consulting were so encouraging, most especially John Higgins and Caryn Vanstone. Joe Howard (then of Saatchi & Saatchi), the sadly departed Richard Marshall (of what has become the Saïd Business School at Oxford) and David Honigmann and Hazel Holker were quick to spot the possibilities of improv and Sue Terry made things happen.

Dr Lynne Maher, Adam King, Keith Leslie, Irwin Turbitt, David Firth, Nicola Phillips, Simon Dane, Andrew Hooke, Emma Botton, Brendan Barns, Dave Lewis, Feona McEwan, Paul Z Jackson as well as Professors Annie Pye, Clive Holtham and Herminia Ibarra gave wonderful opportunities and advice. That list is incomplete, of course. Apologies to those I missed.

Before all that, it was Mike Myers who introduced me to improv, for which I am eternally grateful. We've had so many laughs and adventures together, from sharing the bill with crazed poets in dingy rooms above seedy London pubs to hunkering down in the Four Seasons during riots in LA. Many thanks to you and, of course, to Don Ward and the Comedy Store Players for providing my wonderful improv home for nearly four decades.

Huge thanks to Matt James and Kogan Page for making this book a reality. For your support during its gestation, I am so grateful to Becky Alexander, Daniel Crewe, Simon Lancaster, Adam Kingl and David Taylor. Susan Hodgson has done her best, not just to tidy my typos, but to make it clear and readable. However, nobody but me can be blamed for the blunders that remain.

My wife and children are at the centre of my life, of course: so many thanks are due to you, not least for putting up with hearing my voice booming through the walls during lockdown as I projected at full tilt, grappling with how to engage people in my Zoom workshops.

Thanks also to my Mum and brothers, who've always supported me in my twists and turns. My late father gave me a delicious insight into the absurdities of corporate life but listening to the members of his team at his funeral helped me understand what leadership really is.

My final thanks go to not only the people who have been good enough to hire me to give a workshop, a keynote speech or individual coaching, but to all those participants who played my games and tried my exercises. You have given me such joy over the years and I have learnt so much from you.

CHAPTER ONE

Improv and me

You may never have seen an improv show. Most people haven't. You may not believe it is possible for a team to perform an entire show 'in the moment', based on audience suggestions. I didn't. I had never seen an improv show until I was in one. But now I travel the world teaching improv and other communication skills to business people. Technical skills alone will get you only so far. Borrow from my world and you will be able improve your creativity, communication and confidence to navigate a better career path.

Winging it?

Improv is not winging it. The derivation of 'winging it' is from scripted theatre. If an actor hasn't learnt their lines fully, they might attempt to memorize them while *in the wings* (at the side of the stage) waiting to go on or they might have to go over to the stage manager during a scene to ask for prompts during scenes. Winging it is a state of panic – one that rarely leads to a successful performance because they should have learnt their lines but did not.

Improv is almost the opposite. No 'script' is available. Indeed, to have one in mind may prevent you from being fully aware of what is unfolding. Almost every conversation you have relies upon improv to some extent. It is certainly a mindset, as you accept the external data and respond. Your response and the reaction to it then become part of the external data. In a scripted presentation you should be very prepared, but a good 'ad lib' can work really well, but only if it sits alongside a structured flow. The reality is that moments you've organized and moments that emerge are woven together in life.

Thomas Woodrow Wilson was 28th President of the United States from 1913 to 1921. He was the only person to hold this office and have a PhD in political science. He was very strongly of the view that government was misunderstood. For him it was:

> not a machine, but a living thing. It falls, not under the theory of mechanics, but under the theory of organic life. It is accountable to Darwin, not to Newton. It is modified by its environment, necessitated by its tasks, shaped to its functions by the sheer pressure of life.[1]

I would say the same of organizations. When Woodrow Wilson says that it is not accountable to Newton, he means that it doesn't just follow rules, being predictable and structured. That's what you need when doing a play (or a presentation). But organizations, and you as a working individual, need Darwin by your side.

Things that are Newtonian in this sense are subjects in a coded system, following rules and avoiding risks. But if we are to be creative and innovative, we must look to Darwin, knowing that adaption and risk-taking are essential for moving towards the future.

There must be method in your moments

While I am loath to use a military analogy, most battles feature some hand-to-hand combat, which is unpredictable, but you need to plan where and when to deploy your battalions. You need to have trained your people to face the unexpected. In football (again, another over-used analogy) isn't it basically tackle/dribble/pass/score but with almost limitless permutations? So without a plan or formation, players won't be able to do their best with their 'in the moment' skills.

Everybody talks about the New Normal but nobody knows what it is, except that it's not what came before. Two spectres are hanging over us: Remote and Robots. I've been teaching people how to deal with uncertainty for years. Now organizations are asking me how they can cope with what comes next. It used to be that you knew exactly what your job was, where you would do it and with whom. No longer can we be certain of much. Soon a robot could replace you. Already, your closest colleague could be a thousand miles away. Some things will stay the same. Some things have altered forever.

I have teenage children but I have few technical skills to pass on. They already know how to make PowerPoint slides and are often showing me 'hacks' for my iPhone. What can I teach them about the world of work which they will enter in the next decade? After nearly a quarter of a century of being semi-embedded in organizations, though as an outside observer, couldn't I offer them a user's guide to 'getting on in business'?

This book is less about the future of work so much as how to have a future at work. The 'office' as we used to think of it is history. Mostly. Now we've seen that we can all attend meetings in our pyjamas from our villas in Tuscany, there's no going back. Some are even saying that productivity is increasing. But what about innovation? Doesn't that need face-to-face (F2F) interaction in real life (IRL)? Maybe.

Lots of jobs won't exist soon because artificial intelligence will be doing them. In 2012, a futurologist was speaking ahead of me at a conference. He advised parents not to let their children become accountants, lawyers or airline pilots. I noted that he didn't advise against becoming a futurologist. Or comedian. Or leadership guru.

Robots and rapport?

So will artificial intelligence soon be eating everyone's metaphorical lunch? What's left for us mere mortals? I hosted a charity auction a couple of years ago. Frequently at these events, at dinner you sit next to the great and the good. Sometimes they are neither. That night was different. This splendid chap, with a beautiful Welsh accent that reminded me of family holidays in Brecon, listened to what I teach for a living. For years he had run a software company. He told me I was in exactly the right game because creativity and empathy were the very things that make individuals stand out, especially in our robot future. Hurrah! Maybe, at last I could persuade my mother that I had made a good career choice (my brothers chose accountancy and chemical engineering).

My Welsh dinner companion described his children. The 'cleverest' was the least 'successful'. The least academic had risen up the ladder – because he knew how to rub along well with other people. In remote times we have to be even better at working out how to create rapport and encourage creativity.

Peter Hyman used to be a speechwriter for Tony Blair. Then he trained to be a teacher and set up a school and charity to promote ORACY.[2] Yes, literacy gets all the attention but *verbal* communication skills are so important, aren't they? In meetings, job interviews, pitches, crucial conversations and more. In an article for *The Guardian* on 7 March 2021, Hyman wrote that employers are looking for something broader than that which is currently being provided by school/university: 'Exam grades are no longer seen as a proxy for what is needed, not just in the workplace, but in life.'[3] What really matters are agility, initiative, curiosity, problem-solving, collaboration and emotional intelligence. Improv skills, in other words.

According to a report by the Tony Blair Institute in August 2022, people come out of university and school lacking the four Cs: communication, creativity, collaboration and critical thinking.[4] Or they may be strong on 'quant' skills – numbers, analysis, theory – but so much of getting things done in an organization relies on unquantifiable (or so it may seem) dimensions: alliances, office politics, gossip, legend, fear, diplomacy, confidence, tribal loyalty, patience and niggles about the car park.

How on earth do you teach these vital skills? We assume they just develop by osmosis in the first few years of employment. You can't learn them with a test tube or text book. And how do they work – or not – on Zoom or Teams? If the old certainties around education are changing (would you saddle yourself with a massive student debt to watch YouTube lectures?) so too are those around jobs, which can now be 'location-neutral'. For some roles, what can be done in Guildford can be done in Gujarat.

I operate in the 'space' Peter Hyman and others are talking about – in one-on-one coaching, in workshops, in keynote speeches. Often, improv is my calling card but once I'm through the door I employ other 'technologies' too. I have borrowed from psychology (Jung, Gestalt, even Freud among others), neuroscience, quantum mechanics, management thinkers, educationalists, theatre, story structure, my parents, my brothers, my friends, my wife, my children, but most of all from those people with whom I have worked for nearly a quarter of century, those who do have 'proper' jobs and have shared their fears or frustrations alongside the applications of what I, a mere thespian, have been able to offer them.

Why 'in the moment'?

To some, the idea of 'in the moment' is appealing. It has overtones of mindfulness, authenticity even, both of which are in vogue. To others it's uncomfortable, distasteful even. It reeks of living FOR the moment. It's reckless, not caring about the past or the future, with no plan and with a side order of irresponsible and selfish.

When I am asked to work with an organization, the people who engage me tend to be of the former camp. What they know of my work, generally as an improviser, speaks to them of dealing with uncertainty, of collaborating, of being creative and maybe (aargh!) 'thinking outside the box'. That was fine when I started but it came as a shock to me only recently when, after having spent an afternoon teaching the skills of improv to a group of senior managers gathered from across the globe at a leading business school in France, one of them asked, 'So do you mean, go to every meeting with no plan at all?'

NO.

Go to every meeting and every important conversation with a plan

For a multi-person meeting (*especially* virtual) you need to have a clear agenda, which won't over-run the allotted time. The objective could be as open as 'have a chat', 'find out how they are', 'check in' or more specific, 'ensure buy-in for X', 'update them on Y' or 'stop this disaster now'. Where being 'in the moment' applies is both in seeing how what is being said (or not said) pertains to the plan AND where the plan may have to flex. Does that sound paradoxical? Welcome to my world.

When I started this journey into 'management training' I swore I would not be a 'mere' presentation coach. I'd be the Improv Guy. But much of my executive and presentation coaching now involves making my client *prepare fully and leave as little to chance as possible*. Think Newton for the scripted pieces, then practise with Darwin for the Q&A.

I am often hired to deal with those who need something different. Others can train the conventional stuff – slow down, breathe, keep going to the end of the sentence and more. I am more interested in asking, 'What's the real game going on here?', 'Why don't you sound convinced by your own words?', 'In this moment, metaphorically, are you Cinderella, an ugly sister or Prince Charming?'

Moment, inertia and momentum

For my A levels (which you take as you leave high school – they are the British equivalent of Grade 12 for US readers) I studied physics along with maths and chemistry. We might think that physics is the study of 'things'. Carlo Rovelli (author of *The Order of Time*[5]) tells us that it is the study of change. Reading that made me realize that I am talking about change – how to change, how to deal with change and, perhaps, how to be aware of what may be changing but appears constant.

Newton's first law of motion tells us that an object will remain stationary or continue in a straight line until a force causes its speed or direction to change. This tendency to resist change is called inertia. But where human beings are concerned, is anything actually stationary or moving in a straight line? (And the earth is moving pretty fast and subatomic particles are no slouches but most of the time we act as if objects can stay still.)

There is a bunch of forces acting on us, in all directions, some opposing each other and some which we may not even be aware of. Two concepts from physics seem particularly relevant:

1 **Momentum** is the product of the mass and velocity of an object. It is a vector quantity, meaning that it has both magnitude AND direction. So you could be going really fast but in the wrong direction. *Going slowly in the right direction could be better.*

2 **Moment** as a mathematical concept: think of see-saws. A moment is the measure of the tendency of the turning effect generated when a force (effort) is applied to a lever to rotate it about the fulcrum. So the *moment* depends on both the size of the force and its distance from the fulcrum – the thing in the middle of the see-saw. The further away, the bigger the moment, perhaps surprisingly. Even though the force may be small, if it is applied a long distance from the fulcrum it can produce a *moment* which is significant.

Both words come from the Latin *moveo,* meaning 'I move'. So, for example, a *moment* could be distinct from an instant, which may have no duration. More old-fashioned uses of moment could refer to a sense of importance, weight or value. 'It was of small moment' could mean it wasn't that big a deal. Hence the idea of 'momentous'. There is also the idea of a moment in history or a moment in your life. That could be quite a long period.

Then there might be the notion of 'opportunity', as in *seize the moment.* So think of the moments in your career. The small moments with people or the longer moment that crept up on you as you decided to change job. The important 'moments' from your career that now seem significant might have seemed completely insignificant at the time (a new LinkedIn message that led to a huge career shift, for example). This why we need to embrace an 'in the moment' mentality. Serendipity is not luck. It's about paying attention. I have a whole chapter on that coming up.

Keep the essential idea that a moment has *both* time and movement. What did you do in that moment to move forward the project, the relationship, your career? Or did it move it backwards or create the conditions that meant moving forward became harder? Physicists happily talk of space–time as one dimension, not two. Why can't we? What may not seem right at one moment will be exactly what is needed in another context at a different time or place.

Improv as distinct from improvisation

Improv is a form of theatre in which the audience give suggestions to the actors, who then use them to create a show. It may be sketches, songs or one whole story. This art form has protocols (rules, even) structure and a history. It is a state of mind (and body), an ethos. You might have heard that it's all about saying 'Yes And' instead of 'Yes But'. There's more to it. Improvised music has some parallels but audience suggestions tend not to feature there.

I didn't start out with improv

I wanted to write and perform scripts. After my A levels, I studied Economics and Social & Political Sciences at

Cambridge University. I became President of the Cambridge Footlights, from which have emerged some of Monty Python, Emma Thompson, Hugh Laurie, Sacha Baron Cohen and Olivia Colman, among many others.

We toured Australia before bringing our show to a small theatre above a pub in Notting Hill, in West London. Selling tickets was a man called Mike Myers. You may now know him as Wayne of *Wayne's World*, *Austin Powers*, the voice of *Shrek* and the creator of Netflix's *The Pentaverate*. We talked and he made me laugh.

Soon we were doing a comedy double-act on the eccentric cabaret circuit of the mid-eighties. In 1985, we set up the Comedy Store Players, who are in the *Guinness Book of Records* (for the longest running comedy show with the same core cast) and we are still going strong. In 1999, I started giving management training workshops. I've been teaching improv, communication and more to business folk for nearly a quarter of a century, face to face and remotely.

Improv: Away from the stage

My journey to writing this book started in 1998, when I was taken by the feeling that improv could help people in real jobs in real organizations. I was invited to give a drama workshop at one of my favourite theatres – the Theatre Royal in Bury St Edmund's, a small, ancient town in Suffolk. I arrived early. So did many of the participants. Each person came in one by one to the small backstage room I waited in. I asked what they knew of improv theatre. I gave each a piece of paper saying, 'this is the secret'. On it I had written one word – *Listening*.

Listening

Does that sound too 'woolly' or passive for business? Does the phrase 'a good listener' conjure up some kind of picture from a bygone era of, say, a kindly matron in a hospital? However, it is about awareness and spotting moments that matter. The great improv practitioner is not the one who pulls great ideas out of nowhere but one who takes another's simple notion and co-creates and extrapolates it to joyous heights.

That evening in 1998, I realized how potent improv could be beyond the world of theatre. Lawyers, agricultural workers and high-school students all took to it with ease and delight. Unusually, an audience was invited to observe the drama workshop. A lady, probably in her early seventies, stood up at the end, quite unprompted, to thank me for bringing such joy. I was (and am) merely standing on the shoulders of both the improv giants who had gone before but also the enthusiastic newbies who that night embraced this addictive art form.

Provocative Therapy

It was about this time that I attended an event at the Comedy Store one Saturday where academics shared their research in why and how we laugh, a subject which has always fascinated me. One of the originators of the British alternative comedy boom of the eighties, Arnold Brown, was working with a Harley Street doctor, Brian Kaplan.[6] I can't remember how they described it but I wrote and asked if I could be in their gang. We called ourselves The Academy of Laughter and Health. We did a couple of shows in Hampstead, one at the Freud Museum (where you can see the iconic couch) and one at the New End Theatre (a former mortuary). Rather tongue-in-cheek, we looked at the connections between humour and well-being. One afternoon, Brian played me (on an audio cassette) the recording of his public session with Dr Frank Farrelly (founder of Provocative Therapy), whose 'client' he was for half an hour. It was hilarious and I could see why it would help people over-come their problems – by being able to see them and laugh at them.

It was humour that was emerging in the moment, using what the client was saying, helping them to find a fresh perspective on situations and celebrating our shared human frailty and every individual's unique eccentricity. That's my thing. That is neither alienating nor culturally specific. Humour in business can be so much more than a Dilbert cartoon or making 'jokes' at the expense of others. I was captivated. My literary agent said I should go and interview Frank so I spent a long weekend in Madison, Wisconsin, getting to know this pioneer. I wrote an article, which my agent failed to sell.

I then went to see Frank give workshops in the Netherlands, where I met 'coaches'. I had never encoun-tered such a concept outside sport but these were business and executive coaches. Gradually, I was beginning to see a way that I could bring my world to that of organizational and leadership development. I thought about doing an MBA, but more of that later.

Listening is more than hearing

You can't help hearing, but to truly listen, to be changed by what you heard, to show by your words and actions that you have heard, is quite different. This is an immediately transferable skill. Listening is vital to any relationship, to leadership, to creativity, to customer service. There is a difference between an empty mind and an open mind. In improv we move fast, we take on board what is around. We cannot help but combine it with our own interpretation and then reflect it back to our fellow player. I call it *Intentive Listening*. We *intend* to use that which we hear, not simply leave it fallow as the conversation moves on.

The essentials of improv: offer, block, *yes and*

Improv is about listening, using what is around you, interacting with our fellow player, with the audience, not being fazed by the unexpected. The roots of improv are in Chicago in the 1920s when a teacher and acting coach, Viola Spolin, was working with underprivileged children. She wanted to give them the confidence to speak up in class. She was a follower of Neva Boyd, social worker and academic, who believed that children needed to play. Games and improvisation could help youngsters with language skills, self-confidence and social skills.

Viola Spolin developed it further, for actors. This led her son, Paul Sills, to create Second City Theatre in the 1950s, from which so many talented writers, performers and directors have graduated – not least Dan Aykroyd, Steve

Carell, Tina Fey (and, of course, Mike Myers). Improv is reacting positively in the moment, treating what your fellow performer says (and does) as an *offer* to build upon, sharing responsibility and co-creating with limited resources.

Inspired by this body of work and thousands of nights onstage, I have boiled my approach down to five verbs, summarized in my acronym. Other improv folk will recognize the rules in my 'manifesto' of how to apply skills tested in the heat of stage performance to everyday organizational life.

A typical improv scene might go like this...

A: Good morning, doctor.
B: Good morning, [NAME]. Good to see that your leg is better.
A: Yes, and I'm playing football again.
B: Yes, and I hear you scored three goals yesterday – against my friend's team.

Rule One: Listen

We listen in improv because we know that we need to pick up a hook or cue from our partner to build upon. People – even people who have seen us more than once – often ask me which bits of the Comedy Store Players' show are rehearsed. The answer is simple. None! Every show is different. Every show is unique. They are messy but still people think it looks polished enough that something has been planned. The point is that we really do listen to each other – with intent. I invented 'intentive' as an adjective. It sounds suitably Californian. Intentionality is a thing but it sounds heavy, especially as it has the word 'tension' embedded, whereas *intentive* has echoes of 'active' and 'inventive' and even 'incentive', all of which are pertinent.

An improviser is noticing the words and the non-verbal information. We listen out for when the other person has finished. We give and take focus. This is so important because you want the audience to know where to look. Mostly, that is the person speaking but not always. There is also a rhythm. We encourage short turn-taking. I give you the 'ball', knowing that you will hand it back to me soon.

It's a simple exchange. Dare I say *iterative*? You say something and I respond with something that picks up from what you said. You reply with something that picks up from what I said. You 'accept my offer' and then 'give an offer' based on what you heard.

WHAT IS AN OFFER?

This is one of our basic tenets. When people see improv for the first time, it seems like magic. How did we know what to say and when? An offer is 'something someone gives you that you can do something with'. That is the best definition I have encountered. It came from a group called On Your Feet, founded by Gary Hirsch and Robert Poynton, who started working together after a chance meeting in Portland, Oregon. Their combined artistic and commercial backgrounds meant that improv was the perfect meeting place for them. Robert has written a lot about improv, not least his book *Everything's An Offer*.[7] Imagine if that were your basic assumption in life.

In the improv example I provided, we have the following offers, accepted and given:

Doctor → Leg → Football → Goals → Team

One offer leads to another. That is the improv 'scaffolding', which is nothing more complicated, perhaps, than an 'algorithm' summarized by many as 'Yes And'. The offer accepted is not always the offer we thought we had given. It may be more in the 'eye of the beholder' but that is the joy of openly embracing difference while moving forward together.

Rule Two: Accept the offer

We listen for offers. Build on what your partner gives you. Merely saying yes is not actually our real motto. We want to serve the story. The motto of *Yes And* is not blind acquiescence, passive fatalism. It is that we can contribute. That life is to be accepted (YES) but we can take an active step to move things forward (AND). We have a choice. It's about recognizing reality, not bemoaning it. You can do that with a 'But', though it's not always obvious. And it depends on what happens next.

People fear improv. What if I can't think of what to say? Improv is a form, a mindset, a praxis. It is learnable, it is teachable. It's not just spontaneous chaos. All of our training is about co-creating structure out of what emerges. A chaotic scene is a bad scene. A random set of events is not a story. Perhaps you may be surprised to learn that improvisers are always striving for structure while embracing the uncertain. We look for patterns, just like physicists, like any scientists (including data scientists). We think about how our character changes in the scene – what have they learnt, how are they altered?

FOLLOW THE FOLLOWER

If someone says to you, 'Good morning, doctor' in a scene, you *are* a doctor. But what kind of doctor? We accept the premise that our fellow player gives us, yet we can build on it as we choose, in that moment. Then we see what our partner does with our offer. I picture it not as we each have 50 per cent of the conversation, rather that, at any moment, one of us has 100 per cent of the focus but is passing back and forth so easily that actually we begin to lose sight of where an idea started or which offer led us where. Hence our motto is 'follow the follower'. By accepting your offer, I co-own it with you. It's not two people with 50 per cent 'control' each, but two people with fully shared responsibility for the story.

Yes And is commonly cited as the improv ethos. We use it as a verb: 'I'm *yesanding* you.' It's a powerful way of making sense of the world – embracing the uncertainty and ambiguity and making something positive of it. Improv as a form of theatre has been around since at least the 1950s, so there are decades of practical insights, which make a show work. *Yes And* doesn't quite capture it fully for me. Perhaps better is, 'Accept what you are given and add to it as you bounce it back to your partner.' We know that at any point the scene could go virtually anywhere. We thrive on that, but we are always looking to bring meaning and structure, from what could fizzle into chaos. We frame whatever happens, each moment, each word or action as an offer, to be used with purpose. We are not thinking, 'I want to be the funniest.' Maybe the typical business parallel to this might be 'I am the most right' or 'I have the best ideas'. We are thinking/feeling towards what can help the scene, but only one step at a time. If your character has said my leg is better, I accept that it is.

Rule Three: Give an offer

Turning back to the above example, the doctor scene, I build on the offer of 'leg' – I have a glorious range of options:

How did it get hurt?
How did it get better?
What can I do now it's better?
Is there anything else that is hurting?

As far as the audience is concerned, your leg is better. Undermining that is a no-no. One improviser doesn't write the whole scene on their own. They give an offer for their partner to accept. They are not doing the whole story in one go. Step by step means we can move together, not leaving our partner behind. You give an offer, based on what you heard from your fellow improviser. Start where they left off. So that is:

Listen – Accept – Give: L – A – G

What next?

My fourth letter is E. For a while, that stood for Energy. The energy you bring to a conversation affects the energy you (and others) receive from it. We have all known people who bring little energy to the table or even bring negative energy. We in theatre talk a lot about energy. This doesn't mean just shouting and running about. There is energy in stillness. There's the energy of a character.

John Cremer, a great improv teacher and founder of The MayDays improv troupe in Brighton, has only three rules: Listen, Accept, Commit. There are many improv scenes which flounder because one or more players do not commit, they inhibit the energy. (Does that remind you of meetings at work?) In improv, that can mean not committing to playing the character, the emotion or the 'problem' in the scene. It might even be what we call 'commenting'. You tell the audience you don't like where your fellow player has chosen to take the scene or the offer they have given you or the accent they are attempting. Taken too far it becomes a 'block'.

So why do I no longer have E for Energy? Cowardice perhaps. When I was starting out, trying to persuade the business community that I spoke their language, 'energy' felt too actor-ish, too touchy-feely. But you will find a section on it in the next chapter on the 'Human Connection'.

There is a bigger point though. Mike Myers used to tell the Comedy Store Players, when he was running our workshops, that we must be *specific, specific, specific*. Why today, why now, why are these people meeting in this improvised scene? In the above example, we move to football which leads to goals, which leads to mention of my defeated friend's team and there are many options to explore. 'Why have the gods of improv chosen to give us this story at this point, with these two people?', asked Mike. They must have good reason. *Explore* what's underneath the surface in the scene. **Explore** has grown into a vital element of my pentagonal structure.

Rule Four: Explore assumptions

As the scene moves forward, we may have to let go of where we initially thought it would lead. As improvisers we realize we do have preconceptions but we have been trained to hold them lightly. I may have assumed that the important point was my leg but it may turn out that the football-playing doctor's friend was the very one who broke my leg in the first place.

I believe that there are neural pathways laid down in the improviser's brain, which mean that our focus becomes more external than internal. I may have a picture of a leg and difficulty going up- and downstairs but as soon as you mention football *that* is what matters. That takes centre stage as the leading offer, the emerging spine of the story.

Hence it can seem like magic, as if we have a pre-ordained script. 'Listen like an improviser' is a depiction of being totally in the moment. Often I can't remember what we did in a show the night before. People in the audience remind me of something we did and I can't recall it. My children ask me at breakfast on a Monday what the obscure job was that I had to guess at Sunday night's show or the title of our improvised musical. I struggle to revisit the moment. Onstage my brain is in Flash, not Hard Drive.

WHAT DOES IT MEAN TO 'EXPLORE ASSUMPTIONS' IN AN IMPROV SCENE?

In a scene, two characters meet. We have so much to explore:

Who are they?
How long have they known each other?

What's the back story?

Who else do they know – in common or otherwise?

What's happened since they last met?

What are they not telling each other?

Who has the higher status?

What objects are in the room?

How does that object affect the status?

How does the revelation affect the status?

How does the status change affect what they do with the object?

And so on. Every scene has an (almost?) infinite number of possibilities. But we don't try to do all of the above in one go. I just add a brick at a time, so do you. In the end, we have built a cathedral together, as Del Close, one of the founding fathers of American improv, put it.

So my next letter became E for **Explore** assumptions, which is highly relevant to people in organizations, as we shall see.

What of the last letter? So far we have:

L A G E ...

It could only be **R**, couldn't it? LAGER. If you have ever watched a great sitcom like *Frasier* or *Seinfeld,* you will have revelled in their joyous use of the 'callback', the running gag, the aside, the detail, the coincidence that returns in another context. Then it may emerge again. Sometimes, it may come back as the final pay-off, as the main plank of the denouement, or a coda after the titles.

When I started I lacked courage, as I've said. I wanted an R, so I said Recycle. It worked but when I let slip in a client workshop that the word improvisers use, that Mike Myers taught me, is **Reincorporate,** the client CEO insisted I use that. He felt that it had the whiff of authenticity. 'If that's the word improvisers use, then that's the word we want.'

Rule Five: R for Reincorporate

So you 'bring back into the body' ('corp') some previous offer. It works a treat. When you go and see an improv show, you'll spot how themes, moments and observations re-occur from early in the scene, the story or the evening. It's so satisfying. It gets a laugh. It ties up narrative threads. It may even be the crescendo that ends a scene or rounds off a story beautifully.

It doesn't matter if the original offer was 'good'. Often it's the 'error', the 'oops-I-didn't-mean-to-say-that' moment that becomes the spine of a story. We celebrate the bum note until it becomes the main riff of the sketch. Maybe in the doctor scene above, it turns out I paid my friend to break your leg in the football match…

LAGER

As LAGER gained traction, my confidence grew. People would send me emails saying that, as a result of attending my workshop, they had tried using the *Yes And* approach with colleagues or experimented with a little reincorporation here and there. It had worked.

I used to give a handout. Artist and organizational innovator Steve Chapman suggested I put it on a beermat.[8] Of course! Why didn't I think of that? Sometimes it takes someone else to spot something that was staring us in the face all the time, doesn't it? Steve is but one of the many inspiring people I have met who combine a deep understanding of organizations with playful insights that make a difference. Years after attending a keynote or workshop, people from all walks of life still refer to LAGER or put a picture of their scuffed coaster on Twitter or LinkedIn.

Once they watch an improv show, people see the elements coming to life. We really do listen with intent. I am often asked, 'But what if you're onstage and you can't think of anything?' Those are marvellous moments, not to be feared. Acknowledge them. The audience loves to see that vulnerability. You are not cowed by not knowing. You are transparent. Something brilliant may emerge, your partner may step in or you just may pause and admit the emptiness. This is the very opposite of what our Western discourse would perceive as strength: allowing yourself not to know, admitting imperfection. Surely that is the root of learning? Why couldn't that be part of great leadership – at the right moment?

There is something amazing about being part of an improv show – as performer or audience. In many ways, the performers are just as much part of the 'audience' as those who've bought a ticket. We watch our fellow players to see what they will say. We don't even know what *we* will do, so it's new for us. We 'watch' ourselves and are often surprised (and even embarrassed) by what comes out – but that is part of our shared vulnerability. With improv, you see a team of actors, using your suggestions, grappling with uncertainty, but doing it together. When I read about being in 'flow', a wonderful concept popularized by Mihaly Csikszentmihalyi,[9] I recognized it immediately.

Five simple steps

The steps in LAGER are not linear. It's not Step One, then Two, then Three, etc. Giving an offer may actually be reincorporating or it may be exploring. Or even both. The ethos that most appeals to many in organizations is *make your partner look good,* especially for leaders. It's that simple. *Use their idea, build on it, give them space to excel.*

The 'flow state' of improv means that I feel that I belong – what I say will be accepted – and, in turn, I know that I will accept what you will say. The term 'psychological safety' is bandied about a lot but we *assume* it on the improv stage. The 'magic' is that in accepting your reality, I can begin to shape our shared future. Playing with possibilities becomes a game of imagining, discovering and relating to others. You become part of something larger than yourself by being more yourself. You take risks, you may look silly but you own your silliness. By letting go of the fear of being judged, your standards improve. Improv exhorts us to listen to the other, to affirm it and build on it. That's often summarized as *Yes And.*

How much does that have in common with your environment at work? If it doesn't, what are you going to do about it? Or is it easier to sit back and blame others?

The limits of improv

I am hugely indebted to that initially grumpy guy from an oil firm who said the problem with his team was that they were *too* 'Yes And'. By that he meant that loads of ideas were only half followed through. 'We need a bit more *Yes But*', he said. Not to block off ideas but to give chance for good ideas to be allowed to blossom. Sometimes saying yes to everything is effectively saying no to that flower which gets drowned in the sea of weeds we are busy *yesanding*.

It made me consider 'Yes But' as a creative response. So many times, people have said, 'But what if I can't say *Yes And*?' It's a good question – and one that I will probably spend most of this book failing to answer. The words 'Yes And' actually may not be helpful. More helpful is the notion of offers – accepted, given, explored and reincorporated.

I met Gary Hirsch and his On Your Feet colleagues at the global Applied Improv conference in Toronto in 2003. They ran a session called 'Getting Out of the Temple of Yes'. It opened my eyes to the fact the improv ethos goes much deeper than *Yes And*, and that those two words could be in danger of becoming restrictive if they are seen as the answer only in and of themselves. Plus, it made me realize that offering a simple read-across from stage-work to corporate life could be simplistic and that improv may not be enough in itself. Sometimes you need to plan, sometimes you must acknowledge Newton.

The real world is not like doing an improv show, is it?

There are budgets, structures, shareholders, regulations and so on, but I have found that many people are *already* using these 'improv' skills even if they may never have heard of *Whose Line Is It Anyway* or The Second City. But many are not and they often fail to reach their full potential. In among the spreadsheets and 'to-do' lists and 'org charts', I have seen many teams and individuals crying out for the chance to add these skills to their armoury or to understand why the company's seemingly rational structures turn out to be so unreasonable.

In applying improv and more to leadership and organizational life, my greatest teachers have been my students. They may have started out as wary of this eccentric improv chap foisted on them but soon they are thinking and reflecting as they immerse themselves in the exercises. I have also learnt so much from other facilitators, academics and leaders who have shared their wealth of experience with me. They have seen what I do and, by sharing insights, have elevated it to something deeper yet highly practical. I am grateful to so many people.

When do you need LAGER skills?

There are essentially two strands to applying the broader improv approach:

1 people skills – improv as an interpersonal skill
2 mindset – improv as a broader ethos for interpreting and reacting as events unfold

I do not see these two as separate. If you can 'yesand' in a conversation with a colleague that's a leadership skill – yet it can also bear fruit when you're wearing your 'strategy' hat and other hats.

In lockdown, I couldn't give out beermats. So I changed **LAGER** to **LASER**. *Give* became *Send*. You send an offer back, building the story. 'Send' even implies you're adding *momentum* to the offer. I like LASER because the invention of the laser was based on one of the strangest theories in science. Einstein said that light can behave like *both* a particle *and* a wave. Humans live with such ambiguity all the time. We are both individuals *and* part of something bigger – a family, a team, a troupe or a company. At its best an improv show – and an organization – harnesses these dual identities.

The word laser is often teamed with 'focus' as in 'laser focus', which has overtones of being sharp, targeted, coherent, cutting through. Improv, on the other hand, suggests fuzzy, tolerant, adaptive and pragmatic. LASER connects the best of both: it is a 'left-brain' way of harnessing 'right-brain' creativity.

LASER

LASER cuts through. Over the decades I have shared this, I have become more and more convinced of the applicability of LASER. I started out with the vague feeling that improv had something to offer. My experience has taught me that I underestimated its power and the breadth of its appeal. Leadership theory and strategy are all very well as neat ideas in the abstract, but what does Lesley the Leader do on a Tuesday morning with a person or problem which does not fit into an easy box? There's no ready-made solution. So you *have* to improvise.

It's not just when things 'go wrong' that these skills will help Lesley. It's each and every day. It's when things go right. When I ask my workshop participants if they have ever improvised, they laugh and 'admit' to 'winging it' on occasion. For them, it's what you do when you haven't planned properly, or something you shouldn't really do, that you've let the side down. No, it's as much about making sure that things do go right.

When is improv not the answer? When do you need something else?

Improv might have been the equivalent of Punk Rock that got me started. Soon came along New Wave so I had to learn how to play my instrument. I moved beyond the difficult second album. People liked the new sound I was fumbling for. Then perhaps I became a singer–songwriter with a sound all my own. Okay, so I'm not the Paul Weller of management training, for whom The Jam gave way to the Style Council which gave way to a much longer period of something else, but I have adapted my sound beyond the three-chord, two-minute single I played at the start. I hope you're enjoying reading my concept album.

It's very clear to me that improv is not the answer all the time. If it were, I would be recommending that the Comedy Store Players be running Amazon or Tesco. No, no, no. Please never let that happen. My thesis is that you can blend this approach with your 'technical' skill and then you will really be able to manage your moments better – big and small.

Preparation is key: think Newton

I frequently point out to people that I am part of an improv troupe around which there is plenty of structure. We know who the six players will be; we even do the same games every show; the Comedy Store has organized ticket sales, insurance, food, drinks, licensing, technical and security support and more. All so that when it comes to the moment we ask the audience for suggestions we can then improvise and be fully 'in the moment'.

There must be method in your moments. There are so many moments when you must prepare. I still find it shocking when someone very senior says to me, 'but I don't like rehearsing'. If you are making a presentation, you owe it to your audience (and yourself) to rehearse it. It's bad manners not to, like declining to use cutlery if you are invited to dinner at someone's house. You look slovenly and you get your fingers burnt. It's not just presentations. I encourage clients to rehearse lines for meetings.

I have spent a chapter telling you about improv, so I am not yet an apostate, renouncing my former self, but there will be other 'Maxi Moments', where you need to have prepared for hours, maybe even months and you must use your experience. There will be other moments when it will be most productive to be open and vulnerable, willing to listen and learn. And there will be 'Meh' Moments when you get it wrong for one reason or another.

CHAPTER TWO

Human connection

The best mechanic in a factory may fail as a foreman for lack of social intelligence. EDWARD L THORNDIKE, 1920

That rings true, doesn't it? Technical ability is one thing but there are not many jobs where you don't have to get along with others.

People are using LASER all the time.

They just don't know it. And they may be using it in completely the wrong 'direction'. They are Listening but not to what you want. It could be your tone of voice or that slip of the tongue or their own thoughts. They Accept their own interpretations, then Send an offer that doesn't build on what you would choose, or Explore what could be (for you) the wrong assumption, then they **R**eincorporate some offer which is problematic or which you didn't really mean to **S**end.

People buy from people

Do they? As a consumer, nowadays I rarely do. I buy from the Pret A Manger I happen to be passing. Or I buy online where no human connection is required. However, organizations selling large projects must rely on relationships for business development. To some extent, we are all 'selling' something… 'please do this work', 'please let me be in your team', 'please give me your Instagram username'. You need to be able to get on with people to get on in business. Soon, robot-to-robot transactions may be commonplace. But not yet. Even if you are in a job where you think connecting with others is minimal, surely a little insight will be handy. And anyone can improve, no matter how good or bad you think you are.

Communication

Clients and their teams say to me, 'it's all about communication'. What does that mean? If the boss sends out an email, is that communication? Advertisers tell us that we need to see something seven times before we commit to do anything about it.[1] Film distributors can quantify how many people have heard of their movie. But the number who intend to *actually* see it is often much smaller.

Communication in organizations is often one-way – sending out missives that may or may not be taken in. Are you seeking something more like conversation?

This costs money

'Communication' failure costs organizations time, money and loyalty. A recent study by The Harris Poll and Grammarly found that 'knowledge workers' lose more than seven hours per week of productivity (and hence profitability) due to miscommunication.[2] That's about a day a week, equating to about $1.2 trillion annually in the US economy. What were the main causes of miscommunication?

- People being slow to respond;
- People not understanding the message;
- Too many messages;
- Wrong tone;
- Wrong platform or tool.

How much time and energy does your organization waste? Does it invest in up-skilling its people? Remote and hybrid make this a whole lot more complicated. People are calling you, texting, WhatsApping, all while you are busy on a Teams call. They tut if you don't answer. You fume at them for interrupting.

In a hybrid meeting, never mind the human connection, what about the Wi-fi connection? One client (from a huge, global media company) told me that, if the meeting is important, he goes home, where the Wi-fi is better. In the meeting room at the office he's fighting to get a seat near the camera. At home he has his own camera.

For many teams, little has developed further since those first fumbling footsteps into remote working in March 2020. Have you ever even thought about the picture you present on virtual calls? Or how you sound? Why not? We will come later to how to 'Bring some VaVaVoom to your Zoom'.

Let's start with LASER. You can use the tools in networking, in meetings, with clients and colleagues as well as outside work, in creating rapport, collaborating, negotiations and more, face to face and in person. These techniques are not just for extroverts.

How does LASER apply to life in organizations?

Rule One: L for Listen

People you really need to listen to:

- your colleagues
- your suppliers
- your customers/clients
- the end users or consumers (if they are not your direct client)
- the market
- your rivals (what are they up to?)
- technological changes
- people outside your team whom you may need to influence
- regulators
- other sectors

And listen to your gut. But 'listen' to the data. If they are not in agreement, make a choice as to whether the data is actually applicable, then realize that any decision is not an endpoint in itself. Listening is not a one-off event. Keep an eye on the actions that flow from a decision. How can we know what people are thinking and feeling unless we listen? Both to their words and to their body language. But it's a two-way process. The impact I have on you comes back and, in turn, affects how I feel about you. Think of all the people who have a certain effect on you. What sort of effect are you having on them? How much are you defined by the people around you and the relationships you have with them?

Listening means noticing what is being said, what is not being said, what emotions are at play and what the underlying values and objectives might be. Broadly – in conversations and in broader life – can you see what the 'offer' is?

- Why is my colleague saying this?
- How can I use the particular way this client talks about this situation?
- Can I 'borrow' something from new technology/consumer behaviour to move things forward?

When you intentively listen for offers, you may have to see beyond what you'd already thought, your preconceptions, your biases. What is actually going on? Be curious. Judge later. Accept reality: it's all we've got. For now, at least. And, of course, your reality may be unique to you.

Rule Two: A for Accept

Accepting is not the same as agreeing. It is not passive acquiescence, it's acknowledgement. It needs you to work – parking your ego, noticing your own resistance and fears and filters. We so often override or invalidate what others may offer or ignore data that doesn't fit our existing world-view. Be aware of your own agenda. Put it to one side so you can determine what is really being said, what is actually happening.

In a conversation it may not mean agreeing with all that the other person says. That is why short turn-taking is important. The more you say, the more I may have to pick and choose, the harder it may be to accept all in one go. But one offer at a time means it's easier to weave in ideas from each party.

In a more profound sense, this may mean accepting who you are. But in the same breath that means accepting that what is around you could possibly change who you are. In improv scenes, our identity is created in the moments that unravel in a scene. Cathy Salit, author and improviser, talks about the Becoming Principle© which is 'the ability to experience both who you are and who you are not yet'.[3] It's a dynamic tension.

Tina Fey, the great writer/actor/producer, writes about 'Yes And' in her book *Bossypants,* where she describes one of the rules of improvisation as:[4]

> not only to say yes, but YES, AND. You are supposed to agree and then add something of your own. If I start a scene with 'I can't believe it's so hot in here' and you just say, 'Yeah...' we're kind of at a stand-still. Unlike, if I say, 'I can't believe it's so hot in here' and you say, 'What did you expect? We're in hell.'

Saying yes is about accepting the other person's premise. I think it is about starting from where they are, not where you are. Isn't this a better conversational approach? In the broader sense, it is about accepting what life is throwing at you.

WHAT CAN BE CHANGED OR NOT?

I cannot change the weather. I cannot change technological advances. I can change my clothes. I can change my attitude. I *may* be able to change the attitudes of others.

Accept means:

- be more curious
- note the real data
- talk to other people with diverse attitudes

Rule Three: S for Send

You are specifically adding something to what is said. It needs to connect to what they have given you. I call it *Listen and Link*. We move forward together. It's about building momentum with the other person's idea or perspective. It's really about saying, 'I get what you just said. I am going to use that in my response.' It is one action: Listen-to-Link.

You can still accept the other person's premise – how they perceive a topic, how they feel or what they think they should do next – without agreeing with it. However, if they have said it, *it* is meaningful 'relational data'. It's what they have chosen to say at this moment. Saying, 'you shouldn't feel like that' won't buy engagement.

There are so many nuances. It's about the effect you create on the other person and on the idea. Does your colleague feel listened to? Are you moving things forward?

Is there 'momentum'? Onstage, we HARDLY EVER say the actual words 'yes, and'. Every moment is dynamic. 'What's the offer here?' How my response frames your contribution makes it into an offer or block. I might even start with 'no'...

'No. That won't work. Because that leaves you doing too much. Let's get John to do it.' Note how useful that word 'because' is.

WHEN YES AND GOES WRONG

I worked with a renowned management consultancy. This young consultant came up to me and said, 'Oh I know your thing. You say *Yes And* instead of *Yes But* to get your own way.' His thesis was that just by saying those two words, 'Yes And', at the start of a response the other person would be blinded to any negative intent of the rest of your contribution. I could imagine him saying:

'Yes and... that's a bad idea.'
'Yes and... we tried it last year.'
'Yes and... the CEO won't go for it.'
'Yes and... I don't like you.'

This shows the danger of a simplistic use of 'Yes And'. I'm grateful to him. It was a perfect articulation of the very opposite of what I teach. So I am very careful nowadays how I ask people to try out 'Yes And', and to think of it as just an exercise, like playing scales on the piano before you attempt the concerto, which will be more complicated. You are warming up your improv muscles ahead of the real thing. I point out the pitfalls and how 'Yes But' could be just as legitimate a response. BUT... you still have to be thinking of what you are Sending back. It all depends on the context.

Rule Four: E for Explore

This means accepting that your worldview is merely your set of assumptions. You hold them, just as the other person holds theirs, with integrity but perhaps not full self-awareness. Can you explore your filters, which may have built up over years of experience or may be due to just one highly influential moment? What are the rose-tinted spectacles – or muddy, cynical binoculars – through which the other person sees the world?

Here are some examples of when people fail to Explore:

- That's the way I've always done things.
- That's who I am.
- Never mind what you did at your old firm, this is our protocol.
- Well, you would say that; you're a lawyer/marketer/salesperson.

These are just assumptions. Every day we make assumptions, many of them not subject to any testing:

- This train will take me to the destination indicated.
- There won't be an earthquake.
- My pants won't catch fire.

If you were being strictly scientific, you could find at least one instance where your assumption would have been false. But we just carry on in life as if many things will play out along predictable lines, based on previous experience. It would be exhausting not to.

In human systems, you would be foolish to pretend that there aren't a whole bunch of preconceptions flying around, many of them unconscious, many of them unchallenged. They are not necessarily bad. Or good. They just are. But what are we filtering out because we don't even realize we are making assumptions?

Whenever two people meet, there are really six people present. There is each one as they see themselves, each one as the other person sees them, and each one as they really are. COMMONLY ATTRIBUTED TO WILLIAM JAMES

For some who have attended my workshops, Explore has become the most potent element. In organizations, that could be assumptions about yourself, about the situation, about your team, your client, your organization. Or it could be assumptions you have about the other person or what you assume that *they* assume about *you*. It's just about an awareness of the filters. We should remain curious.

When I introduced the Explore concept to a bunch of pharmaceutical sales reps, they piped up that this was like that clever wordplay they had been taught when they started out:

Never ASS – U – ME anything or you'll make an ASS out of U and ME.

Geddit? I can see that's useful to an extent. However in reality we cannot help but make assumptions – but are we aware of them? Natural science is full of assumptions. So is economics, as in 'assume perfect competition' – which cannot exist, by the way. We might assume a reaction is happening in a vacuum, or in mechanics we assume there's no friction. These are acceptable because they are explicitly stated (and actually possible under certain conditions), but they make the calculations more straightforward. With human beings, there are so many variables at play – in the observer and the observed – so any extrapolations could be unreliable. Ask Darwin or Einstein.

That's why medical remedies are tested alongside a placebo. You need to eliminate as many variables which may affect the outcome as possible. And one variable is the patient thinking (or feeling), 'I'm enjoying being part of drug research and this nice person in a white coat has given me a pill. I feel better already!'

COGNITIVE DIVERSITY

I am no expert in DEI (Diversity, Equity and Inclusion) but I like that a B has been added now – Belonging. There are all sorts of historical and systemic reasons that various groups are under-represented but I work with leaders and teams who should be more aware of how there could be different ways of perceiving situations and arriving at different outcomes. Some people call this 'cognitive diversity'. I do often refer to Daniel Kahneman's work on all the biases we have, many of them unconscious. His book is called *Thinking, Fast and Slow,* representing two types of thinking.[5] 'Fast' (System One) – habitual, instinctive – very helpful in saving time and energy, for example when driving, riding a bike, remembering your times tables. However, the danger is that we may not be aware that we are relying on an automatic reflex, rather than on reasoned reflection. 'Slow' (System

Two) requires effort and deliberation, even seeking out new information before making decisions.

In organizations there is plenty of 'system one behaviour'. You quickly learn what and how to do things. That can be very handy and the new person may feel more comfortable 'fitting in' but what is being squashed by conformity? Professor George J Sefa Deia of Ontario Institute for Studies in Education at the University of Toronto said, 'Inclusion is not bringing people into what already exists. It is making a new space, a better space for everyone.'

As I noted before, in improv scenes we are continually exploring assumptions. One of the protocols for newbie improv performers may surprise you: 'Don't have your character ask questions.' Saying something like:

'Why are you doing that?'
'Who are you?'

could be seen as not committing to the scene or even as blocks. The story would have more impetus if a specific offer were made:

'Nice whittling' or 'You're making pasta.'
'Don't worry, she will come back to you' or 'I was hoping you'd be here. I've not seen you since that party.'

In business, especially in coaching, I have found that questions can be helpful, open questions in particular. But it can be illuminating to make a bold assumption and see how the other person reacts. Making (possibly unwarranted, maybe even humorous) assumptions means they have to put you right or qualify what you've said. So you learn more than by simply asking a direct question which may not open things up as readily. This is a technique I learnt from Frank Farrelly, creator of Provocative Therapy (see Chapter 1). You might make more headway or go deeper by making the other person actively step up to put you right or (sometimes) agree that you've serendipitously hit the nail on the head. With straight questioning you might not get there or it could take longer.

CASE STUDY   Exploring assumptions

I was working with the marketing department of a global energy firm. As usual, I asked them to give examples where they found it useful to Explore assumptions – their own or others'. A woman (let's call her Jill) told us how just one word she uttered had ruined her relationship with a colleague: let's call him Jack. It wasn't just any old word but the name of an advertising agency: let's call it Jeepers. One day, some time into the project, Jill said she had worked with someone from Jeepers and thought nothing of it.

Three weeks passed, during which time Jill found things rather fraught. Jack had changed. He was unfriendly and difficult. Exasperated, she eventually asked him why. Jack told her of his bad experience with Jeepers. When he had heard her mention them he had altered his view of her instantaneously, despite their previously good relationship. Jill was flabbergasted. Even though his 'Jeepers incident' had been some time previous to Jill's moment with them and with different people, Jack stepped back from Jill because she cited them without disavowing them. He did not explore his assumption that *anyone* connected to Jeepers in any way was bad. Before that moment, Jill and Jack had got on just fine, over a long period. Wasn't it brave of Jill to ask? Often we don't. Even if we did, I wonder if the other person even knows why they've taken against us – or even overly in our favour. That can happen too.

Rule Five: R for Reincorporate

On the improv stage, this is a major plank. We bring back elements from earlier in the scene, the story, earlier that night even. It can raise a laugh, it can tie up loose threads. In meetings, strong ideas may be lost by the wayside. Looping back to them can be creative, finding new combinations. And, on a personal level, don't we love it when somebody remembers what we shared with them about ourselves?

This is applicable to networking or chatting to relative strangers. Let them talk. Every now and again, gently waft one of their own previous references back at them. It means you're not short of something to say, it proves you were listening and – it's fun! It can be about hobbies, holidays, family, education or their likes and dislikes. On a video call, it can be about what's in their shot, their background. Why wouldn't you deliberately put something in your background to 'humanize' yourself? When a child/pet/partner wanders into your shot, we forgive you. It creates a commonality. What might have been considered 'unprofessional' in the past is now part and parcel of the virtual dance.

Once you have a tiny topic, either in face to face or virtual, people love it if you ask about it later once in a while – perhaps later in the week, month or year. It needn't just be social. In business if you recall someone else's idea later on in a meeting, it makes them feel good – and could be just the right time for it to herald a creative breakthrough. You could call it the *delayed Yes And*.

I read a story about Sir Alex Ferguson (former manager of Manchester United). A young footballer, who left the club fairly early in his career, still felt able to ring Sir Alex to ask for advice. Not only did Sir Alex take the call but he would also ask about the player's three sons – *by name*. That's Reincorporation – playing back a previous offer from someone to them, in this case a profound personal offer which can only have enhanced trust. Sir Alex knew the names of all the staff at Carrington (the club training ground) and their partners. Asking after people who matter is an example of Reincorporation as a social 'tool' – creating rapport. When I introduce this notion in my workshops, people often cite an inspiring leader who did this effortlessly yet brilliantly. You can do it too. Make yourself write little notes as reminders.

What about when you have to say No?

I've talked about 'Yes And' but what about when you have to say 'No'? This is vital. For me saying *no* to A could mean saying *yes* to B. If you had said yes to A (which is where a simplistic reading of 'Yes And' would lead you) that means that B – an opportunity, a person, an idea – would be lost. 'No because' will have a better impact than just 'No'.

Saying no is sometimes essential as a way of managing your energy. This is often overlooked, be it the energy of the team or the individual. Jenny Campbell of Resilience Dynamic, through years of research with many executives identifies it as one of the four pillars of resilience.[6] Energy cannot be overlooked – not just physical energy but mental, emotional and spiritual.

A great leadership coach, Kate Tojeiro, told me she found the most successful senior folk work on conserving their energy. David Ogilvy, the famous advertising guru, said he always gave 100 per cent in meetings. But he made sure that he had nothing else to do once he had left. He could not do the former without knowing the latter in his mind. It takes energy to listen to another person. You need to carve out time *not* to be available.

Mike Myers told me that Lorne Michaels, legendary producer of *Saturday Night Live* and many movies starring its alumni (including *Wayne's World*) would say to his stars, 'It's your duty to take a vacation because that's when the ideas come.'

Many people have told me that managing their time and energy in remote times has been very hard. It's felt less like 'working from home' and more like 'homing from work'.

TOOLBOX   Tips to conserve energy

- Have a nap: 15 minutes can work wonders or even 10, just shutting your eyes.
- Set boundaries (time: when you can't be disturbed; topic: I don't need to okay that decision).
- Turn down meetings. Or say you would love to attend but only for 10 minutes.
- Work out when you are at your best for meetings (mornings?) and when for reflective work (Friday afternoons?)

You don't have to be always 'on'

You might be in the supermarket. Or filling up the car with petrol. Or reading a particularly terse text message. Or you've just been dumped. You can be forgiven for not being the Best Networker in Town. Well, I'd forgive you anyway, much as I have forgiven myself when I didn't give a lovely smile to the delivery driver as I stood dripping in a towel on the front door step.

The problem with working from home is you feel like you're being watched for eight hours a day – because you are. There's no downtime between meetings. We need time to be NOT on. So that we can be fully on in meetings and so we can let our mind wander in other moments (see the chapter on 'Serendipity').

Separate lives

Perhaps you don't miss the commute to work. Since Roman times, we have travelled roughly half an hour each day. It provides physical and mental distance from work.[7] It helps our mind decompress. The British cultural commentator Julia Hobsbawm disagrees.[8] For her, not commuting saves time and money and the planet. Many of my clients share these contrasting perspectives.

Personally, I would hate to have to go to the same office on the same train to see the same people every day. I chose a career which did not involve the 9–5 routine. Only now is everyone else catching up with me. However, for a workshop or keynote, I much prefer knowing that I have travelled and arrived early to be physically present. I dislike the juddering return to home life after a Zoom workshop. I need to do more than walk downstairs before being convivial with my family. How do you ensure you separate home and work when they are in the same location?

One client puts on a tie 'at work' when they're working from home. Another tells me that, in lockdown, his friend would put on a suit, get in the car, drive round the block and come back 'to work'. Of course, he would repeat it at the end of the day. Luckily, there wasn't too much rush hour traffic. I wonder what he put in his sat nav?

Remote and WFH

We are not going back. Just moaning that 'face to face is better' is pointless and defeatist. It may be preferable for you and for certain things but we must learn to make this new medium work. Stop complaining, start working at it, for yourself and others. 'Every desk must be occupied' is not useful and there is evidence that any such edict is simply ignored. According to *The Guardian* in August 2022, some Apple workers are saying no even to three days a week.[9]

How do we bring some humanity to Microsoft Teams? 'Virtual' is an amazing way of connecting people across the world. It needs to be treated as a new medium, combining video and audio and text – all in real time. You are closer to people's faces than in real life. You are in their houses, in their lives. Make it social, make it fun and enjoy not having to be stuck in traffic for hours for a 30-minute meeting which may turn out to be a bit of a damp squib. Having spent years in TV and radio, I know it is possible to engage a remote audience. It's a new medium. Not as fast-moving as TV, maybe with more in common with radio, but with added interactivity through the spoken word and the chatbox.

How do you inspire, lead, decide, recruit, choose to promote, mentor, stay close to customers and have difficult conversations remotely? You have to manage your moments. Virtual meetings require more preparation than face-to-face meetings. First of all, your set-up. Do you really want people looking up your nose, squinting because you have a bright light or window behind you, rendering you no more than a silhouette? You wouldn't turn up to a client meeting wearing flip-flops, smoking a cigarette, would you? So sort out your set-up.

Teams and the like are exhausting. Make your meetings shorter. Do you even have to have a meeting? I heard the phrase 'Zoom Fatigue, Netflix Intrigue'. The latter refers to the fact that we are used to the grammar and pace of television – frequent edits to keep up the pace (close-up, wide shot, two-shot). Music and lighting keep us engaged.

Compare that with your last Teams meeting. Was some dullard droning on through some congested slides that someone else had made? No wonder you furtively check your emails and catch up with a fascinating crochet enthusiast's Instagram feed or something equally non-urgent. You need to get this right. Please see my lists of tips at the end of the chapter.

Can we make remote more human – humane even?

Many people have told me it was the informal interactions they missed in lockdown. That could be in sharing the 'up' moments of triumph (birthday/successful date/won the pitch) or the 'down' moments (unsuccessful date/lost pitch/ being bawled out by a boss).

What about the half-formed idea that blossoms from a brief aside in the coffee queue? The serendipitous moment that happened as you hovered at the end of a meeting? Each day I hear of a new way to replicate this – the virtual bike shed or cyber smokers' corner.

Most people tell me that they are hoping that they'll spend two or three days in the office at the most. (This trend has adopted the catchy acronym, TWATS: Tuesday, Wednesday and Thursday.) Big employers are planning to reduce office space. However, the boss of Goldman Sachs (who went into work in Manhattan throughout lockdown) wanted all his employees back. Jamie Dimon, boss of JP Morgan, opined in 2020 that productivity was slipping in 2020 and in 2022 that 'in person' would enhance diversity.[10] Agree or not, we can all wonder how new joiners can learn and understand company culture.

Was Andy Haldane, chief economist at the Bank of England, right when he asserted that people are having fewer conversations that spur new ideas?[11] That trust and relationship can't be built virtually? Yet Ford announced around the same time that 30,000 office-based workers can work from home for good.[12] Is 'office culture' a thing of the past? Many virtual teams have found ways of creating rapport. Is Haldane right when he says that remote working is just about avoiding the commute?

The new nimble?

Did the invention of the telephone herald the death of the face-to-face meeting? No. It will be the same with video calls. But we could do so much better. During lockdown people were happy not going to work or attending meetings in pyjamas, or being able to take the dog for a walk at 11 am or put the washing on at 2 pm. Everybody is saying we can't go back to how it was pre-Covid. But we can't even go back to what we did in lockdown. It was an emergency. For many, the initial freedom became frustration. But for others, the thought of having to go to the office AT ALL is daunting.

I ran a session for a government department of 30 people. It's divided into seven teams. Of course, some teams are bigger than others. A couple of teams have one and a half people (yes, really). But they just don't know what the New Normal looks like. Around 70 per cent don't want to go back, and 30 per cent do. Though surely there's no point the 30 per cent going back if the 70 per cent aren't there? Tricky, isn't it?

CASE STUDY   We can be sociable on Teams

The NHS really cares about leadership. I have run many workshops for their leaders who have to cope with uncertainty, deal with interconnected systems and make tough decisions where there's no clear 'right' answer. During lockdown, training was severely reduced, so any organizational developers were re-assigned during the lockdown to answering phones. One of them told me that they sometimes logged on to the Teams Chat – *when they were not on duty* – simply to catch up on the gossip. Humans will always find ways to share moments together.

Zoom, zoom, zoom

According to a report by Zoom from May 2022, Britain is well placed to take advantage of the new hybrid world.[13] Zoom 'talk their own book' of course, but 82 per cent of employees at surveyed UK SMEs said they used video-conferencing tools – a greater take-up than the United States, France, Germany, India and Japan. Some 89 per cent of UK businesses surveyed either agreed or strongly agreed that video-conferencing tools helped maintain social connection and affiliation with colleagues during the pandemic.

No wonder there is talk of a 'great resistance'. A Stanford survey from summer 2021 found that nearly 20 per cent of employees in the United States who can work remotely were not coming into the office as much as stipulated by their employer.[14] What do managers do to enforce the rules? More than 40 per cent do nothing. Organizations should just accept that people won't come in unless it's worth their while, for things like training, group discussions, mentoring, client meetings and social events. Some are offering yoga, free food, etc. Really?

WFH: burnout can happen

However, many of the people I encounter found enforced continual working from home extremely stressful. Whether the divorces I know about were due to this or not, I can only speculate. Some longed for solitude. Others, who lived alone, longed for company. But several simply demanded that they go to the office. Are you surprised to know that they were all men? How much of the family slack did mothers pick up during that time?

Let's not overlook the millions who had no choice but to work in person. Some were lucky enough to be able to make a choice to go to work, perhaps because their employer understood that working from home wouldn't produce the best results. But what about the many people who have no choice – they cannot do their job via Zoom? Many were happy to save on commuting costs but not so happy when they had to pay for more electricity at home.

On 11 August 2022 I watched a webinar by Professors Andy Cross and Debbie Bayntun-Lees of Hult EF Corporate Education about their report *Rethinking Leadership for The Hybrid World of Work*.[15] It raised lots of questions about ways of working. People have strong views about this. Of those interviewed, 73 per cent wanted flexible working to continue but 67 per cent wanted more face-to-face opportunities. How do you square that circle? It seems to be that it's going to come down to bosses. Many head honchos have decreed one thing or another. But what if people take no notice? Or decisions tend to be made by line managers according to what suits them. Nearly all of what has emerged since March 2020 has been by default rather than by design. For some, it has been good 'improv', working with what people can give and want. One company I work with has supplied adjustable laptop stands so people didn't have to look down all the time. Another offered screen covers for those for whom looking at a blue-ish screen all day doesn't play well with their mind. But for others it's often been a clunky mess. They have been winging it, stumbling through with little intentionality or empathy, trying to stick to an old script, ignoring the momentum since 2020.

Sometimes leaders ask what is good for the business, others ask what is good for employees. How often do we think about the customer? As someone who has waited for hours on the phone for customer service or weeks for an email reply, all of which has been explained away 'because WFH', I'd say not enough. WFH is just an easy excuse. If implemented well, it shouldn't be a barrier to good customer service.

New skills

What skills are needed? First some tech and practical skills, which I list in the next Toolbox. But the human connection is vital. You need to listen better in video calls. Who's hogging it, who's said nothing? New leadership skills are needed. How do you check in with people without them feeling that you're checking up on them? I know one very senior person who loves going in on a Friday – because nobody else will be there.

What kind of work is better done at the office and what type of work is better done not there? 'Together stuff' for the former, 'solo stuff' for the latter? The Cross/Bayntun-Lees study found that actually, some people go to the office to get their head down alone, a bit like I would go to the library at university (except I was mainly going so I wouldn't be distracted by coffee, biscuits or listening to the latest single by The Human League).

How much do we need to know that there is a 'mother-ship'? A physical place with a massive logo which represents us? Where we were inducted/onboarded? From where important announcements are beamed? That is a physical representation of the 'culture'? Many organizations closed offices outright and had gone fully remote/digital before the pandemic as well as since, and seem to survive. Yet plenty have not. I have spent quite a lot of time helping in those moments of 'it's our first moment back together'. They are needed. But whether our time together physically is every day or once a year there has to be more to it than, 'we're meeting because we can'. There has to be real value added if people do come together.

Experimentation

Science is all about trying things out. Disproving a theory can be just as illuminating as proving another. In improv scenes, we let go of a strand if another seems to have more momentum. So with hybrid working, keep experimenting. But also with your interpersonal skills.

It's important to have the right emotional parameters. You've got to care and it's got to be enjoyable when you put it into practice, maybe even fun. Make a game of it, whether it be noticing others' people skills or trying something out, just to see. At a networking event, imagine it's your job to put everyone else at ease. Or to let someone else talk as much as possible. Or to use the word 'cheese' seven times before leaving.

There are plenty of ideas to try on virtual calls which can make them more fun, more humane and more effective. Let someone else run the meeting. Try cameras off for short periods when you need to reflect and listen more deeply. In face to face, sit in a different place. Book an informal chat with someone you may not know too well.

Recent years have taught us that we do have more in common than we thought and how life is diminished when we are deprived of human connection. Let us embrace the moments we have, on whatever platform. Let us think of ourselves and our relationships in the parameters of improv, with possibilities in even the smallest of moments as we find out who we are and what we are capable of, on our own and with others.

TOOLBOX Bring some VaVaVoom to your Zoom

Prepare the look

- Tidy your background. No window or bright light silhouetting you.

- Camera at eye-level. It's indicated by the white or green light. You will have to raise it with books or boxes or a laptop stand. Counter-intuitively, if you look at the camera, it will feel to the audience that you are giving them direct eye contact.

- If you use slides keep them simple, so that they can be visually digested in the first moment, not some spider drawing that confuses or a tumult of text.

- Keep screen-sharing to a minimum. We want to engage with you, not your thumbnail.

- Have a source of light in front of you, to light your face. A window is best. No need for a YouTube-influencer million-watt light.

Keep the momentum

- Circulate the agenda in advance.
- Don't overfill it. Wouldn't it be great if you finished ahead of time?
- Assign roles: facilitator, note-taker and 'producer' (running slides, checking the tech, chasing late-comers or no-shows).
- Circulate the notes afterwards. Who committed to what?
- Change the dynamic every 3–5 minutes. Yes, our attention span is that short now. Pass the baton to another speaker, or ask for responses in Chat, or show us a different slide.

Keep it efficient

- Don't overfill the agenda. (Did I say that before? Because it matters.)
- Don't invite the world.
- Does it have to be a meeting? How about an email or even face to face? For one-on-one it could be a phone-call.
- Be a good host. Bring people into the conversation by name.
- If it gets tough, allow silence. During a negotiation or creative session, don't be too eager to fill it.
- Acknowledge when it's difficult.
- Prep your content: shorter sentences, simpler phrasing, minimal jargon.

Keep it energized

- Shorter meetings.
- Allow different voices to be heard.

- Stand up every 20 minutes. (Have you heard of the 20/20/20 rule? Every 20 minutes stand up, have a break of 20 seconds while looking 20 feet away.)
- Speak up. Emphasize your key points a little more than in face to face.
- Invite participation – asking people for thumbs up or down and other physical cues, plus comments in Chat and 'throwing' to someone who looks like they have a point to make.
- Use gestures. Stand up when presenting. (This means raising your laptop even higher.)

Keep it fair

- Tune in early to chat, especially if it's your meeting.
- Everyone has their camera on, most of the time.
- Find ways to engage all voices – maybe some prefer to put things in Chat.
- Keep an ear out for who's spoken too much and who's spoken too little.
- Keep getting feedback afterwards – what could be better, what did others like? Talk about the way you have meetings, not just the content.

Why not try these?

- Bring 3D objects into view. It creates visual engagement. Even ask participants to bring one to a meeting to illustrate a discussion. Or to go and get one during the meeting.

- Put yourself slightly off-centre. Look at portrait paintings, TV and film. The most interesting thing in shot is rarely in the middle of the screen (except police mug-shots). The eye is drawn elsewhere, looking for movement.
- Zoom tip. Use the space bar to mute and unmute quickly.

To summarize: OLÉ

- **O**rganize – the tech, the content, the casting.
- **L**isten – to yourself and others; what's being said or not.
- **E**nergy – yours, that of the conversation and the momentum of what will happen as a result of the meeting.

CHAPTER THREE

Collaboration

'Better collaboration' is the most obvious application of improv and one for which I am often in demand. Lack of collaboration is a big problem for many organizations. LASER works well here. Better listening is key. If you're managing a team then you have to Accept that every individual in the team will have different priorities. You need to Explore the different assumptions that teams have. It might be that Sales must collaborate better with Risk or IT with Customer Service. Corporate HQ needs a better understanding of how their diktats land at local level. Things look very different out in the field.

People with different ideas and different personalities thrive on the improv stage. That very diversity gives improv energy: listening, saying *Yes And*, adapting, working with people who are different from yourself and from each other, thinking laterally. The same should be the case for business. Organizations are desperate for these skills. The improv concept of the offer ('something someone gives you that you can do something with') opens people's minds.

Soloing and supporting

There is also the concept of 'comping' (this is from free-form jazz but is applicable to improv theatre and beyond). It means *accompanying*. In music someone may play a solo and others support it or keep the rhythm going. In the theatre, someone may be playing an 'out-there' character or plot while their partner is calmer. We let them run with it. But it's understood that we share it around. There's joy to be had, for example, when there is a switch, so we learn that Mr Calm is actually the murderer...

Being in the moment, co-creating through uncertainty means you accept and work with the offers of your fellow players. There is a joy in not knowing, celebrating error, sharing vulnerability. Sometimes I'm working with a firm just for 'teambuilding': an afternoon of experiencing this way of being can have a real and lasting effect. People tell me they have explicitly cited a tiny moment in the session where they realized they were blinkered by their own thoughts. Opening up to another person's idea gives greater cohesion. It's as if you 'double' your brain capacity by embracing their offer. That's when it's done well... As I said earlier the same LASER dynamic can go wrong if you listen only to yourself.

Teambuilding

Improv is a pleasant activity with lots of interaction and laughter. But I always smuggle in more reflections on how they communicate day to day. The combination of laughter and learning is potent. Sometimes I don't get the teambuilding gig because they fear anything involving laughter will frighten the horses. They think it's all about telling jokes and making people look stupid. No. It is *neither*. Improv is not stand-up comedy, where an individual delivers a largely scripted monologue (but isn't really about making people look stupid either).

Improv is co-creating story in the moment with others, with 'Funny' emerging organically. Those who impose their own gags in a scene are not intentive listeners. Isn't it fascinating that 'gag' means both a joke but also something used to stop someone speaking? Often I am asked if I would like a list of 'likely candidates' to be guinea pigs in my workshops. I always decline.

'Trust me', I say. 'After 20 years of working in multiple sectors across the world I know how to choose the handful of volunteers I need.' Improv at its heart is about making others look good. I do not want the 'usual suspects'. If someone knows they have been nominated they and others wonder why. They will feel it's a trick. My choosing must be transparent. I ask the audience lots of questions before alighting on a few people. I invite them to join me. I give them chance to say no. And the audience loves it when their 'unexpected' quiet colleague proves to be brilliant – all because they listened and trusted the LASER process.

All sorts of activities are included under the catch-all guise of 'teambuilding'. What I offer requires a commitment from the sponsor. Ten-pin bowling is cheaper than hiring me. I even lost out to smoothie-making once. How about building a raft together? Quite how that helps those whose real job is not actually building a raft but sitting at a computer organizing things evades me. I have seen people get mightily cheesed off with teambuilding activities and just check out. But maybe that is just like at work.

(A senior military fellow told me how much he annoyed his MBA tutor on Day One of his course, by taking charge and giving everyone clear instructions. Their raft was built in double-quick time, to a high standard, much to the irritation of the other teams and the academic in charge. Mr Military then spent a year understanding the power of not taking charge. He accepted he had to learn when to be Mr Bossy and when to be Mr Touchy-Feely Flat Hierarchy. When to be accountable to Newton and when to Darwin.)

My point is that just calling something 'teambuilding' doesn't make it so. How we speak to one another and share our energy day in, day out at work is what makes a team, not dragooning us to do karaoke.

The arts tell us that we can collaborate – that we *must* collaborate. People with different ideas, different personalities and different skills can contribute. That is central to the endeavour. You don't begrudge 'giving away' your idea or taking on board another person's.

'People are our greatest asset'

Really? Isn't it the *relationships* between people – inside and outside the organization? Your organization is nothing more (or less) than a network of conversations, a miasma of meetings. Getting people to collaborate is not easy. It may well be harder in a hybrid model. Or easier. A leader can't go to every meeting but if it's asynchronous collaboration – i.e. a document which people annotate now and then – maybe they can keep a keener eye on things. But should they?

How do you know if you are doing well at collaboration? You can measure the number of emails your people send or the number of hours they were online but that is not productivity. How do you calibrate 'teamwork', 'relationship-building', 'critical thinking', 'innovation', 'listening to a client's gripes' or 'avoiding a copper-bottomed disaster'? You should be thinking about 'outcome not activity' says Professor Andy Cross of Ashridge whose research on hybrid working I noted in Chapter 2.[1]

(Going for a walk on your own may be the most productive thing you do all day but it may not look great in your calendar. A study by Buffalo University in 2017 showed that deliberately seeking solitude can facilitate creativity.[2])

How do you keep people accountable? Sam may have good sales numbers but be rubbish at answering emails or Slack messages, while Alex might be always available to help and offer advice. Who gets a bonus? We have all been frustrated by how work is assigned and rewarded:

'Well done mate, you win a prize for answering an email at 3 am on a Sunday morning.'
'Hey, this award is for the most number of meetings attended, without having accepted the invite.'

How do you measure collaboration? Is it always a good idea? If you are a manager how do you make sure it happens but does not become perceived as an end in itself or be derided by some as weakness?

CASE STUDY   The dangling customer

I once spent an amusing afternoon at a Gatwick airport hotel with a commercial finance company. They lend money to people who want to start or grow a business. Seems straightforward, doesn't it?

So I set out to create a moving tableau, from left to right, starting with the customer. It became harder and harder to physically represent the process. Sales had to ask Risk. Risk had to ask Compliance. Marketing had to ask Compliance to speak to Risk. Governance put in an appearance too. We weren't sure where to put IT in this chain. And the customer was left dangling. We all had a good laugh but they used the video of that event to change their systems and in their induction process thereafter, to try and bring simplicity and transparency to their processes.

Is collaboration always a good idea?

Real work isn't like theatre and movies, is it? Collaboration sounds humanistic and positive but what about outstanding performers who are lone wolves? What type of projects are better achieved by individuals? If we are working at home two days a week, what does collaboration look like?

Fairly early in my adventures in corporate training, I was asked to do some work for the National Health Service. People were working too much in 'silos'. Oh dear. I knew the word silos; it's where silage is stored – or nuclear weapons were kept. I had never heard 'silos' applied to organizations. 'People are working in silos... there's silo-thinking... we have to break down silos.' I realized it meant that different departments were not working well together, so I soon embedded the word in my sales pitch.

We live in a connected world. So we need to work together, don't we? In teams and across teams. So, who you gonna call? Mr Showbiz with his improv shoes! The Silo-buster! In improv, diversity rules. You can do a scene with someone you loathe. You can do a scene with someone with whom you have nothing in common. You can do a scene with someone you just met.

And you can really kill someone else's scene stone dead. We try not to do this in the Comedy Store Players. But if we do it by accident, we often call it out, breaking the scene momentarily to address the audience directly, making the misstep into an 'offer'. It can then bring a whole new energy as the subtext is brought to the fore. This theme can bubble under for the rest of the evening. Most improv text books would consider such behaviour reprehensible. But I work with many teams where collaboration is skin deep and 'polite'. Lack of apparent conflict is not creative. Acknowledge difference with respect and the assumption of good faith. Then you can call yourself a team. How you argue is actually part of how you work together.

I've been wheeled in as an outsider with my LASER toolbox to all sorts of teams over the last quarter of a century, all in the name of working better together. I always ask about the different tribes/silos. Labels matter – which office are you in? Which function? Which floor are you on? Near senior leadership? Hidden in the basement? Maybe you're in a different time zone and that urgent email I sent last night lands without fanfare in your inbox. If I'm lucky you'll take a look after lunch following your busy morning of meetings and getting your gym membership renewed for another year of not going, or you're busy checking your hashtag crochet Instagram.

If you are really unlucky, someone will send you an invite to a Teams or Zoom call, with a subject that could be as innocent as 'Jim/Jane Catch-up' or something more accusatory like, 'Dealing With My Issues In a Timely Manner, You Unfeeling Brute'. And there in your calendar, completely without your say-so, is a shaded entry – daring you to decline it.

I often host sessions where a bunch of teams have been rearranged under slightly different banners. The group designations keep changing, in name at least. 'Operations' has become 'Operations Excellence'. 'Technology' becomes 'Digital'. 'Enterprise' becomes 'Performance, Enterprise, Technology'… commonly known thereafter as 'Enterprise' (wouldn't 'PET' have been great?) All the while, the courtiers swap seats, some fall by the wayside, new ones are crowned and the peasants simply wait for their new queen or king to fall foul of inertia or boardroom shenanigans. Then I come back, three years later and 'Operations Excellence' has become 'People and Operations'. They are no less excellent, I am sure. They have a new target and Mission 2020 has been usurped by Vision 2030.

CASE STUDY   On the bus

I have a fond memory of working with a team in a financial services firm in a very posh hotel in the English countryside. Only they weren't a team. They were several teams, lumped together for 'org' reasons.

('Org' means organization; an abbreviation particularly useful when looking at the new 'org chart' or even 'organogram'. It's a beautifully visualized work of fiction, which sums up a neat theory of who is supposed to work alongside/above/below whom but with little to say about what they really do or the messy bits that don't fit readily into a box or even into two dimensions.)

So I came up with the metaphor of a bus. I arranged the chairs in rows to represent it. Who was driving the vehicle? We all knew he was leaving soon. I nicknamed him 'Daddy', such was his influence and the frankly Freudian concern about his imminent departure. It is no surprise that many fables and morality tales are about changing family dynamics: loss of a parent, a new step-parent or sibling, a fairy godmother. I playfully impose these archetypes on corporate characters. People rarely disagree.

Uncle and Auntie were going to take over. But who was really going to be in charge? Where did they fit? One team admitted that they felt they weren't facing the same way as everyone else on the bus.

There was a group called 'Other'. Literally, that was their *official* title. There was no room for them on the bus. They didn't know where the bus was going. They didn't even know there *was* a bus. They vaguely knew about Daddy but Uncle and Auntie wouldn't affect them much. We put some barstools nearby but not adjacent to the bus. Soon after that session, I was told that group had been split up, rent asunder in the name of, um, streamlining or something. The 'Other' contingent was cast adrift, once more wandering the org desert in search of the land of management milk and honey.

Is it any wonder that people are cynical when yet another top-down edict is issued? They mistrust a restructure, with new departmental names and possibly painful changes in headcount. People often tell me that 70 per cent of 'transformations' fail. (I failed to find any justification for this oft-quoted figure, repeated even by the likes of McKinsey.[3] Perhaps the figure is about a third but for many the working assumption is the higher figure.[4])

Do we really need culture in the gig economy?

Talking to a leader in a small financial services firm, we wondered whether certain people ('tech' people, maybe?) really needed to feel part of the culture. Even pre-pandemic they might be behind a firmly closed office door. They are so in demand that they can and do move about easily. Just give them a puzzle to solve and maybe they're happy. Loyalty is not a thing for so many freelancers. Neither is a company pension.

I read about some tech types who are exploiting the WFH culture by working 'full-time' for two or more organizations at the same time.[5] Why not? The San Francisco programmer who started Overemployed.com ('Secret Door To Financial Freedom: a community of professionals looking to work two remote jobs, earn extra income, and achieve financial freedom') has tens of thousands in his Reddit group.

I am being increasingly asked to do team-build sessions for project teams – contractors and staff from several organizations. This is the way of the future. Several firms I work with are explicitly looking to have fewer but better customers where the relationship goes deeper and longer. The supply chain becomes more co-operative than transactional. The unit of collaboration now is framed by time and project rather than employer or office.

Collaboration is king?

At one leadership retreat for a management consultancy at a former abbey in rolling hills by a river, I was lucky enough to join a session run by a very clever chap who had worked with NGOs, different governments and big companies. He pointed out the qualitative difference between *collaboration* and *consensus*. You can collaborate with someone – or another organization – on a project without agreeing on anything other than what is required for that project. The project tends to have finite limits in terms of time and scope.

He talked about how very 'woke' Western charities had worked in Africa on a project with a large US corporate, which would have been deemed a 'baddie' in Britain. As far as this project was concerned, however, the company's participation was vital and came with no strings attached. As it happens, years later, that company now has a less controversial image. I'm lovin' it!

Consensus is something else. Consensus might mean that everyone settles for their least worst option. Nobody is particularly happy, perhaps, but they can rest assured that everyone else is equally not-quite-dissatisfied.

In improv, we don't sit and discuss options. The show unfolds in the moment. We make offers. We take offers. We make choices for the scene. You accept mine and I accept yours. We make it work, we don't mourn where it might have gone. We are too busy moving it on. You might think that I am just talking about compromise. No. It's deeper than that. We hold a conviction that the co-creation will win out, not our 'idea'. To me compromise is conceding, settling for something second-best. We do not hold our ideas that highly nor that firmly.

Lucian Hudson has spent many years as what he calls a 'reticulist', one skilled in navigating different networks and brokering collaborative outcomes. He worked for the UK Foreign Office, writing the first-ever international report on what makes for effective collaboration and partnership, particularly between governments, business and NGOs. For him:

> Effective collaboration turns on genuine deeper engagement, listening and properly understanding the needs, interests, concerns and expectations of others. This is often not visible or conscious, to oneself or to others, so planning for conversations, though useful, is radically deficient without people taking time to interact, be more spontaneous and surprise themselves with what actually emerges. This forms the basis of greater trust and opens possibilities of collaboration that adds value to what might not be immediately apparent.[6]

That is something akin to the improv mindset, something more radical and dynamic than 'compromise'.

I wrote a sitcom[7] with Tony Hawks (now a successful author even if he isn't an accomplished skateboarder like his near namesake Tony Hawk).[8] Co-writing comedy can be ghastly and wonderful. You curse your partner for dissing your apparently brilliant idea – but only momentarily. Soon you are thanking them for improving it. We would often use the metaphor of a 'pontoon' – a makeshift bridge. It would soon be swept away but it had helped us to reach the other side and maintained our momentum. Similarly, software folk talk about 'kludging', a quick and dirty fix that you're not proud of but it gets things moving. Your culture needs to have an acceptance that evolving innovation is messy.

This is the kind of collaboration that teams might envy. Or at least their leaders think they should envy. It's practical, it's non-hierarchical and the customer – the audience – comes away happy. As do the performers. We can't recall how we as individuals might have initially imagined how a particular scene would unfold, because we only held those notions lightly, if at all. They are quickly dispelled as the team move things forward and we don't look back in anger.

Is collaboration a good in its own right?

Collaboration sounds warm and lovely, doesn't it? But is it really an end in itself? What's the shadow of collaboration? The dark side? Jung wrote of the *shadow,* the dark side of your persona. The Mr Hyde that Dr Jekyll dare not admit is part of him. That part we repress yet which still makes us who we are. I first heard about it in terms of strengths and weaknesses. Courage sounds good but its *shadow* is recklessness. We yearn for decisiveness yet when it goes rogue, we decry it as insensitivity. Every 'strength' has its weakness. This is the basis of Myers–Briggs and other personality profiling systems that abound in business.

Of course, the idea of *the shadow* appealed to me because nothing is as it seems, I've come to believe. It's how we choose (consciously or not) to see it. Accepting that yin must have its yang, that seeming opposites are complementary, means you accept ambiguity and may even actively look for it, for therein lies the truth. An electron is paired with another spinning the opposite way. A thesis has its antithesis, said Hegel.[9] Put them together and you have synthesis...

So what is the *shadow* of collaboration? The other side of the coin? What dare we *not* say when collaboration is being foisted upon us by a new regime or set of 'values' or 'behaviours' handed down from on high, by the new occupant of the driving seat of our beloved business bus?

What stops us collaborating?

I do all the work, you get all the credit.

More and more meetings.

Working with people I don't like.

Working with people, period! (Just let me get on with it on my own!)

I give away my secrets/knowledge/contacts/power/soul.

I have to 'report back' more often.

I cover up your mistakes, tidy up your mess.

The team gets the bonus that is rightfully all mine.

Dumb compromises.

Sharing my limited resources.

I can't tell you what I really think of you.

I have to collaborate with you when I was quite happy collaborating with Jean and ignoring you and your silly spreadsheets and targets and ROIs and KPIs.

In general, collaboration can mean 'play nice' and possibly waste time doing so. A professor at Berkeley, Morton Hansen researched collaboration for years and concluded that there *is* such a thing as bad collaboration.[10]

Some tasks and some projects simply don't require people to work together.

They are better done alone, or mostly alone. Once teams start collaborating, accountability can go out of the window. A problem shared is a problem halved they say. But a project shared could mean productivity is halved. It can fall between the cracks… 'It's not my/our problem – it's theirs.' Is this worse in our new hybrid world?

TOOLBOX Tips for collaboration

Encourage collaboration when:

- tackling a complicated problem that needs insight from several people from different domains
- the solution will need several people to enact it, so they need to be invested in how the problem is defined
- it's a big thing about the organization's purpose or strategy

Discourage collaboration when:

- it needs deeper thinking
- time is short – you are in a position to make a decision now

---

Nowadays, there are lots of digital tools for collaboration. I don't even have to talk to you, but I can collaborate with you anywhere in the world, by cutting and pasting my bits into your homework, via a Google Doc or Teams. We used to have face-to-face meetings (maybe with biscuits and coffee laid on if there was a senior bod present) but we also had emails and Skype. Maybe we had heard of Google

Hangouts, Blue Jeans, WebEx or we used some internal thing like Slack or Yammer. I had even used Zoom a few times, with some bloke in Italy.

And then one day... that was ALL WE HAD. We had to get used to it in three days or less. Now we cannot imagine being without these as the new hybrid reality emerges.

You have to be able to work in a team to survive in any organization, don't you?

A *Financial Times* survey from 2018 is but one survey which shows that employers want new MBA recruits to be able to:[11]

- work in a team
- work with a wide variety of people
- build, sustain and expand a network of people

So why don't they teach this at school? I think they *think* they are. They set group projects. The truth is that one of the group ends up doing nearly all the work. Or their Mum does (yes, Dads, you need to pick up more of the slack). There is no actual coaching of *how to work in a group*. It is not easy. It is hard to lead a bunch of disparate people into working together effectively.

Just setting a task to multiple players without any guidance is NOT teaching them to collaborate. The raft will get built or the Henry VIII project will be handed in because one or two of them pull their finger out but the biggest learning for people might be that Jim is a lazy so-and-so or that whatever happens you can rely on Jane to sort it out.

I know business schools that do focus on this but whether you are in education or the wider world, collaboration can be learnt.

> **TOOLBOX**   Tips for better collaboration
>
> If you want better collaboration:
> - assign projects clearly
> - 'cast' the team carefully, with overlapping skills
> - set guide rails
> - check in regularly
> - most importantly: model the give-and-take required, with your peers and your team

But what about groupthink?

You can have too much of a good thing, can't you? You could be too 'teamy' and nobody wants to rock the boat, to speak out of turn. None of those courtiers wanted to be the first to tell the Emperor they could see his birthday suit. There is a phenomenon known as 'pluralistic ignorance', first coined as a social construct in the 1920s by psychologist Floyd Allport. People go along with what they thought everyone else agreed with only to realize later that lots of colleagues also thought it was a *stupid* idea all along. The herd mentality is real. So there is the actual group norm but also the perceived norm, which is what everyone incorrectly assumes are the attitudes of the rest of the other group members.

How is this affected by remote working, when we can't perhaps 'read the room' so well? It's hard to pass a note under the table in real life saying, 'this stinks, doesn't it?' But we can send illicit WhatsApp messages to each other during virtual sessions, can't we?

Is groupthink bad? What about the wisdom of crowds?

Actually, crowd is the wrong word. Large groups have wisdom, says the research, but only if the guesses are independent – i.e. a bunch of individuals not a motley crew who might be swayed by those with the loudest voices.

I read of a study (by Ethan Bernstein of the Organizational Behavior Unit, Harvard Business School and others[12]) in 2018, where three groups were set the task of solving The Travelling Salesman Problem.[13] They were given a list of cities and the distances between each pair of cities. They had to find the shortest possible route so the salesman visits each city exactly once and returns to the original city:

- Group One were to act independently.
- Group Two saw others' solutions at every stage.
- Group Three were kept informed of others' views intermittently.

The result may surprise you. Or not. All of us may broadly fall into one of these groups, and each approach has its strengths and weaknesses. Group One (individualists) reached the optimal solution more often than Group Two who were collaborating constantly but had a poorer average result than intermittent collaborators in Group Three. This latter group found the right result as often as individualists but had a better average result. Okay, it's an experiment. Not every task will be like that but it seems perfectly rational to say that we need a bit of space but occasional collaboration is helpful. Not only do we need to be aware of our own preferences but also of the nature of the project. I love improvising on a Sunday with the

Comedy Store Players, but there are so many things I would rather do on my own – writing this book being one. I do use LASER as a solo method – listening to an idea that pops into my head, accepting it without knowing where it will lead. And I am always looking for chances to reincorporate.

So remote working may be advantageous if it allows for the right mix of group and individual processing. But how do we allow for the latter if we have to make a diary invite? It used to be so easy to pop by someone's desk to ask for or to offer advice. Now there is extra negotiation to be done – when, which platform, how long?

JUST SAY NO

It's too easy to send an invite for a video call. It's not easy to say no. Just ringing someone up feels a bit rude though, doesn't it? Like knocking on their door when you can hear the shower running. So, after saying hello, we now say, 'is this a good time?' There are so many ways you can get hold of me now – phone, iMessage, Slack, WhatsApp. I will know and be stressed if I refuse the call because you know that I said no.

FLEX YOUR STYLE

In my work, I have come across all sorts of psychometric tests and models and ways of helping you understand both your style and that others may be different. You might be a colour or a type. But essentially they all boil down to archetypes such as 'you're focused on the details', 'you look at the big picture', 'the task is all that matters'. People find them helpful but their usefulness is limited if you define yourself as only one trait and unchangeably so. The best ones show us all that we are a mixture but to be aware of other people's dominant preferences.

Onstage, improv performers are constant collaborators. Magic happens because we don't know what is going to happen next. And that is the essence of this delightful, throwaway art form. But when the Comedy Store Players did a tour many moons ago – onstage virtually every night with lots of travel – we became weary and a tiny bit tetchy. That level of interdependence takes its toll.

The comparisons with the arts and other industries don't always hold up. Every theatre show has a finite run. And it's less stressful after the first night. The movie will finish shooting. In the arts, we may not be creating long-term supply-chain solutions. We are not always solving complex problems (though figuring out Shakespeare may turn out to be easier than how to make Jim not quite so irritating). But we understand that problems can be addressed in a group situation or one-on-one with the director or alone. However, if from the example above, you are a 'Group One natural' yet some things need a Group Three approach, how can you cope? You need to learn some collaborative skills, such as LASER, and when to apply them.

How do we do collaboration?

You may be very uneasy about sharing your views. Or you may be the type to steamroller others with your superior notions. I find that these two types are equally common.

Of course, there are some who are very good at spotting which is a Group Three-type problem versus one that needs a Group One- or Two-type approach. Some might call that *leadership*.

How do we keep everyone engaged without producing a flabby result at the end which pleases nobody? Collaboration means taking the best of different people and making it work. It may involve compromise. It will involve persuasion. As with all of the 'soft' skills this is trainable. Why wouldn't you want to improve at this? But does your organization offer lessons in collaboration?

I often coach people who are very bright, perhaps very technical. Plenty are willing to work just as hard at their people skills as they did at academic subjects. They know that's how to get on. It's fascinating to see them humbly roll up their sleeves and take on the task of learning how to improve in these seemingly 'lesser' skills.

Others think their 'collaborative coefficient' is set in stone:

'Let me get on with what I'm doing. I'm good at it.'

'All this "politics" stuff is for other people.'

'Others are naturally good at this.'

Nope. Nature/nurture may have something to do with people skills. But I have seen adults who have nurtured this area and developed and improved. It does not require huge amounts of effort, like being an Olympic athlete. But it does require focus and willingness to experiment, which as any scientist will tell you, is the way to learn. Intentive listening is the key.

It's not me, it's you

What if you are good at collaborating but everyone else is rubbish? What if you are a leader who knows how important collaborating may be and the superior results it can produce, but you don't know how to get your team to do it well? You need to articulate exactly what is meant by collaboration and what is not.

A study published in 2010 found three factors which determine the 'collective intelligence' of collaborating groups of two to five people:[14]

1 Social intelligence – how good are people at rating emotional states of others?
2 The extent to which members took part equally in conversations. The more equal the better.
3 The proportion of women in the group – the higher the better!

Groups ranked highly in these areas co-operated better than others. Is this any wonder? They found the 'c factor' wasn't strongly correlated with the 'intelligence' of the individuals but with the social sensitivity.

However, can anyone be a perfect citizen all the time? Doesn't our inner Mr or Ms Hyde want to be appreciated as an individual while Dr Jekyll may present as the perfect team player?

Interestingly enough, when Nigel Nicholson, Emeritus Professor of Organizational Behaviour at London Business School, saw me give a workshop on improv techniques, he saw collaboration but noted there is an element of competition. Could we call it friendly rivalry? Pushing others to the top of their game? Great sports players lift their game to match others. Performers too. When an improv scene is soaring, when the audience is in the palm of our hands, the flow could have started with a moment of individual brilliance. You may have started the fire but I can stoke it.

This is the joy of being part of a theatrical troupe, a movie cast/crew or sports team. We follow the same ethos yet we are still individuals. I am fully me and I am fully part of the team. Just as light can be a particle and part of a wave. Just as music can be a moment (a single note) and have momentum (the melody or indeed the entire concerto). I believe that human fulfilment is down to this twin, possibly paradoxical conclusion, that we want to make our own contribution (and have it recognized, even quietly) but it's great to be part of an ensemble.

I want to be recognized for who I am but I also want to be in the gang.

I don't see why organizations cannot achieve this. I have seen it done. Managers can stand in the way of this or can really enable it but they have to be empowered beyond the boardroom. It is easier to achieve in small organizations. But every large organization is made up of smaller organizations. Yet, when I ask people to name such moments of personal/collective achievement, they often talk about one-off or 'off-desk' events, like putting on a conference or organizing the charity day. Perhaps those moments are easier to discern. A new five-year strategy may need to be broken down to give a weekly or daily sense of achievement.

Wait a minute! What about the shadow? Too much collaboration?

Rob Cross, Reb Rebels and Adam Grant researched this in 2016 for an article called 'Collaborative Overload' in the *Harvard Business Review (HBR)*.[15] They looked at 300 organizations and found the collaborative ethos is not evenly distributed. Things are decidedly lop-sided.

In most cases, 20 to 35 per cent of 'value-added collaboration' came from a mere 3 to 5 per cent of the staff. These people soon gather a reputation as 'go-to givers' and they can have a huge effect. Just one of the super-collaborators – Extra Milers – can improve team performance more than all the other members combined.

Hurrah! But remember how much I like looking for the flip side? The virtuous circle can become vicious. Helpful Horace can actually become a bottleneck. A project may not move on until Collaborative Carol has been involved. Or, at some point, Carol and Horace get fed up with pulling much more than their weight. They may find themselves stuck in Zoom meetings from 8 am to 8 pm. Because they've set the bar so high, if they say no it's taken much worse than if Lazy Lesley had said it. The Overburdened Helper is someone we've all met. 'No good deed goes unpunished.' *Collaboration Fatigue* can set in.

Collaboration is a bit of a woolly term, isn't it?

In the arts, no. We have good listeners. We have generous performers who willingly share the stage or screen and leave room for others to shine. But sometimes in improv we have gag-merchants who aren't really 'scene-builders'.

We have all heard stories of selfish stars. It's a fact. Nice guys don't always finish first.

The authors of the *HBR* study above identified three types of 'collaborative resources' that can be seen as an investment in others:

1 informational: your knowledge or expertise – it can be passed on
2 social: your awareness, access to others, your standing in a network
3 personal: your time and energy

These three are not equivalent, from the giver's point of view. I can share information or a social resource in an email or a single conversation. I still retain what I pass on and can use it later myself. But if I give you my time – getting stuck in to help you out – it has gone. I have sacrificed my energy and hours of my day.

Which one are *you* prepared to give? You might find that there is one that seems to be more your style. Can you begin to flex? Think about others. That other person who has given of themselves, perhaps to the detriment of their own to-do list?

Collaboration just means more meetings, doesn't it?

A simple request becomes a diary invite becomes a flood of back and forth and some executive assistant tries to get the right people in the right place at the right time. Once the ducks are in a row, the most senior person ducks out right at the last minute, possibly making the meeting redundant.

In 2013, Dropbox cancelled all recurring meetings for a fortnight. They called it Armeetingeddon.[16] Two years later, with nearly three times as many employees at its San Francisco HQ, the number of conference rooms had actually only doubled.

Rob Cross (co-author of the *Harvard Business Review* piece which covered Dropbox's meeting approach) wrote in a 2021 blog for TED.com that:

> the most efficient collaborators have an expansive tolerance for ambiguity. They focus on being directionally correct, making sure they are moving in the right general direction on the project. They remain open to adapting their ideas and plans as new information comes in.[17]

They focus on going in the right *direction*. Remember moment as a vector?

Where does the collaborative buck stop?

Some moments need the same skills as the arts and some don't. So in technology we know developers have to talk to the testers and to the end users. But there are moments when people will say, 'Can I just have a bit of peace and quiet for now? I'm not ready to collaborate until I've got my own answer or have run out of options.' I have seen script writers who want to go away and work on the script and others who are happy to play in public. This is mirrored in business.

One French advertising executive came all the way from Paris to London to attend one of my workshops. She could see how others were able to give of their best in meetings – gathering thoughts, suggesting ideas on the spot and able to articulate their arguments. She felt she could not. She knew she had plenty to contribute but something eluded her in those public moments. She was very bright. After a day of playing with intentive listening and the ethos of *Yes And* (*Oui Et* en français) she became more confident.

The improv world thrives on difference, immediacy, you-take-my-input, I-take-yours. My great idea may get lost by the wayside or developed beyond recognition, but that's okay. However, that is not the type of collaboration frequently required in business. We need to hear the quieter voices. They might prefer to put something in Chat rather than un-mute.

Surrounded by familiar items, perhaps in your slippers, do you feel more able to jump in on video calls? There is a whole new set of parameters to play with in the virtual dance. Because I also notice how some people, even when I clearly haven't finished my conversation with them, mute quickly. Too quickly. It's the remote equivalent of holding your tongue or apologetic language such as, 'it may just be me' or 'can I say...'.

We know that collaboration is not always the answer but...

Many of today's challenges are complex and can *only* be tackled by people with different skills and expertise. You need to harness ideas, people and resources from different disciplines and across organizational boundaries.

Recently, I spent some time coaching a doctor, now working for a pharmaceutical firm. He was up for an award and was preparing for the final hurdle. Three people would present their story and then be interviewed about the project for which they had been nominated. The whole process for him had depended upon collaborating. Nothing else. He'd had to persuade reps, legal types, marketing folk and others to believe in the idea and to do a lot of work to make it a reality. All this, just two months after arriving. And all in lockdown.

For how many people is their job 100 per cent collaboration? For whom there is nothing *other* than gathering people and nudging them to do stuff that helps others? It may or may not surprise you that Cross and his team found that there is 'an overlap of only about 50 per cent between top collaborative contributors and those employees deemed to be the top performers'.[18] Plenty of people hit their targets by helping nobody else and are rewarded for it. So there is what I might call a 'collaboration deficit'. How do you reward those who may be contributing to someone else's end-of-year numbers?

A *Huffington Post* survey in 2013 on how people 'give back' found that men were more likely to share knowledge, information and expertise – primarily 'informational' collaboration.[19] Whereas women were more likely to help others by doing some work – the 'personal' collaboration I mention above. They give time and energy which they could have spent on their own projects. Though some tasks can only be achieved this way, perhaps think about that before you ask for (or offer) this, think about a form of collaboration that won't deplete someone's resources.

A 2005 study by New York University found that 'the same altruistic behaviour can result in different performance evaluations' depending on whether you are a man or a woman.[20] A man staying late to help out got higher ratings than a woman who did the same. When they didn't, there were unfavourable reactions to the women, but no disadvantage to the men. It seems to be expected that women will help out and a surprise when men do. Let's change this with a bit of push and pull. Recognize and reward those who do help out – but make sure you ask as many men as you do women.

Things may be moving. In many organizations, being helpful or collaborative is now explicitly part of the annual appraisal. In sport, they don't just track baskets or goals scored, they track assists. Maybe there should be a place at the top table for a Chief Collaboration Officer? Their job would be to make collaboration easier, check that it is happening and perhaps step in when there is a deficit. Plus they would help focus on where collaboration is NOT needed. They could check that meetings are not acting like those autoimmune diseases, which attack the host's body.

It shouldn't be underestimated how much your feeling about your team can matter. A team can be the reason you might feel more engaged (and more productive) at work. Or not.

What's your collaboration style?

Do you speak up in meetings or go away and think about it?
Do you agree to stuff in meetings, 'Yeah, yeah, I'll go along with it'? Then do nothing but gossip later about how rubbish it all is?
Are you shouty? My way or the highway?

Are you more Tantric? 'Let's just sit in a circle in silence for three days until the moment feels right and we can hug and reach a new level of consciousness?'

Do you only offer information when actually wisdom is needed?

Are you too ready to offer too much of yourself and take on a task you should not?

Could you spare some time just to listen and reflect?

Improv teams are often held up as great examples of teamwork. I have even been in a workshop where the Comedy Store Players were held up as a shining example. Ah, if only you knew, I blushed. We can be brilliant onstage, but we only have to do it for two hours a week. How about if you could take the best of our world and overlay it on yours? I find the best leaders and teams are already doing this but what if it could be codified rather than ad hoc? Plenty of teams actually spend time talking about how they 'do meetings'.

TOOLBOX   Lessons from improv

- Everyone has the chance to talk.
- I wait until you have finished before I speak. But we don't take up too much airtime when it's our turn.
- Everyone's contribution is welcomed and used.
- There is a common goal and it doesn't matter who came up with the idea. We value and add to it.
- I can say something even though I don't know where it will lead, or where my fellow player will take it.

- I hold my agenda lightly. (In the improv scene, I gave you what I thought was a (mimed) cup of tea but you saw a cup of coffee. So it is now coffee.)
- Each person can shine, by being a great team player. The audience loves seeing the interplay, the collaboration, the shared joy.

What about robots?

Pretty soon, will we be able to make robots do all the dirty work? No emotional intelligence will be needed when you're dealing with artificial intelligence, will it? I've read about the idea of 'Collective Intelligence': the best of humans with the best of machines. That sounds good, doesn't it? But what happens when the robots become bored during budget meetings? Angry in appraisals? Or grumpy because the task assigned is 'beneath them'?

Data may be more sophisticated now but it still needs human interpretation. You need to ask machines good questions and make sure they are learning useful things. I see no diminution of the need for 'working together' skills. I see adaptation. If we are not in the office all the time, the moments when we are all together must be used wisely. 'Awaydays' will still be important. Building a raft not so much. Finding ways to make our Teams meetings fun should take centre stage. And I'm not talking about miming to *YMCA* or making cocktails.

Recruitment may often be location-neutral now but what about the person – or levels of people – for whom being in among the action is vital for career development?

What if your boss doesn't want to go back and you do? Or they do and you don't? Will there end up being favourites because of these choices?

I believe that face-to-face interaction offers something that Zoom doesn't (and Teams most definitely doesn't). However, I worked with so many companies that had taken on new people in lockdown that it didn't feel that odd. If I have met you face to face, will we work better together remotely? Perhaps meeting someone over video calls increases our interest in meeting in person?

So what now? Just like one dog year is equivalent to seven human years, is there a virtual coefficient? One Zoom hour is a seventh of a face-to-face hour? Big conferences can take place online. Hundreds of millions of pounds (and tonnes of carbon) have been saved by reducing conference and business travel. I don't think firms will be willing to pay that kind of money again. Face-to-face contact will be more localized, more regionalized.

A study of over 60,000 Microsoft employees from the first half of 2020 showed that the collaboration network of workers became 'more static and siloed'.[21] What active steps are you and your organization taking to make sure this is not the case? Unless you do, it becomes a vicious circle. We focus on the people we know, because we don't know who else knows what. And if we haven't met or worked with someone, we are less likely to ask for or offer help. We need to talk to people who have different mental models from us. Spending too much time with those who agree with us isn't effective. You have to find a way, especially in hybrid times, of working with different disciplines and making sure each team has a wide variety of backgrounds.

TOOLBOX   Making collaboration effective

1 Ask yourself: Is collaboration needed at this moment? If so, what type of collaboration?

2 Grab the chance to use new technology as an opportunity for connection rather than see it as a 'poor substitute' for face to face. Create new rituals for interaction with social moments, not just 'task conversations'.

3 Focus on team culture more than company culture. But that is not just the half dozen or dozen people the org chart says and it could well include outsiders (e.g. suppliers and contractors). Include them.

4 If you get numbers 1–3 right, you can have a varied hybrid mix in the group. Right person beats right place.

5 Better collaboration means that you should be having fewer meetings, but each of them will be more focused and productive.

Two questions

Just having more collaboration isn't the point. It's not an end in itself. It's about knowing:

- when to collaborate
- how to make it work

When does collaboration work?

Depending on your job, you may only need to collaborate with colleagues at the margin – with updates and so on – because crossover is minimal. Sometimes those silos I mentioned reflect what needs to be done and how it's best achieved. You can and should be making decisions without recourse to others.

Just because more people are involved doesn't mean productivity increases or diversity of approach is achieved – sometimes meetings create the opposite. I will look at that more in Chapter 6. I would say that there are times when you should think about the coefficient of collaboration. In our improv shows, many of the scenes are two-handers. That is so much easier to manage. More than that and things can become messy. Of course, when you do have six performers all sharing the stage on song (sometimes literally) effectively it is beautiful and joyous but it needs each of them to be self-aware and generous.

In business, working with one other person is really productive. So for some situations you may think about the issue, go to one person, then go away and think about it and then look for larger group buy-in. (I will talk more about side-meetings in Chapter 6.)

When something radical or disruptive is needed, you will need to find allies one by one. So I recommend one-on-one moments as the 'nursery slopes' or testing group for larger collaboration (when it is needed). However, don't always go to the same person. There will be diversity of thought each time you work with someone different. That person need not be an obvious choice, so not just the colleague 'next' to you, but your boss, or someone from a different department, or even another firm, or even outside your sector.

Should leaders be better at facilitating solitude as well as collaboration?

When are you most creative – walking outside, being on your own or sitting in a meeting being frustrated at the politics? Perhaps you actually need to get away from people to think more creatively? It's not fashionable and possibly seen as rude to seek time alone. I am an introvert. I spend a lot of time with other people – often filling an extrovert role – but I find it exhausting and I have to build in time before and after. It used to be wonderful to be in a foreign city and have no cell-phone coverage. I knew that I simply could not be reached by anyone. How do we harness the creativity of introverts? They may not speak up in group meetings and others may speak too much or not be open to ideas expressed more reflectively.

I was taken by the idea of the 'rhythm of collaboration' in an organization, put forward in a 2019 piece by Ethan Bernstein and others (as a follow-up to their research on intermittent collaboration).[22] It's really a question 'of whether the task primarily requires co-ordination or imagination'. When we are on Teams all day, or easily contactable or expected constantly at meetings, there is less ebb and flow of connectivity. If we are 'always on' there is little room for solo learning: 'During periods of separation, people naturally struck out on their own and tried new and diverse approaches to the problem – but when they came together again, they could learn from these different solutions.'

It seems to me that each of us must take care of our own rhythm of collaboration, sensitive to different moments. Each leader and each organization must be aware too. It's the quality of the output that matters, not the quantity of collaboration.

CHAPTER FOUR

Creativity

What is creativity?

There is plenty of froth generated around the notion of creativity in organizations. I don't think people really know precisely what they mean by it. I never considered myself a creative person yet now I am often called in to business for being just that. People can now think beyond the lone geniuses like Picasso or Mozart, but at the start of my sessions they are very quick to dismiss themselves as not creative. They soon demonstrate how wrong they are by what they do when we work together. Then I find out more about their career and personal lives: they have brought people together to complete plenty of projects or organized a sports team or run a marathon or put on an event, all of which should be considered creative.

Along with the misconception that creativity is something limited to those special people in 'creative roles' is the assumption that it is limited to special moments like the occasional brainstorm.

There is no lack of creativity in each business I have worked with. But it's not always adding to the bottom line or in service of the firm's objectives. Think of the phrase 'creative accounting'. 'Creativity' could be mucking about or mocking the head honcho or the arcane expenses system. But creativity is really about *being open to possibilities*. It can be about new products, new services and 'big ideas' but it could also be about everyday things – how you run meetings, arrange the coffee cups, start your Teams call, what you choose to discuss, how you engage new recruits and much more. Everybody can be creative at any time, but not all the time. You may have read that we can be productive only four hours a day so that's why we tend to knock off easy items from our to-do list: tidying up a spreadsheet, cutting and pasting things or deleting old emails.[1] Many may actually feel that their job is limited to these kinds of tasks but everyone should have the opportunity to pipe up now and then to suggest new ideas or even to simply ask 'why'? A creative company culture should mean that these types of conversations occur often.

Everybody thinks they want creativity – especially leaders – but they may not know what it is. If they did, they might not want it. It might lead to changes they cannot control. On the other hand, I find that it is often the most senior executives who desperately desire it from their troops. It's the middle managers who gum things up. Sometimes.

How do you make your team creative when in a group setting and how do you keep creative as an individual? LASER is the answer in both cases.

LASER and organizational creativity

Listen – to members of your team and more widely to customers, suppliers, the market, the changing technology, the regulatory environment.

Accept – what the new reality is, the data, people's perceptions, what you cannot change.

Send – use what's happening to move forward, to try something, a small experiment perhaps, to develop in light of what has changed.

Explore – what are the assumptions, filters, biases behind perceptions – yours and others? What's about to disrupt the prevailing wisdom? What if we can look at this problem working back from the answer?

Reincorporate – what happened before? What has worked in other sectors? How can we use this to move things on? What was available before but wasn't ready to be used? What are your customers and suppliers telling you that you can then incorporate into your product?

Remember, LASER is not sequential. Keep looping back, using the incoming data, some of which is a reaction to your 'offers'.

A note about Reincorporate

I felt emboldened to keep using this word when a great 'corporate writing' coach used the same word –

reincorporate – to describe the borrowing of a concept from another sector. This is a great way to clarify your message. I was once helping a construction company improve its customer service. It's not a sector renowned for its high standards in this area but it must improve its game, especially now that, within seconds of a pipe bursting, it can be on social media and endlessly shared. This firm was doing very well, but it wanted to do better. It wanted not just to have the best customer service in the building industry, but to rival Apple. A social housing organization wanted to be compared not with others in their field but with a hotel chain.

I often use the notion of analogy with clients. It is a powerful method of helping people understand their own world better. If you were not in the sector you are in but, say, a car maker, what would you be? Some go straight to Rolls-Royce but I point out that means you would be beyond the budget of most people. More recently, Tesla has been mentioned but plenty more electric cars are available. Or I ask about hotel chains. Would you rather be the upmarket boutique brand with fluffy robes and home-made cookies or the no-nonsense budget brand which has many more outlets and you know what you will get whichever town you are in. We use metaphor all the time in improv. You can often say so much more by not saying it...

In a business sense, there are many ways of using reincorporation as a creative technique:

- What did we do before?
- What used to happen in earlier societies?
- How would this be viewed in another cultural milieu?
- Could we borrow from another world, another sector?

Certainly, I note that a lot of public-sector organizations borrow from the private sector. They talk about their 'business' or 'business unit'. It is not necessarily an easy 'read-across'. I recall Sir Terry Leahy, under whose aegis Tesco made great advances, suggesting that the National Health Service could not be run in the same way. His wife was a doctor so he knew what he was talking about. Organizations in the public and private sectors are continually looking to explicitly reincorporate the 'offers' of their customers, clients, service users, patients, employees, suppliers and, um, voters. It can be effective to reincorporate ideas and approaches from other sectors but it should support your main strategy rather than supplant it. Just calling people 'customers' doesn't mean you treat them better.

CASE STUDY   PLUSSING IN SILICON VALLEY

At Pixar, *Yes And* has become 'Plussing'. You can't just criticize an idea: you must add a constructive suggestion. You build on the other person's work. This, of course, means you are talking about their notion, not criticizing the person. You're not undermining them. Separating 'it' from 'you' is always productive.

The words 'Yes And' are not the answer on their own. Understanding the ethos behind them is revelatory but just talking about it isn't enough. It only becomes meaningful when people mean it. 'I don't always want to say yes to someone', said a very bright woman from a leading software firm in Palo Alto to me recently. She had attended a *Yes And* workshop before. 'Do I always have to say 'Yes And?'was her downcast question.

NO! You don't always have to say those actual words.

She had been badly taught. *Yes And* is an exercise you can practise. Then it becomes a mindset. Many people have this mindset who have never heard of improv. We don't have a monopoly on this practical wisdom. If those two words become a stick with which to beat people, count me out. It is so much deeper than that. It's an attitude. That is part of the reason I am writing this book. People have heard that improv is simply just about saying Yes.

No. One of our main rules is 'Make your partner look good'. Practising saying Yes to their idea is a good drill. You make them look good by accepting and 'plussing', hence building upon their ideas. But in real life, you can still accept their offer without agreeing.

Overcoming fear

Fear inhibits creativity: 'Should I really be doing this or even thinking that?' The LASER mindset opens things up, sees possibilities and challenges assumptions and uses restrictions as enablers. Creativity doesn't need to be something huge or daunting. It can just be how we organize ourselves or make our Zoom meetings more effective or even what we decide to *stop* doing. What's for sure, though, is if we feel we can't explore assumptions about small things, bigger innovations may be harder to come by.

Once you overcome the fear of being seen as Mad, Bad or Wrong, then you can become an improviser. KEITH JOHNSTONE

Keith Johnstone was one of the gurus of improv. He literally wrote the book – or one of them at least.[2] It has so much to say beyond its own world. I have seen it on the shelves of many non-theatre types. Keith was at the Royal Court – the theatre for new writing – when he became more and more drawn to non-scripted theatre. I once gave him a lift back to his hotel after a workshop on his brilliant improv show format which is called *Life Game*. Keith told me that he wished he had never said 'you must take the first suggestion from the audience'. It's okay, I replied, we often don't. The audience – bless them – don't always know what will lead to a good scene. We do. So we listen out for suggestions that we know will have more life, more energy. And they are often better if they are not funny. Some of the most innovative business ideas come from the most generic or dull suggestions.

So are we 'blocking' if we don't take the first suggestion we hear? Or could taking that not-so-good-suggestion actually be seen as blocking the better suggestion that came a moment later? Just saying Yes to anything is a simplification of improv.

There are some purists who say 'there are no such things as bad ideas'. Yes there are. But it depends what you do with them. In improv, we talk about 'choices'. It's what your fellow player chooses to do with your offer that makes it good or bad or better or worse. And what you do with theirs. Saying 'What are you doing?' isn't a great offer. But replying, 'You can see what I'm doing, Nigel, I'm packing my bags' could lead somewhere interesting…

The creative process

Creativity: that's brainstorming, right?

I am not a fan of brainstorming for two reasons. First, I don't think it works. Second, creativity should not be confined to a cordoned-off time. Every interaction, every meeting, every email is an opportunity for creativity. Parcelling out people and time to a platform which is separate – the brainstorm – implies that in normal hours we are not expected to be creative. Why do I dislike brainstorms? Tomas Chamorro-Premuzic in a 2015 *Harvard Business Review* article found research that showed brainstorming was not as productive as solo work.[3] Why?

1 We make less of an effort when in a team.
2 We fear others' opinion of our ideas.
3 'Regression to the mean': great players sink to the level of mediocre players in the group.
4 Only one idea can be expressed at a time. With more than six or seven people, suggestions get lost.

They can happen all too often in business. When improv teams are in the zone, the very opposite of points 1–3 is true, because we are not judging, we are open to others' ideas, we love to support others moving the story forward and we are all contributing. Granted, once you have more than two players onstage it is harder to maintain focus but not impossible. Our ethos is, 'make the other person look good'. But we are not trying to come up with multiple ideas which can be evaluated later. We are trying to tell one story and only one story, in that moment for that audience. The story is a springboard for ideas. We don't mind if a possibly 'good' offer falls by the wayside since we can never know how it would have played out in the unfolding process of building the narrative, just as separating one bird from a murmuration (a flock) to calculate its individual aerodynamics wouldn't encompass the whole.

So creativity is an everyday thing?

'I think people are in danger of conflating three things: innovation, collaboration and culture' wrote Paul Taylor in a blog from 2021.[4] He is a wise innovation expert. When I first read that, I agreed and was glad he had said it. It's possible to say these are three separate dimensions. Innovation can happen in spite of poor collaboration or culture. The context is all. It depends on what type of organization you are in: public, private, small or large, dispersed or not. A leader can force through innovation, people can leave (and I have seen leaders explicitly stating that 'this is how things will be, so you can be part of that or not') but the intent is *towards* a culture of collaboration leading to creativity even if the journey there is anything but. Returning to such outfits a couple of years later, I note the change in personnel. Either lots of the team have gone or the leader has. When you throw all the pieces on the board up in the air, you don't know how they will land. But when things are going well, once the pieces have landed perhaps, culture, creativity and collaboration are inseparable.

There is no formula for creativity. It's about curating the right atmosphere. Leaders can affect this but responsibility goes wider. A 2021 study by Signature Consultants connected a culture of kindness to innovation.[5] That's the Pixar model. That's LASER. In a *Harvard Business Review* article from 2021, Amy Edmondson and Per Hugander define psychological safety as 'the confidence that candour and vulnerability are welcome'.[6] It is essential to creativity. I am sure we have all encountered non-creative environments where these pillars were absent. We can learn this but only in the sense that you learn how to rock-climb. It's not something you can do 'in theory' but you can also feel yourself dangling in mid-air sometimes. You need to work at it, one conversation at a time, prioritizing intra-team dynamics in a way for which no school or college has prepared you.

What if you are not in a position to shape your environment? Are you better off finding a new one? Reader, it's your call. This is why I couldn't imagine myself having a proper job. But I am fortunate to be freelance. What I have found is that it's quite comfortable to complain – and that comfort should not be dismissed lightly. However, I have met small teams that have made their own micro-environment. After all, you may not be able to influence very much, but you can never influence *nothing*.

Innovation?

I once heard a rough definition of the difference between creativity and innovation. Creativity is coming up with an idea. Innovation is making money out of it. Is that a bit icky? Innovation is how you deploy an idea; how you present it to others; how you give it a purpose; how you extract value from it. But I have found some frustration in teams who have no shortage of ideas but nothing actually seems to get done.

'Making people feel more included' as a creative output is hard to measure. The hard-nosed among us might say, 'so what – we are not social services'. But it's what it can lead to that matters – or what the lack of it is costing you. You can measure things that may correlate with a creative culture – retention of staff, recruitment, staff satisfaction – all of which affect the bottom line. So do endless dull meetings, sabotaging others' projects, email squabbles, going round and round in circles because the people who could have helped didn't... these all happen day in, day out and they do matter.

Making a new product seems more tangible. LASER skills may have helped come up with the initial idea. But months and months of testing, possible frustration with prototypes and consumer reaction require hard slog which an improviser like me couldn't bear. However, creativity is still essential along the way to finding novel ways to adapt the device or product, based on real-world feedback – whether from people or devices that don't behave themselves outside the lab.

The chief innovation officer of a global company that develops an array of products told me about the 'breadboard'. It's a software term for rapid experimenting, seeing humans and nature interact with the idea. In the early days of electronics, people put nails into actual breadboards to connect circuits. He likes to use the term more broadly. Will the idea that worked in the lab work in the actual conditions for which it is intended? Such as... Can we build more than one? Can non-experts operate it? The innovation process isn't finished until the product is out there, being made and used regularly in ordinary life. At each step, lateral thinking is required. It isn't really finished even when it does become available more broadly, of course, because competitors will come along and make it cheaper or more accessible. Or the whole market disappears. Fax machine, anyone?

I am often called in to run creativity workshops, under the guise of *convergent* versus *divergent* thinking. Convergent is finding the right answer. Divergent means opening up the questions. Convergent is asking which car we should go in. Divergent is asking should we walk or go by bus or by horse; or do we even need to go; or why doesn't what we're going to *come to us*? Convergent thinking can hamper organizations because people may only see the established process and no more. You might say that convergent is exemplified by the quote by Henry Ford: 'If I had asked people what they wanted, they would have said faster horses.' The car could be claimed to be divergent thinking, which disrupted the 'transport market'.

The trouble is that he didn't actually say it. Patrick Vlaskovits in an article for the *Harvard Business Review* in 2021 reveals not only that Ford never said it but was guilty of not listening to customers when he should have done.[7] His Model T was very popular. But soon rivals were introducing updated models, different financing options and even a second-hand market. So Ford lost out.

So you need both divergent and convergent thinking. It is foolish to say that creativity is all about game-changing innovations. It could just be imaginative tweaks. Today, listening to customers may seem easier when there is so much data about their behaviour. Too much, in fact. Who can be sure how to interpret people's behaviour? No matter how much empirical evidence there is, some intuition may be needed about asking the right question or understanding the story behind the data. That's why pilots and prototypes matter.

One of my favourite stories of innovation – perhaps apocryphal – was of a new internal tech platform for employees. The developers were very pleased. It had so much functionality. It gave access to the data that employees had requested. But hardly anyone used it. It was too difficult. The developers didn't understand why. So they put a big red button labelled 'Press to Start' on the front page. It cost hardly anything to add but suddenly usage increased hugely. Those who create new ideas need to put themselves into the non-expert shoes of those who will have to use it day to day.

In-the-box thinking

Often leaders come to me because they want their people to 'think outside the box'. Why? What's wrong with the box? Who knows what's actually in the box? Why not make a better box? Okay, I'm being silly now but I often think, in these circumstances, of the box that contained Schrödinger's Cat, which was both alive and dead at the same time, until you opened it to find out.

It turns out there was a Russian chap who found that most novel solutions were not new at all, but an adaptation of a previous one. This is the **Reincorporate** of LASER writ large. He was a Soviet scientist/engineer called Genrich S Altshuller. Between 1946 and 1985 he and his team came up with TRIZ (pronounced *trees*) which is the Russian acronym for the 'Theory of Inventive Problem Solving'. Whatever problem you are facing, someone else has solved something like it. There are 40 principles and 76 standard solutions.[8] That's a lot. TRIZ seems to be most applicable to engineering and process management. Mostly it's about defining the problem, especially by the contradictions you are trying to resolve.

Then you find the solution that fits and apply it to your situation. So Thinking In The Box could be handy. For example, Principle 27 is 'Dispose'. The solution is 'replace an expensive object with a cheap one, compromising other properties (i.e. longevity)'. Principle 11 is 'Cushion' and the solution is 'compensate for the relatively low reliability of an object with emergency measures prepared in advance'. Not unlike movie sets, where they have stand-by props and lots of spare lights and bulbs, in case a quick replacement is needed. They often go unused but you have them there anyway.

Looking at the TRIZ list, you have to work quite hard to define the actual problem. In doing so, the solution may be clear. But this presupposes the problem is definable in such a way that a solution exists. What if you can only define it in a certain way? What if you cannot see the TRIZ for the wood?

Big isn't so beautiful

It may be obvious, but I find that smaller organizations tend to be more creative. Everyone knows everyone, there is psychological safety because the founders are still part of the gang, everyone in the firm can talk to the CEO, anyone can make a difference. With large firms, process and structure are necessary but become restrictive. So they seek to instil a 'challenger mindset' or something like that. Speaking at a conference for one of the world's largest tech firms, I followed a small businessman dressed in a milk carton. The business was small but the carton very large. It was him, a mate and a van. What could these corporate business people learn from him? He was a great speaker but the parallels were hard to draw, I felt. He didn't have to worry about stock price, pensions, inventory, cyber security, appraisals, recruitment, retention, succession planning and all the rest, including, ahem, anti-trust lawsuits concerning monopolistic practices.

There is a lot of lip service paid to creativity. Steve Blank, who's been involved with eight tech start-ups, wrote in 2019 about 'innovation theatre'.[9] You might bring in some dudes with floppy hair and T-shirts to run a hackathon or design thinking workshops. There might even be some posters put up in the elevator. There's a flurry of activity which looks cool in a report to the board and gives great opportunities for a week's exciting work experience for teenage offspring of the C-suite but it may lead nowhere. If it's not part of the everyday fabric, it's just a side-show.

When Don Sull[10] was a professor at London Business School we had several conversations, one time by the duck pond in Regent's Park. He said, 'You know, Neil, I think improv is the answer. I'm just not sure what the question is yet.' For me the question is about how to be more creative and collaborative and thus more aware of possibilities.

I taught a session for his MBA class. After 15 minutes, one student, for whom English was not his first language, asked, 'So you're talking about lying?' For him, improv meant 'making it up', which meant telling untruths, rather than optimizing the best of less than perfect conditions, which was how I hoped to frame it. In Don's book, *The Upside of Turbulence*, there is a chapter on improv in which he argues that turbulence actually throws up many opportunities.[11] LASER isn't just about making the best of a bad job, it's about spotting moments for taking action.

A creative culture is one that takes time to ferment and needs to be curated. It requires patience because results may not come overnight and collaboration is essential. Just saying from on high, 'everyone collaborate' or 'stop silo thinking' is not enough, especially, as is often the case, if the leadership team are firmly entrenched in functional funnels.

People need to disagree but in the Pixar way, assuming good intent, with ultimately shared purpose. There needs to be a clear commitment to following through with ideas, experimenting to see where they will lead, giving them the best chance to succeed and being open to the idea that not all will, as well as being bold enough to call time on some. Those that don't fly have to be seen as part of the learning process. Often in our improv scenes, a possible seam is dropped early because something else emerged that seemed a better choice. Judging ideas too early chokes off future possibilities.

Do you feel creative?

Too often people think that creativity is something that only others can achieve. But teams can; maybe even Teams can. And so could you. You can use LASER with yourself, to facilitate inner dialogue. It's always the first offer that is hardest. Picasso said, 'The paper defends its whiteness.' Want to draw something? So do a squiggle. Turn the paper sideways or upside down. See what it is telling you. A shape may be emerging in your mind's eye. Mostly I have talked about team creativity but what about you, as an individual? Creativity is a muscle. Whether or not you believe in the 10,000 hours thesis, actually making something happen in that first hour is often the greatest creative challenge. (I have to admit that before writing this next section, I spent a lot of time avoiding it. Emptying and stacking the dishwasher, replying to emails that have hung around a while, putting out the recycling and more). So find ways to keep your hand in. Start a journal for half-formed thoughts or unfinished sketching.

The power of solitude

The most creative thing you might do is go for a walk. Solitude, if a choice, is very good for mental health and creativity. I ran Zoom workshops for some public-sector organizations during the Covid-19 lockdown. I called them 'An Island of Sanity'. So many people in multi-person households said how much they missed their own company. Unsurprisingly, the opposite was true of those who lived alone. I remember one very senior medic, whose entire practice had shut down, had moved into his new house but had not been able to have a single visitor. I suggested a great idea borrowed from Liz Kentish, a very inspiring consultant in the facilities management world. I divided the virtual workshop into pairs and told them to go for a walk. 'Screen on, shoes on' is a great idea. Using FaceTime or similar, you go for a walk but you turn the camera away from your face and point it where you are looking. So you don't feel the intrusion of being looked at but you can share the view of the street or the park. Of course, Dr New House showed his conversational partner round his place. It helped him feel human again.

Solitude, if curated well and intentionally, can help us process, reflect and 'rehearse' the future. It has historically been seen as part of living life well. It means we will cherish those moments that we do spend with others. On the other hand, so many people in lockdown did not have the luxury of choice. 'Shoes on, screen on' was a great way to use the resources available to bring people together. I might add that Liz is also a huge fan of writing letters and postcards. For one of her friends, who had not touched another human for eight weeks, Liz got her husband to draw an outline of her shoulders and arms from the fingertip of one hand to the fingertip of the other. She folded and mailed the long piece of paper. Her friend was able to give herself a hug with it, knowing that it represented love and care.

Creative attitude

This is just one example of having a creative attitude to life and how it can help us overcome the barriers and obstacles along the way. Put yourself in moments where creativity can visit you. Sitting alone, walking, talking to friends; just having a shower opens your mind. Of course, those are the very moments (of 'meditative distraction' as our conscious mind is disengaged), achieved by meandering or chopping vegetables or gardening, that we find hard to timetable perhaps. Using our 'intelligence' or getting busy-busy with work often means that creativity and inspiration leave the building. Intuitive moments, or what psychologists call *incubation*, are all about the wandering mind. And guess who can harness this professionally? Improv performers, of course! (*Disclaimer: we may not be unique in this.*)

I often describe the state we are in as 'relaxed concentration' which is similar to Mihaly Csikszentmihalyi's idea of Flow. The majority of people, when they hear what I do, say 'I could never do that. I can't imagine anything worse.' This includes lots of 'creative' types – actors, writers, stand-up comics – as well as those in conventional careers. They frame it as being thrown, unprepared, into a situation where you will fail in front of a large number of disappointed people. Whereas I characterize it as the chance to work alongside others, without having to bother to write or rehearse, in a highly creative state, to entertain an audience, who know what they've come to see and are ready to be delighted. And whatever I say is 'right'. I can't forget my words, because whatever I say is the 'script'. What freedom!

I describe my LASER approach as a left-brain way to access right-brain creativity:

Listen to the notions that pop into your head.
Accept that you don't have to justify them but use them to…
Step into somewhere you didn't expect.
Explore the reasons why you think they are wrong or why something wouldn't work.
Reincorporate them.

Keeping a journal will act as a catalyst to help ideas pop up. Some might say have one notebook for creative ideas and another for non-creative to-do lists. I say just have one notebook. But maybe a waterproof one for those moments of 'shower inspiration'.

A study of freestyling rappers was published in 2012.[12] It was led by Siyuan Liu with Allen Braun of the National Institute on Deafness and Other Communication Disorders. It showed that when we improvise, certain other parts of our brain take a back seat – those that make decisions, plan and regulate. The 'medial prefrontal cortex' area, which is responsible for associating, emotional response and context, starts working overtime. 'We think what we see is a relaxation of "executive functions" to allow more natural de-focused attention and uncensored processes to occur that might be the hallmark of creativity', says Braun. There was a sense, to which I can attest from my improv work, that you don't know where the ideas were coming from. And that's okay.

TOOLBOX   Tips for being more creative as an individual

- Arrange oases when you are not having to make decisions or plans; so that your mind can wander (or improvise).
- Find ways to capture your mind's output at unexpected moments when it does wander.

For many people, an obvious moment when they need to be creative is when preparing a presentation. Or it should be. Too often senior folk delegate it to their team to make about a hundred slides which leave their boss daunted. So I always let the leader talk me through what's been prepared. Then we put it to one side and I 'interview' them and record the audio of the conversation. I am looking for what gives them energy, which will in turn enthuse their audience. We talk about what's keeping them awake at night: a notable success; a fraught failure; stories which could be used to illustrate the wider point; pet peeves; something personal which may engage the audience. We need to decide what we want the audience to go away with. Too often, the reason for doing the presentation is given as something like: 'Because I was asked and now my direct reports have gone and made some slides.'

One such time I was talking to a supply chain director. Not many laughs there, huh? But when you delve, there are stories. I kept digging until I found that the message he (let's call him Mike) really wanted to spread was, 'Procurement needs a seat at the top table'. It should be a fundamental part of strategy. So I probed. How does it feel *not* to be there? My method is warm provocation: 'So what you do really is try and save 10 per cent on the price of paperclips?' I always dig for a metaphor which people use to describe (or dismiss) a team or function: 'Yeah, we're just seen as cost-down monkeys.' This is gold.

Guess what, as I write this, I realize I was looking for contradictions, just as with the TRIZ method. We needed to find the opposite of 'cost-down monkey'. As I pushed Mike, he kept using the word 'entrepreneurial'. That's not how Procurement was seen. Everyone gets excited about strategy or the big new project. Then they send in the procurement police to screw the suppliers.

I listened and listened. Just like Karl Marx, TRIZ tells us to look for contradictions. Entrepreneur and Procurement seemed to be opposite ends of the spectrum. So, having Listened and Accepted, I Sent an offer back, Exploring why Procurement should spearhead strategy, embracing entrepreneurship. I **R**eincorporated and a compound word popped into my head – *Entreprocurial*. It seemed cheeky, silly even, but it was bold and brave. But we needed a case study to back it up.

At Mike's previous (large, global) firm, a new idea for chilled meals emerged. The usual strategy story would be: prove concept, agree business plan, build factory, eventually product comes to market. That could take years. The real 'offer' was actually 'produce tasty, chilled meals', not 'must build factory' which would cost time and money. So Mike talked to suppliers, who already had the technology and hardware to produce the meals. The project was launched in half the time, at half the cost. Entreprocurialism in action. Mike's consulting firm thereafter used the word in their marketing, at exhibitions and in keynotes to promote their services.

But what about making money?

As you can imagine, plenty of the people I know in show-biz bemoan the influence of 'the suits'. This is a disparaging term, also used in advertising, to characterize people who are deemed not to understand creativity but to care only about the bottom line. But isn't that their job? You don't want to run out of money such that you can't make *any* movies – good, bad, artistic or popular. The point, though, is how do we allow creativity while making it accountable? Someone with an MBA might not understand movie-making but they do understand budgets and distribution. In my brief forays into Hollywood, I did find some brilliant people who could appreciate both sides of show-biz – the show and the biz – and they are much in demand. But, as the legendary screenwriter William Goldman wrote in his book *Adventures in the Screen Trade:*[13]

> Nobody knows anything... Not one person in the entire motion picture field knows for a certainty what's going to work. Every time out it's a guess and, if you're lucky, an educated one.

So how do we make creativity pay? Can we make it adhere to some sort of process? Big firms might buy smaller firms to nab their ideas; they might hire in consultants; or they have 'intrapreneurs' (see, I'm not the first one to make up silly words). Ideas are great fun – don't we all love Post-it notes and flip-charts and different colour pens and wacky thoughts? But what about getting something out there that customers want? And 'scaling' it? That means making lots of whatever it is and distributing it at a price which means people will pay for it and you can keep making it.

A cautionary tale is one where the 'suits' could have had something to say. The biggest-selling 12-inch single on vinyl is New Order's 'Blue Monday' from Factory Records. The radical and brilliant sleeve design was based on a floppy disk (which younger readers may recognize as the icon used now for saving things on your computer). Sadly it cost 10 pence more than the record's selling price. The more they sold, the more money they lost. But maybe it was a loss leader? Or just an apocryphal tale to enhance the myth of Tony Wilson, the entrepreneur behind Factory Records, who did often wear a suit but was not everyone's idea of a 'suit'.

So how do you encourage intrapreneurs while keeping their feet on the ground? In a blog from 2017,[14] the author and innovation consultant Tendayi Viki suggests 'incremental investing'. Expectations change as the innovation teams progress or not. So they must show that:

- a real customer needs the product or service
- the product satisfies the customer's needs
- there is a profitable business model to deliver value

These might not be sequential steps but, when starting my own business, I really had to work hard to establish the first two, to explain how LASER could help organizations. Whereas if you are mass producing widgets – or chilled meals – the third is likely to be the toughest.

Hybrid working: more opportunities to be creative

The telephone didn't signal the end of the face-to-face meeting but became a useful platform for when people were physically distant or needed a shorter or more immediate or different sort of conversations or interaction. Virtual, if used judiciously alongside face-to-face interactions, will become a great tool for better creativity. We can see someone's face from across the world for a short meeting. No need for flights and jet lag and carbon off-sets. The key is to curate a creative climate. As soon as lockdown happened I experimented with Zoom. Soon it became clear that it was possible to use it playfully. I make people stand up during sessions, to wake up their minds and bodies. I continually ask for contributions in Chat. I ask them to bring an object – or to go to get one during the session – to talk about. It's amazing how much more energy and emotion (and hence creativity) people bring when talking about (and holding) something real and tangible, especially if it means something to them. Just putting on a hat means they react differently. It's a standard creative game to ask people, 'What would Richard Branson/Jeff Bezos/ Madonna do?' But ask them to put on a hat, then ask them and/or others to describe the character they now appear to be and inhibitions leave, as ideas flow.

I found some research from 1994 (and it still rings true today) that the generally held idea that groups are more creative than individuals is incorrect.[15] But it's hard to quantify what is meant by 'creative' – number of ideas or 'quality' of ideas or something else? They say that 'the evidence suggests that the productivity loss in idea-generating groups is caused mainly by mutual production blocking due to the constraint on groups that members can talk only in turn.'

Remember that word – constraint. In improv we are only working on one idea at a time, developing it. We tend to have only two or three people in a scene at any moment. Any more is harder to create focus but when it works (i.e. some are playing 'background' to add to the drama or singing a chorus) it is glorious.

Management professor Leigh Thompson says:[16]

It's widely believed that synergy among group members generates more creativity than individuals can. But virtually no research supports this. In fact, most studies have found that 'per capita' creativity declines precipitously as group size increases.

So beware brainstorming. But remember Pixar. If handled well, groups can be very creative but the point from the Stroebe and Diehl study was that we are *constrained* because we can only speak in turn.[17]

This is not the case in virtual. Use the chatbox. When I ask a question on Zoom, I ask for responses in Chat. I start easy. Where are you? Not just where in the world, but where in the house? Are you wearing socks? Get people accustomed to putting things in Chat – creating a non-judgemental space for play, establishing psychological safety – and more voices will be heard.

One of my clients – the UK part of a global automobile manufacturer – told me that plenty of those who had been seen as 'shrinking violets' were now blooming in virtual meetings, because they felt more relaxed at home, in their own environment. (And it was the same firm who told me that their caterers were having to get used to Fridays being unpredictable and that the default length of meetings was now either 25 or 45 minutes. The tyranny of the hour-long meeting was over.)

Creative constraints

I was asked recently to host a session based on a book by Adam Morgan and Mark Barden called *A Beautiful Constraint*[18] for a 'challenger' in the UK fibre optic market. The book cites plenty of examples where a constraint became an enabler of creativity. Many cultures have a version of 'necessity is the mother of invention' or 'every cloud has a silver lining'. There is a French word, *bricolage*, and in Hindi, *jugaad*, which is about making do with what you have. Remember Tony Hawks and our 'pontoon' from Chapter 3?

Barden and Morgan give lots of examples of where a constraint actually means that *better* practices have arisen. Southwest Airlines is now very successful, but in the early seventies was not doing well. It had four routes and four planes. They had to sell a plane but were determined not to lose the route so were forced to find a workaround – which meant 10-minute turnarounds and unallocated seating (now industry standard). They describe how to create a positive culture which encourages finding the solutions.[19]

Barden and Morgan found that there were over 70 academic studies looking at how constraints relate to creativity. They spoke to Colin Kelly (Global Technical Quality Director at THG at the time of writing) who told them of his time in Russia. His team were very good at looking at a problem and finding reasons why it couldn't be solved, saying, 'We can't... because...'. So he just made them start sentences with 'We can if...'. It was transformational and now Barden and Morgan's consultancy, eatbigfish, uses this simple verbal hack to change mindsets in organizations. It's about breaking 'path dependency', where you just stick to old routines and can't see constraints as opportunities. Challengers in a market often lack resources – like a marketing department or R&D function – so have to, um, improvise. Along with two other improv performers, we demonstrated this approach for the employees of the firm at a huge event. We found that you needed to bring in several 'Yes Ands' between each 'Can If' but it is highly creative.

So in Stroebe and Dieh's study, having to wait to speak in turn was a constraint.[20] But what if you see that very constraint as an *opportunity*? In improv, we speak one at a time and it works. Why not bring that focus to your organization? Barden and Morgan give five reasons why 'Can If' works so well in finding the potential in a challenge. And, guess what, they apply equally to the LASER approach:

- you're talking about what is possible, rather what isn't
- optimism and inquisitiveness are central
- everyone is involved, taking responsibility to move things forward, rather than finding blocks
- people see themselves as 'solution-finders' not helpless victims of outside forces
- mindset changes: any 'failure' is actually a helpful step towards a solution

All of these depend on how you curate and facilitate interactions. As I said in Chapter 2, virtual meetings should be fun and human, but well organized. Pre-pandemic, when we asked people to bring a meaningful object to a workshop, it would be constrained by what they might be able (and not embarrassed) to bring in hand luggage. Now, they can go find something (or someone) that will help them reach a creative state. They can get up and move about. You can take a short break in a virtual meeting that you wouldn't face to face.

Of course, I am not saying everything should be virtual. In-person encounters need to happen but should be much more valuable and their worth fully appreciated.

Conferences should be creative not cumbersome

As I write in late 2022, every in-person event is still a celebration. People may not have seen each other for three years. But don't waste that time and don't fall back into bad habits. That 75-minute teleprompter speech by the CEO? NO. Make it 10, 15 max. You could have conveyed more detail through a webinar or email – or let it 'trickle down', so have managers share information with their own teams. Those un-rehearsed 'round-ups' from each department at your away-day? Tighten them up. No more than five minutes each, please, and rehearse them. Give people time to talk to each other informally. Spend time and effort on the catering and logistics. Don't stint by having crummy food or lengthy queues at the buffet. Face-to-face events can catalyse innovation but they can also teeter towards truculence if poorly planned.

A study in 2022 by King's College London found that half of us feel like our attention spans are shortening.[21] Certainly, with the advent of TikTok we don't want 45-minute one-man (yep, that's still often the case) PowerPoint parades. However our attention spans can be lengthened by more engaging, stimulating content. TikToks may individually only be 15 seconds or so long but people often spend hours on the platform. How to emulate that?

So don't have just the senior bods talking. Bring on others, maybe in pairs. Have them talk about a recent project they did or something outside work. Make sure everyone is rehearsed. Make sure senior people role-model this. They must commit time and energy. I have seen this approach work with some of the busiest executives at the most successful companies in the world. It makes a huge difference for months if not years after the event.

Creativity is not something that can be doled out like a goody bag. It has to be modelled, talked about, nurtured and continually curated. That's why you must make those annual conferences matter, but also the everyday meetings, whether virtual or face to face. Morgan and Barden talk about the 'conversational climate'.[22] What is that like in your team? In your firm? Is it open to risk, to difference and to seeking solutions? Some of this is down to legacy. Much of it is down to leadership, the subject of my next chapter.

CHAPTER FIVE

Leadership mindset

Leadership is too important to be left to individuals. So 'leadership' should be dispersed to everyone in the organization. It's about more than mission statements or 'charismatic' CEOs. It's at all levels, with everyone thinking both about improving things today and rehearsing a better tomorrow. You may be in a leadership role or you may want to be in one or perhaps you just want to cultivate a 'leadership mindset'. It comes down to our old friends – confidence, creativity and communication.

I am often asked in to help with leadership teams. I humbly bring my LASER model and others often find the parallels they need. Dr Nick Pope of the Academy of High-Performing Teams, when introducing my sessions for his clients, talks about letting go of the need to be the smartest person in the room, being comfortable with not knowing, embracing difference, the power of making the other person look good, being able to cope with uncertainty and when things don't go to plan.

In 2018, Paula Mackenzie had just become the boss of KFC UK and Ireland. She is currently at Pizza Express. I have worked with her a few times. She was interviewed for a piece in *The Times* in November 2018 in which she said, 'Chief executives only do two things – people and strategy. The magic is identifying the potential in people and helping them to flourish.'[1] Brilliant. There are lots of books on leadership and plenty of courses (reader, I have taught on them). But Paula nailed it. (I'll say more about strategy towards the end of the chapter.)

In my early forays I was pleasantly surprised to find that several management models chime with improv. The more I delved, the more I found that improv demonstrated these leadership theories and people were keen to bring me in. For example, have you heard of VUCA? It was popularized by the US military. We live in a world which is:

Volatile
Uncertain
Complex
Ambiguous

Have you ever seen an improv show live? That's pretty VUCA, isn't it? We improvisers are past mistresses/masters at dealing with such situations – effectively and creatively – to the joy of our customers. The audience is bewitched and delighted by the seeming magic of our spontaneity, as we navigate the unpredictability and even celebrate it.

I found that improvised music was often used as a metaphor for leadership. But lots of people don't like freeform jazz. Still fewer can play an instrument but I find it worth borrowing their jargon. Management professor (and accomplished jazz musician) Frank J Barrett wrote a book called *Yes to the Mess: Surprising lessons from jazz.*[2] Sometimes you are 'soloing' and sometimes you might just keep the rhythm going or fill in gaps (I am not musical, did you guess?). This is the 'comping' that I mentioned in Chapter 3, as in 'accompanying'.

So, is it a leader's job to solo all the time? No. Should they *never* solo? No. It's about taking turns and embracing the notion of comping when needed. Just like in improv theatre, when someone's on a roll, others keep the story going. That might mean not exactly playing the straight man, but keeping some plates spinning if the other person is knocking them off or setting others to start. Good leadership is stepping back in a meeting when someone wants to present an idea or giving them a chance to run their own project and giving them autonomy when they need it.

What goes wrong with leadership?

As in other areas, there are two, seemingly paradoxical problems that occur:

- Leaders 'lead' *too much*. They dominate and possibly domineer. They (probably unconsciously) close off opportunities for the team to contribute ideas. Team members stop bothering – through fear, frustration or boredom.

- Leaders don't lead *enough*. It's about seeing where collaboration is required and where being directive is essential. It's about harnessing individual talents and how best they contribute to the overall impact of the team.

There are three things that a leader brings to their job:

- their values
- their aspirations for where to take the organization
- what they actually do

Of course, only the third one is properly observable and may not cohere with the other two. Basically, how self-aware are you? Leaders need to know what effect they are having on their team. Many leaders do a great job of uniting their teams – by being the one thing they can agree on: they all loathe the boss. In 1924, the US sociologist Mary Parker Follet wrote: 'Leadership is not defined by the exercise of power, but by the capacity to increase the sense of power among those led.'[3] That sounds good. But what if not all of them want power? Some just want to have a clear outline of what is expected of them and then they go home, on time, without having to fret?

Very early on in my first forays into management training, I was thrilled to find my LASER model being reflected in established leadership theories, which acknowledge that human organizations are not like machines but are messy and unpredictable, but adaptable: more Darwin than Newton?

First, I discovered complexity and Ralph Stacey (Professor of Management at Hertfordshire Business School, who sadly died in 2021) along with the concept of 'Emergent

Leadership'. In any team or organization, there is some disagreement over what should be done and a degree of uncertainty about how things will play out. Too much of both and it is chaos. I introduce this idea after they have played a story game (where they say one word at a time) that could be brimming with 'ideas' that have no connection, making no sense, perhaps not even grammatically, usually because individuals are too busy following their own agenda. Or it ends up being dull because nobody takes the initiative to introduce something novel. Somewhere between these two extremes, teams will find the space for collaborative creativity as the story unfolds, but it is fragile and subjective, with each individual feeling differently about how much the team is veering from a norm. There may not even be clarity about what the 'norm' is in an improv game; for some, it is keeping the syntax on track, for others it's about concluding a pleasing narrative closure, for others it may need to be dramatic and full of action. This diversity of opinion is reflected in people's attitudes to their work.

Stacey created a matrix summed up in a deceptively simple diagram, bringing the idea of complexity to leadership.[4] I have drawn my own version (see Figure 5.1).

The top right corner, with lots of uncertainty and lots of disagreement, tends to chaos but what about the space between? Where there is *some* disagreement and *some* uncertainty but not an overwhelming amount? That middle area in Figure 5.1 was first described to me as 'bounded instability' but I soon grabbed this potent piece of real estate and renamed it 'LASER leadership'.

FIGURE 5.1   Leadership: LASER

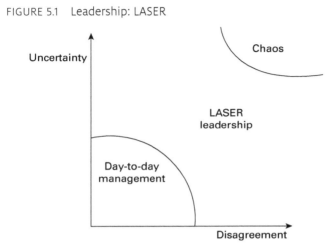

Note: With apologies to Ralph Stacey

What if you reduced uncertainty and disagreement to a minimum? I ask my workshop participants to describe that place from their own experience. They offer a range of words – from harmony or perfection to boring or stasis. All of which could be true, depending on your comfort with disagreement and uncertainty. I have drawn various different versions of the diagram which reflect the variations in how people have told me they feel. Figure 5.2 has harmony in that bottom left corner; is that where you'd like to be, since you're not comfortable with too much uncertainty?

For some people (see Figure 5.3) that bottom left corner is boring; I find that marketing and sales types may well use that word but far from exclusively.

FIGURE 5.2   Leadership: From harmony to Aargh!

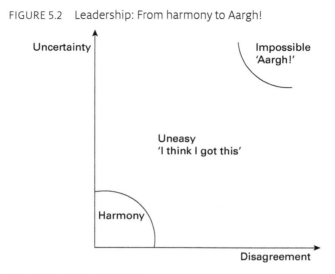

Note: With apologies to Ralph Stacey

FIGURE 5.3   Leadership: From boring to Ouch!

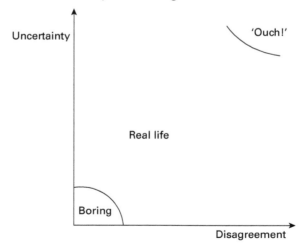

Note: With apologies to Ralph Stacey

I'm being a little cheeky with Figure 5.4. There are times when a leader is making decisions in the bottom left, or discovering in the middle of the graph, but trying to avoid disaster in the top right. How would you describe that very bottom left-hand corner? No uncertainty, no disagreement? Is it even achievable? One mobile phone salesman suggested 'North Korea'. I pointed out that there may be disagreement even there, though perhaps it may not be regularly aired. That bottom left-hand corner may not be possible or only fleetingly so.

Then I read about 'adaptive leadership' coined by Ronald Heifetz and Marty Linsky of Harvard in a 2002 *Harvard Business Review* article called 'A survival guide for leaders', where they wrote: 'Leadership is an improvisational art. You may be guided by an overarching vision,

FIGURE 5.4   Leadership: The 3Ds

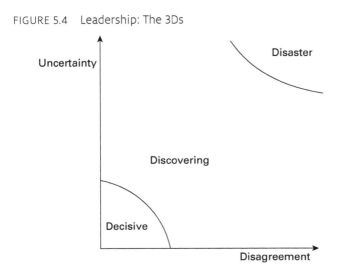

Note: With apologies to Ralph Stacey

clear values and a strategic plan, but what you actually do from moment to moment cannot be scripted.'[5]

For me, there is no better quote on leadership, backing up my hunch that LASER skills are essential. Heifetz differentiated 'technical challenges' (to which you apply existing solutions or knowledge) from 'adaptive challenges' (which need novel solutions).

Ralph Stacey similarly differentiates between ordinary management and extraordinary leadership (see Figure 5.5). You need both. There are plenty of occasions when the leader knows the answer. There is a 'script'. They have been there before, they have expertise. Why pretend otherwise? Pass it on. Save us all a lot of time. Don't let your team wallow in improvisational mud. Be direct, be clear and then

FIGURE 5.5   Ordinary management versus extraordinary leadership

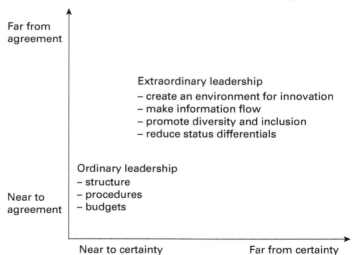

Note: With apologies to Ralph Stacey

we can all go home early. Heifetz calls this type of moment a technical challenge.

On the other hand, what about a novel situation? One the leader has *not* seen before? Suddenly, the leader has to cope with uncertainty and ambiguity. The team looks to her. Her job is not knowing the answer but encouraging curiosity – curating the questions. Suddenly, emotions, status, risk, politics, collaboration and a whole lot of human mess and fuzziness – discomfort – are at play. It's hard to know what it means to lead in an adaptive moment. It may be harder even to identify *when* it is upon you. A big mistake is tackling an adaptive challenge as if it were a technical one. If I am in a play, I'd better turn up at rehearsals, learn my lines and attend the costume fitting. In organizations, it's tempting to lament 'if only we could re-organize the team' or 'we need more money'– easy ways to frame a problem.

This is where my distinction between improv (being responsive in the moment) and 'winging it' (panicking because you forgot the script) is vital. Newton and Darwin again? I have put them in Figure 5.6.

In my workshops, I demonstrate the adaptive environment by having small groups tell a story, one word per person, at a time. It's fun but a bit messy. So I take one out of the group. He or she is now the 'director'. They are not in the game any more as a participant but can offer advice on content (bring in a chicken, forget the sausage, the prince meets the princess) or style (speed up, shorter sentences, switch direction). Then I ask the group to give feedback on their 'leader'. Some leaders do barely anything

FIGURE 5.6   Leadership: Beware Mr Bean

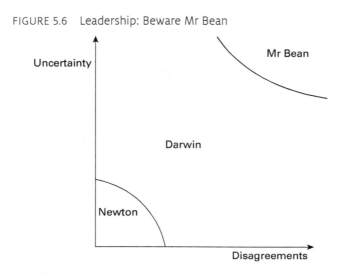

Note: With apologies to Ralph Stacey

and the group are happy. Others think that isn't 'leading'. They'd rather have the type who writes the whole story themselves. Some leaders are sad they are no longer in the gang and want to be playing again.

These are all reflections of real-life leadership dynamics – how much to jump in, how much to step back? Heifetz talks about being on the balcony, watching the dance, as opposed to being in the thick of it. Just as in an improv scene, someone watching from the side might want to wade in to 'solve' the scene, right at the moment when the players onstage have a breakthrough. When to say 'yes to the mess' and when to impose procedures? The emotional toll on a leader, trying to navigate the tricky parameters, can feel overwhelming. Interestingly, when I show leaders the Stacey matrix (Figure 5.1), they relax. They forgive themselves for not knowing, understanding that it is part of their role.

Ever since studying physics, with its uncertainly principle and paired electrons, or Karl Marx and his contradictions (by way of Hegel) I have been a sucker for a paradox. Give me a binary choice that sort of isn't a choice and I'm happy. Then I was introduced to the work of Professor Keith Grint and his topology of problems, power and authority.[6]

This was through my work with the public sector. I have rubbed shoulders with clinicians, health administrators, directors of children's and adults' social services, teachers and education administrators and found enormous talent, integrity and sacrifice among their number.

In late January 2020 I ran a communication day for those who had recently become or were about to become directors of public health. They were having to take phone calls from GPs about how to deal with patients who were showing the signs of what became known as Covid-19. 'Don't send them to hospital!' was their exasperated advice. Having worked with similar groups before, I remember that some issues were due to the fact that they had recently been moved to be under the aegis of the local authority, away from the Department of Health. They had to justify themselves in this new environment and were seen as 'boffins' with slightly ethereal concerns – how do we help people become healthier in general (stop smoking, reduce obesity, exercise more – 'yeah, dream on, mate') or how do we cope with an epidemic ('it'll never happen, who cares about your spreadsheet?').

Wicked problems, clumsy solutions

Grint has three types of problems: critical, tame and wicked. Researching this book, I was disappointed to find he had not coined 'wicked' but then delighted that it (and 'tame') had first been used in 1973 in an article with the thrilling title 'Dilemmas in a general theory of planning' by Horst Rittel and Melvin Webber.[7]

This is a more nuanced picture than Stacey's so the diagram is more complicated (see Figure 5.7). Having done no figures in the book until this chapter, I am now over-whelming you with them. That's because this is the nub of

FIGURE 5.7   Leadership: Wicked, tame, critical

Note: With apologies to Keith Grint

how LASER applies to leadership, and Grint and others have done so much research that it would be churlish not to wallow in it. And it makes sense to those who are grappling with leadership. Actually, these diagrams come as a relief to many of those with whom I have worked. They realize that their job is to be comfortable with moments of not knowing, yet clear when the moment demands that they do adopt a more conventional model of leadership, that it's okay to be 'directive', even if they've attended workshops where 'command and control' gets a very bad press.

A *critical* problem is where the leader just tells everyone what to do. No discussion, no democracy: I'm the boss, the building is on fire, go to that exit now! Then there's a *tame* problem: we can discuss it rationally and find a process to sort it out. We can organize a rota so that there's enough food and room in the canteen; or create a 'reporting line' or gather a team to work on a project with a deadline and budget.

Then we come to *wicked* problems. There is no answer that won't disappoint one group or another. You can see why this is especially relevant in the public sector, with competing aims, varying interest groups and ultimately votes up for grabs.

It is also applicable to the private sector, even though the profit motive may seem to be the only motivator. It's not. Even if it were, it's unclear what may happen in the short term or long term when people are involved. Emotions are at play, 'animal spirits' as John Maynard Keynes would have it. You cannot know the ramifications of decisions in advance. Improv skills are needed. Grint even uses the French word *bricolage* (putting something together by using whatever comes to hand). It might be that you use things for purposes that they weren't originally designed for. It's all about clumsy solutions – multiple partial solutions. You don't just press a lever. You make a move. You curate what Heifetz called the disequilibrium. Unless it's a bit uncomfortable, people don't move or change.

Improv scenes have rocky moments. You have to navigate them. You trust the process. You take the appropriate amount of time. 'The productive zone of distress' is a phrase I love. Distress is when things are out of kilter, perhaps you are (or feel you are) heading towards that top right-hand corner in my uncertainty/disagreement diagrams.

Note that it is *productive*. Distress can be destructive if it goes too far. But without enough of it, will people actually put in the necessary work? 'Never waste a good crisis' says Irwin Turbitt, slightly mis-quoting Winston Churchill.[8] I have learnt so much from Irwin, a former police officer and fellow of various business schools, with a keen eye for what people busy themselves with instead of doing leadership.

Leaders should experiment, testing and learning as they go. Real life is not a series of straight lines. Improv scenes are much more like reality than any 'strategy document'. If your prism is *Yes And*, you need to be much more aware of what you are saying Yes to – what is actually going on, how things are perceived and what people are doing with the 'offers' that come their way. Then there is the And element – what are you actually going to do once you have acknowledged the reality?

Leaders have a responsibility to give everyone a chance to solo – fully expressing themselves – while comping should be celebrated just as much, recognized as an essential part of the job. This all takes the leader's time and energy and is unlikely to show up on a spreadsheet as it involves listening, encouraging, uncomfortable conversations and sometimes no apparent movement. 'Riffing' needs to be prioritized when the temptation is only to measure tasks. People need to be fully aware of what others are doing. Shadowing a colleague for a day should be part of everyone's job. It means we understand the pressures they face and gain a new perspective on our own. Asking team members to try something they haven't done before all adds to a culture of *Yes And…* Yes, this is the reality And we can make something of it.

During the Normandy landings, the Allied forces were able to make decisions at local level, unlike the Nazis. They could be more agile as they became aware of conditions on the ground. I have heard military types mention 'mission command' when I share the improv ethos. Micromanagement is out. The local leader is given the task, the 'why' and the resources but *not* a detailed plan. This fosters autonomy, empowerment and engagement. Why not in business? Give people close to the action power to take decisions. As a customer, I love it when someone on the end of the phone can make something happen just as much as I loathe being fobbed off by 'well I'll have to talk to my manager about that' and the like.

This 'mission command' approach was also used by David Marquet, author of *Turn This Ship Around.*[9] He devolved decision-making down the chain of command on his nuclear sub. He didn't want to be the only one thinking with everyone else following orders. On Twitter in June 2022, he wrote, 'In healthy cultures people take responsibility for their behaviour and leaders take responsibility for the environment. In unhealthy cultures people blame the environment and leaders blame the people.'[10]

Do you really want to be a leader?

During lockdown, I hosted several virtual sessions for a global consultancy for those who had been recently promoted. A great piece of advice was to stop doing a third of what you used to do and find what you should be doing instead. For some, leadership means jettisoning much more than a third of the 'technical' stuff they used to do and entering a place where the majority of their activity is interpersonal – coaxing your team, advocating upwards on their behalf or spending time seeing what is going on elsewhere in the firm, outside the firm, in your sector and beyond.

That doesn't suit everyone. I saw an old video of Laurence J Peter, the Canadian educator, talking about the Peter Principle, an initially satirical notion that people are promoted to their level of incompetence. He cited his local garage, where the brilliant mechanic who looked after his car so well then became the boss of other mechanics and was found wanting. So we need to find a way to help people to be rewarded for doing what they are good at. For some that may not mean leading a team.

> *Managers should ask themselves, 'What can only be done by me?'… It's amazing how little you end up with.*[11] ROBERT HELLER

Groundhog Day

I run an extended workshop called 'Leadership in the Moment'. I share LASER and the models I have described above. Then I make it real. Each participant has to think of a conversation that is coming up that they would like to 'rehearse' and crowdsource some wisdom from others. I suggest it may be a conversation which they keep having but which feels 'stuck'. Like the movie, *Groundhog Day*, things are repeated and they feel frustrated. It might even be a wicked situation, though those tend to be communal with more than one team and a lengthy cast list, with some lead actors but plenty of walk-ons.

For about half of the participants, it is 'How do I manage this person who isn't performing?' For a quarter, it's 'How do I manage my boss' The former is an ever-present part of leadership, so I like to use one such situation to help the whole cohort consider their leadership style. I use a mix of Frank Farrelly's Provocative Therapy (offering absurd options, questioning why this is a problem, literally 'teasing' out what the real issue is) and 'acting it out', my own mix of Keith Johnstone's improv show format *Lifegame* and Augusto Boal's Forum Theatre. (Boal was a Brazilian activist who developed 'Theatre of the Oppressed' in the 1970s. Audience members can speak up as they identify with the situation onstage, so they become 'spect-actors'.)

By 'putting it on its feet' – enacting the conversation – rather than endlessly talking about it, we can gain a new perspective. The volunteer talks a little about the situation, just enough so we can set the scene for another volunteer and me to act it out. I always ask the 'so what' question.

Does it matter that much? What if you did nothing? Why upset the apple cart? 'Do nothing' isn't a bad motto, is it? At least you may avoid making things worse. They normally say they must do something – so I ask, why not sack the miscreant? Wouldn't that be easier? Nope, they don't want to do that either. Invariably we discover that what might be seen as a one-on-one conversation has ramifications across the organization. It's not a machine. It's a living, breathing mess of people, playing for power, consciously and unconsciously.

You've got to suss the system

Office politics

Do you avoid office politics? Well, you can't. Not getting involved is itself a political choice, however much you'd like to be 'above' it. You have to be politically aware for your sake and your team's. You need to get buy-in. You need influence, so you need to understand the power structures – explicit and implicit. The latter may be more 'real'. Alliances may exist between senior and junior folk that cut across the apparent hierarchy.

It means you must be aware of organization-wide issues and longer-term implications rather than simply whether your particular project can be justified rationally. There are often counterintuitive links and loops. It's not just that the boss is friendly with someone you wouldn't expect. Or that you have been brought in specifically to undermine someone else because the CEO doesn't know how to confront the situation. Remember, even if you don't like the smell of such shenanigans, they are going on and you have to be aware of them or you may become a victim of them or accidentally identified as the perpetrator.

Gossip

This is an inevitable part of organizational life. Is it inevitably bad? No. You may have read about mavens in Malcolm Gladwell's *The Tipping Point*.[12] They are people who spread word of mouth. Ahead of me at a conference I once saw the manager of a flagship store for a national brand in Oxford Street, with a turnover of over £30 million a year. Like in many places, there was an assumption that 'something' was being kept from people. It's not *always* wrong. But the idea of 'they' is very potent. Every communication from on high is presumed to be hiding some truth, so staff take it with a pinch of salt. What do they actually believe? The stolen mutterings of those in the know. So this store manager, deliberately and openly, dispensed with edicts from on high and just invited the known mavens to a regular meeting to tell them what was afoot. These people were known to be trusted and listened to by their colleagues. What an efficient, inexpensive and authentic way to distribute your message. It rewarded chatty folk. Why not? It's a good example of understanding that an organization is a human system. Use the momentum that already exists, capitalize on existing networks, choose your moments to be 'top-down' judiciously.

Lots of the models I quote above (and others) see an organization as a 'complex adaptive system'. Or even 'complex responsive processes'. Sounds spooky, doesn't it? It means that each individual, each action is part of the system, affecting it and being affected by it. People talk about their organization or team in the third person. It's not necessarily helpful.

Humberto Maturana and Francisco Varela, the Chilean biologists, came up with the idea of 'autopoiesis'. They applied their concept only to biology. An autopoietic system is 'a network of interrelated component-producing processes such that the components in interaction generate the same network that produced them'.

Then a German sociologist called Niklas Luhmann applied it to social systems. (Bear with me on this.) He said that a social system consisted not of people, or roles or even acts, but of *communications*. And that's what drew me to this – that organizations and teams are but an aggregate of conversations (and emails and texts and more). So whatever you think you are doing or who you are, it is the nature of those communications that matters. They are hard to measure, impossible to be outside of – and it's not obvious how to change the system. Conversation may be your only tool, gossip even – which is just another word for viral communication.

Communication, says Luhmann, involves three inseparable elements: utterance, information and understanding (which also includes *mis*understanding). You choose what information to share and what *not* to share. The utterance is both the how and the why that you choose to share. The understanding is the distinction between the first two, utterance and information. Whatever the intended meaning was, it's what the recipient *understands* that is the reality. And this is ongoing, of course, because any utterance can affect, retrospectively, what we understand of previous communication.

There is a fourth element:

Acceptance or rejection of the meaning of the communication. This fourth selection is already part of the next communication. Understanding does not imply acceptance![13]

Hence why improv is about *Yes And,* not just Yes, why my acronym isn't just **LA** for Listen and Accept. It's what you make of it, what you **S**end back and your **E**xploring assumptions behind the utterance and behind the hearer's context.

Plenty of people dispute whether this concept, which is mostly applied to biology and computer science, translates to business. But I note that so much 'change' is discussed in terms of the existing system yet nothing much actually changes, regardless of the alterations in personnel, org charts or car parking arrangements. People at all levels rail against the system, seemingly powerless to alter the existing rhythms. Does that sound a bit like your company? Did they mention that at the interview? Or in the onboarding?

Whether or not you buy into the scary idea of autopoiesis and complex adaptive systems, I would urge you, at the very least, to entertain it as a useful fiction or model to help reframe how you see the 'game' of office politics. Nothing happens in isolation. There may be reasons to change nothing. But if you want to change things, you have to think of your organization as an ecosystem. Your team may be part of that or apparently separate. At any point the system is evolving in ways which are not linear, coping with the ambiguity of what it is, combined with what it might be. Think of it as organizational ambidexterity, an idea coined by Michael Tushman and Charles O'Reilly in 2004.[14] How good is your firm at 'both exploiting the present and exploring the future'?

You want equilibrium in your operation and production routines, while there may be disequilibrium as customer and staff behaviour alters. I once followed a presentation by a software firm who not only did payroll but looked at who might be a 'flight risk'. That's clever, I thought. Losing people is a pain to the business. They take their expertise and networks with them. Replacing them costs thousands – and you may end up with someone not as good, either technically or in terms of fitting in with the human systems established. So why not look at who has been in the same job for a while, or even at their domestic situation or a recent re-location? These algorithms are a little scary but in hybrid times it's more about the person than the place, isn't it?

So data is handy, but you need to think systemically. What is happening in the system? What is my role in that? What effect is it having on me? Complexity is a splendid buzzword now bandied about but your firm is a system, in which employees, bosses, customers, suppliers and even competitors interact with laws, strategies, ethics, regulations, personal networks, profit (all of which may have their own 'rules') in an evolutionary, dynamic way. There is no such thing as objective truth. Managers can't control people but they can aspire to influence and inspire them. Reframe 'office politics' as diplomacy. Think of it as a positive way to enhance connectivity and inclusion and share good news stories – in front of people, not behind their backs.

Sounds like an improv scene, doesn't it? Actually, it sounds like a whole bunch of improv scenes going on at the same time, with different casts and backstories and audiences, drifting from theatre to theatre. You'd better be humbly optimistic. There is only so much you can do. But it's not nothing. Get on that stage, work with what you have, side-coach where necessary, call a halt to a story that's run its course. Encourage different people to connect and start a new story. But listen out to what is happening and take small bets on what might be emerging.

TOOLBOX   Tips for the LASER leader

- accept what you cannot control
- connect diverse minds
- question habits and assumptions
- reduce differentials in power
- listen to emotions

Does this sound exhausting? I think it is incumbent on senior leaders to find simplicity where they can, while navigating complexity. There are ebbs and flows. Remember the vital 'scaffolding' around the edifice that is the Comedy Store Players' improv team – running order, casting, start time, bar, food menu, insurance, sound and lighting, security and more. Don't denigrate mere 'management', which might include creating simple structures and procedures, orderly decision-making, co-ordination, accountability and giving guidance.

Is leadership fairly simple?

You cannot change things by diktat. Rebrands and change programmes and mission statements and purpose posters have their place but the only really effective way may cost little money but plenty of time. What the boss does and the way they hold conversations day in, day out will be the main predictor of change. So says Roger Martin, Professor Emeritus of Strategic Management at the University of Toronto. He says:

> People watch the leadership and do what the leadership does. Literally the only way that I've seen culture change in the 42 years since I graduated from business school is when a leader sets out to demonstrate a different kind of behaviour and makes that behaviour work.[15]

Too often, leaders go for wholesale change: Professor Martin encourages a 'retail' approach, one conversation at a time.

Some CEOs I work with send out regular communications. Sometimes there is a bit of eye-rolling, 'Oh he's off on one again' (yes, it is still too often a he). But a Stanford study from July 2022 which talks about 'communication calibration' says that under-communication is the bigger sin.[16] Leaders are 10 times more likely to be criticized for that rather than over-communicating. They are seen as less qualified for the role and lacking in empathy.

CASE STUDY MBAW (management by walking around)

I worked with the middle management of a very large team who were building oil rigs. It was a joint venture between an energy conglomerate and a construction firm, though many were on short-term contracts of a year or 18 months. The younger folk had complained of lack of feedback. It had been fairly old school – 'get on with the job and I'll tell you when you've gone wrong.'

For me, it was a daunting first session: a workshop full of men, all of a certain age who had grown up in an era where 'soft skills' weren't a thing, probably not for engineers, anyway. One of them admitted that he thought the session was going to be about how they manage 'up' (feedback to bosses) rather than 'down'. But I ploughed on. I asked each of them to think of some piece of feedback that had made a real difference – perhaps from a parent, relative, teacher, mentor. I was able to bring out what my research had told me – that feedback needs to be timely, authentic and personal. Not generic, not six months later, but with the presumption that it could be put into practice. By the end of the day, the tough crowd I had experienced in the morning had warmed to the task and come up with their own list of five top tips. The participant I had found most difficult took it upon himself to write up the list and circulate it within an hour of the end of workshop.

We did talk about senior leadership. I asked my usual questions. Are they on a separate floor? How often do you see them? Do they have a better coffee machine? Answers – *yes, not much* and *definitely.* I ran the session for a second cohort at the end of which the top bods popped in. Chatting to the Big Boss, I asked if he had ever thought about just popping down to the floor below and wandering about. Just for people to see him would be great, I said.

'Me?' He asked. 'Why would they want to see me?' I tried to be diplomatic and explained that they may say nothing, or it might be just a hello or they may feel they could approach him with something substantive. It was clear that he didn't think that was his job.

Contrast that with Vittorio Colao, who was Group CEO of Vodafone. There was a shop at the bottom of their HQ in Paddington in London. Every day, I heard, he would pop in to chat with the staff about what customers were wanting. I also liked the idea that no matter how senior the executive, they still had to go through the normal retail process when ordering a new phone: no VIP treatment, so they experienced what it was like to be a real customer if things didn't work out.

Leadership deficit

So often, I observe that the leadership deficit is due not to nasty, Dickensian, crack-the-whip-type behaviour but because people don't step up. They need to put on a mantle – for the sake of their team – but they seem unwilling. Perhaps they don't think they are special or think they don't even deserve to be in charge. But people need to know that there is someone in charge. I guess this is why there are so many leadership books and courses.

Leadership energy

It may be as simple as the *energy* you bring as leader. In a *Harvard Business Review* (*HBR*) article from April 2022 Emma Seppälä and Kim Cameron state that 'leaders are the single most important factor in accounting for an organisation's performance.'[17] They talk about 'positive relational energy'. (Does that make you feel uneasy? Be Positive is a dangerous motto. It can lead you to blame yourself if you listen only to those motivational gurus who tell you *that you can do anything if only you really believe it.* Not true. It doesn't mean you shouldn't put your mind to it though.)

Dr Cameron says that it's not about being extrovert either, that anyone can develop this energy because it is about showing 'compassion, gratitude, kindness, forgiveness and integrity'. A leader's positive energy is the single most powerful predictor of organizational performance.[18] The good news is that, unlike physical energy, it tops itself up when spread.

This reminds me of 'surgency', which the *Dictionary of Psychology* defines as a personality trait that features cheerfulness, spontaneity, responsiveness and sociability.[19] I came across this word in a brilliant book called *Messengers* by Steve Martin (not that one) and Joseph Marks, which looked at why some people are listened to and some are not – regardless of whether they are right or wrong, intelligent or not.[20] It seems that charisma is associated with people who have surgency, use metaphor and story, use expressive body language and... *can improvise.*

All of these can be taught. But you have to want to learn. Now we are in a hybrid world, where we've realised that the big, swaggery, gung-ho CEO speech in an enormous auditorium isn't the only way of doing things. So the introvert leader who prefers small groups or even giving presentations from their own home can feel more comfortable.

New leadership skills

Raffaella Sadun (Charles E Wilson Professor of Business Administration at Harvard Business School) and colleagues, writing in the *Harvard Business Review* in summer 2022, said that things have changed.[21] An executive search firm examined 5,000 job descriptions that it had developed for clients from 2000 to 2017. If you wanted to be in the C-suite, you still had to be good at the finance and operational stuff but they were becoming less important in favour of interpersonal skills – self-awareness and awareness of how others think and feel, listening, ability to work and communicate with different people. This isn't just for CEOs; it's true for CFOs and C-*other-letter*-Os.

With large, complex organizations the senior folk can't just do the technical stuff. Ironically, as automation takes over, they have to cope with a diverse workforce, unexpected events, and make decisions where there may be conflict or uncertainty. The idea of a 'servant leader'[22] who prioritises 'listening, persuasion, access to intuition and foresight, use of language, and pragmatic measurements of outcomes' is appealing, but we should not overlook that, at certain moments, the best service a leader can deliver is to stand at the front of the room and be seen.

So there's a big focus on these skills when recruiting people – psychometric testing, simulations and references. But is it crazy of me to ask: if there is a technology – improv – out there which can help develop these very skills, why not use it?

The benefits of humble optimism

This was the title of a side-bar in an article in the *Harvard Business Review* from May 2003. I bought a hard copy and have kept it. Humble Optimism is just what we improv performers have. We can't do it on our own, each performance is novel and risky but we have trusted the process enough times in the past that we can feel positive about the unknown outcome. The side-bar was from an article entitled, 'The high cost of accurate knowledge'.[23] Amusingly, in the same edition of the *HBR* was an article entitled, 'Don't trust your gut'.

The thrust of the first piece was that if top executives accepted that they couldn't control their environment, then their firms changed and *the better* they did. Their mindset (or 'interpretative orientation') was 'consistent enough to filter information and focus attention but loose enough to allow improvisation and speedy adjustments'. So they knew they couldn't know everything but felt confident they could cope with change and they passed that confidence down to their teams. For middle and junior managers, it's good to have accurate data. For senior leaders, it's about managing ambiguity and creating momentum, whatever incoming flak they receive from outside. But I remember Don Sull asking that MBA class at London Business School if they had access to up-to-date 'close of day' figures in the mid-2000s and none did. I spoke at a Gartner conference once and one of their senior folk confided that there were plenty of examples where data was used well – for example, in not recruiting too many of the same type of people – but plenty where there was so much data that nobody knew what to do with it or even knew it existed. Data is always in the past tense. I know that now, with analytics and dashboards and the like, it can be very recent but there is still something of the 'rear-view mirror'. So when dealing with the future, you can never know. You are in the improv arena so why not have the humility but boldness to borrow some LASER skills?

Strategy

There is a lot of guff talked about Strategy. Is it even a thing? It certainly sells a lot of places on business school courses and gives rise to mountains of internal PowerPoint presentations. Strategy is intangible. Execution is real. What goes wrong between strategy and execution?

I once shared a cab on a long journey back to the airport in Switzerland with a strategy professor from a top US university. We discussed what this S word means in reality. The essential argument could be polarized between 'do you just stick to your guns and ignore reality or do you just blow with the prevailing winds?' He assumed that I, being an improviser, would go with latter. I pointed out that, for a show, the externals are well structured (start and finish time, cast, insurance, security, as I have said) and that we tend to have a 'microstructure' in scenes which is story: what is the quest, what are the obstacles, how are they overcome.

'Strategy is running as fast as I can', said the UK CEO of a large global management consultancy at a private meeting I attended. Don't pretend things are predictable and stable, when clearly they are not. The LASER mindset can cope with, and capitalize on, disruption.

Is 'efficiency' a flawed strategy? It may mean you have no room for manoeuvre. 'Culture eats strategy for breakfast' is the quote often misattributed to Peter Drucker.

Certainly, no amount of PowerPoint and 'town halls' will make a difference if people haven't bought in to your plan. Often I am invited to run a session where a shiny new 'strategy' is being unveiled by the CEO. To most people it means nothing. Half the exec team ignore it anyway. Then two years later the CEO has gone, never to be mentioned again and hey presto – there's a brand new strategy to underwhelm us all. You might think an improviser shouldn't opine too much on strategy but let me quote a military man and former president of the United States, Dwight D Eisenhower: 'Plans are worthless, but planning is everything.'

You have to have a plan; you can't be in the moment all the time; you need to budget. For me it means that you have to adapt, but that doesn't mean you don't prepare. The brain cannot help wanting to predict the future so it makes sense to guide that process a little. When I worked alongside Don Sull at a London Business School MBA session, he counselled against anything as clear as a three-year plan. Just have some woolly 'mission' with some vague sense of the direction of travel. Anything too specific is a hostage to fortune. In early 2020, who knew we would have to rethink all our working processes? Yet the most agile organizations moved fast. Even the simplest adaptations can make a difference – just something easy like sending laptop stands means your people are less likely to ruin their posture and think better.

I still don't really know what strategy actually means – other than 'stop doing this and do more of that'. One very clever partner at a Big Four consultancy told me it was about making sure you are playing on the right pitch. Do you know what you are actually good at? Often, it seems to me, strategy comes down to energy. Where are we putting our energy? Strategy shouldn't be the preserve of just the top table. But it should also be translatable into everyday actions. Your business strategy may look great on paper but do you have a *leadership* strategy – that encourages the right relational energy – that fits with it?

Leadership in hybrid times

This is the new frontier. How on earth do you lead people if you rarely come into contact with them? You have to work even harder on the 'soft' skills. When some jobs are designated as remote and others as 'we expect to see you in the office quite a lot' it can be tricky. Whether in person or remote, isn't it about the outcomes you expect? Leadership priorities in lockdown apparently changed to be less about technical things, more about well-being. Why did it take a pandemic for that to happen?

I think that ultimately, team leaders are going to have to decide on the mix of virtual versus in-person arrangements. Democracy and surveys can help, but be humbly aware of your own priorities. What is the sweet spot for you? Three days in the office? Don't make it something that doesn't work for you. A knackered, truculent leader is a useless leader. Ultimate flexibility is not possible, transparency is. With all of my clients, there is still plenty of letting the dust settle as the right balance is found.

There are many reasons why I dislike Microsoft Teams. For my workshop purposes, Zoom is way better for half a dozen reasons. But a major issue for those on Teams much of the day is that you can be contacted too easily, via another Teams channel. People ignore Do Not Disturb prompts. One person told me she was in a Teams video meeting when she was called on Teams by her CEO. She didn't want to leave the meeting but was scared to turn him away. He could see she was on Teams, so why wasn't she answering? She couldn't see a way out other than by logging out completely.

I mentioned the report on the future of work before (see Chapter 3) by Professors Debbie Bayntun-Lees and Andy Cross. They came up with the idea of the 'connecting leader' for whom the new skills will be much more 'relational' and 'facilitatory'. Leaders need to role-model collaborative behaviours. 'Intervene for inclusion' seems a wise idea. They need to think about ways to redistribute power and create 'ways of working' which fit the person and the purpose.

A leader divides their time between one-on-ones, team moments and external moments. For each, they need to choose face to face or virtual. Updates, analysis, co-ordination and information-sharing can be done virtually. It's generally thought that innovation, trust and 'culture' need face to face. But does this mean there is a tendency to wait till everyone is together? The proactive leader should find ways to create the psychological safety and sense of play in virtual team meetings. By the same token, the leader should be out there advocating for their team. Again, don't wait for the in-person moment to do this. If people are working 60 per cent or even 80 per cent virtually they simply must find ways to forge trust and connection virtually – a cheery email, a tight video call or phone chat or LinkedIn message have to be part of the networking nexus.

As far as your team is concerned, you may need to have difficult conversations about the new arrangements. How do you discipline someone on Teams?

Can you hear me?...
You're on Mute. Well, never mind – you're sacked.

I'm just putting that in writing – in Chat. Cheerio.

Appraisals, feedback, performance management, yada yada...

The whole way organizations manage performance has always struck me as strange. It's often a long time after the event and counterproductively formal. Yearly appraisals? We in the creative world don't wait months to give 'feedback'. It's central. It's part of the daily discourse. I was part of some research for Korn Ferry who found that conventional 'performance management' really isn't working.[24] So they looked at worlds where it isn't just a ritual performed now and then, looking backwards, but rather a constant part of a dynamic process, as the 'leader' (say, the director of a show) judges the moment, the tone and the forum to share feedback so as to create momentum for a better outcome for the individual and the team. They spoke to dancers, actors, chefs, musicians, sports people and the military. In our world, feedback is built into the day-to-day rhythm of work, not stored up (or vaguely remembered long after the moment) to be shared in annual performance reviews. I drew upon my experience acting in and directing scripted plays, being in movies, as well as performing improv.

We know that feedback is highly personalized. The director gives 'notes' and takes responsibility for how they are enacted. The rest of the cast can help ('I'll move earlier so you can get into position') too. It's not just that we are used to taking feedback, we would be surprised if it were *not* given. It is part of the daily rhythm (that word again) and the director 'owns' the notes just as much as the performer. It is assumed that the performer receiving the feedback *can and will* adapt or improve and that the director will be there to notice and adapt if needs be.

There is always a (possibly split-second) decision for the director: how ready is the recipient for this feedback, what's our shared history up to this point, can they put it into practice? You don't get that by everyone writing it down in some 360 feedback process. Giving feedback is an essential part of leadership. Lack of feedback is always construed in some way.

Timing, context and content are vital. Don't assume that the way you like to receive feedback is shared by others. It is an imprecise science but you will not be serving your team if you do not actively look for moments to give praise and ways to address below-par performance. This is where a few well-timed words – spoken, texted or post-it noted – can have a great effect. And the opposite is true. So if you are a leader or you are led, whether giving or receiving feedback, bear this in mind. None of us is perfect and we can all express ourselves badly on occasion.

Leadership with a small L

The job of the leader is to 'capture the moment', to frame the story of where we are and where we are heading. Are we steady as she goes or hurtling down a helter-skelter? Is it a time to buckle down, to relax, to think afresh, to expand or not? You need to be able to gain the attention of the right people – your team, your bosses, your peers, your clients, your suppliers. You need to be comfortable with ambiguity, making sense of the now, yet creating momentum for the future. Can you read the room *and* lead the room?

CHAPTER SIX

Meetings

Three stages of career development are:
I want to be in the meeting, I want to run the meeting,
I want to avoid meetings.[1]

Is that how you feel? I had this nagging feeling that I should write a chapter on meetings. My other chapter titles are all 'big picture' but there's no getting away from the fact that 'meetings' are the main conduit for so much. You can't achieve much without them and they are often the forum for all the big topics I've looked at so far – where creativity, collaboration and communication can actually happen or be stifled. So you need to make sure you are having the impact you want. That may mean changing your tactics where before you just turned up, without a plan and not enough awareness in these meeting moments.

Meetings: Why? Just why?

From over two decades of paddling in the murky waters of corporate life, I know that people find them frustrating. Yet so much time is spent having to endure them, now with the added complication of remote etiquette. Surely they can be improved? Wouldn't you like to feel a sense of accomplishment after a meeting rather than a sense of angst? Do you feel you have too many meetings or they are not effective enough and that much of the real business of your organization could be done elsewhere?

Meetings do not have to be boring, unproductive or unpleasant. But they require work from you and your colleagues. Not just the boss, but certainly including them. Does anyone actually keep an eye on whether the organization's meetings add up to something of real value? Apparently, in 2020 a middle manager spent 35 per cent of their time in meetings and an upper manager even more – approximately 50 per cent.[2]

You can find all sorts of stats about how much time and money is wasted. There are various methodologies but Steven Zauderer (CEO of CrossRiverTherapy) found an impressive array of numbers.[3] Just a few choice ones: there are around 55 million meetings held each week in the United States (over 1 billion a year) and 71 per cent are unproductive. But, apparently, people think 15 minutes is a good length of time for a meeting and a majority prefer them in the morning. Wouldn't that be a useful starting point?

Maybe some meetings are okay when in person, because biscuits are laid on, maybe even free tea and coffee. Plus you have a change of scenery. But for virtual meetings you have to bring your own refreshments. A meeting can be the arena for showing off. Or for your idea to take flight – or get squashed in a snake-pit of politics or a marsh of misunderstanding.

You need to be good at meetings

You may be good at spreadsheets. You may be up to date on the latest cross-border digital rights law. But if you can't win at meetings, your prospects will suffer. You need to get good at meetings – internal and external. By meetings I mean more than two people. One-on-one is a different game, as I have said, and can be really effective.

CASE STUDY   Lean in, sit up

I worked with a management consultant who was enormously clever, accomplished, respected. But he came across as diffident, apologetic even. His field was life science, a huge opportunity for successful investment. He was about to go to persuade some money people to back a project. He had a compelling case. Under my cross-examination he dared admit as much. But I had to draw it out of him. His demeanour played down his strong story. We tried various things. I 'acted as' him for a moment, just repeating back what I had heard, but as if I were of high status, imagining these financiers to be my equals.

A lightbulb moment. 'Ah. I see', he said, 'You were sitting up.' Was I? He showed me that I had put my hands on the table, rather than resting them in my lap. And that was it. That was not all I was doing but for him it unlocked everything – voice projection, pace, eye contact. He was transformed. (In fact, I had been speaking slower, taking more breaths, with no disfluencies and strong eye contact.)

How many millions of dollars are wasted by meetings?

A 2022 survey by Steven Rogelberg, of the University of North Carolina, found that 'organizations could save an estimated $25,000 or more per employee per year by reducing "unnecessary" meeting attendance.'[4] Professionals spend over a third of their time in meetings but they'd like to decline about a third of those, but only actually decline 14 per cent. Not many people talk about the option of declining. What if they cut out unnecessary meetings? Rogelberg estimates that firms of a hundred people would save $2.5 million a year. For those of 5,000 people, he reckons the number is $100 million. Crikey.

Has remote working meant that meetings are better organized now? Or worse? How many hours a week do you spend preparing a status update for a meeting? How many of the people in the meeting already know the information being shared?

Do you 'multitask' during meetings? Are you more distracted in virtual meetings? Do you feel okay if it's a work thing that's taking your attention? It's not like you're on Tinder or TikTok during the CFO's insightful update on 'Risk Profiling Going Forward', is it? Do we try to multitask less on video calls than on phone calls? Some people have told me that, for them, video calls are actually *more* focused than in-person meetings. Do you find external or internal ones easier? At least with a client meeting, you might have someone on your side. In internal meetings, it could be everyone for themselves.

At Amazon (as reported by *The Times* in 2018), meetings start in silence.[5] There's no PowerPoint. People read the documents/memo for the first half hour. Then discuss them. How would that change the power dynamics in your organization?

Often I am brought in to firms to cope with the phenomenon of bright and capable people who contribute plenty in one-on-one conversations or with their peers, but fall apart in front of senior folk and at larger meetings. So, extrapolating from that, does that mean that those who DO rise up the ladder are good at meetings? Does being good at their actual job count for less? Maybe. But being good at meetings IS your job, isn't it? So you need to up your game. And you can.

What are your frustrations with meetings?

Perhaps you feel that not much is achieved or that they meander on after the real business is done. Maybe loudmouths dominate and you feel your time and energy could be better spent elsewhere. Some people argue the same points over and over again or the opposite – they just check out. Good ideas may be lost as point-scoring is prioritized.

Unless you do something, these frustrations will continue. You have to be proactive to make sure, whatever the systems and structures and personnel, that you put in the work to ensure your meetings are productive, whether you are running them or not.

How to be a meeting maestra or maestro

I will look at two different roles in a meeting: the meeting organizer and the meeting attendee. The leader of the team should not always be the meeting facilitator. Someone else will run things differently, perhaps bringing in different voices and giving you chance to listen better.

I'm thinking of 'bread & butter' meetings: those internal gatherings where you report back, discuss future project and tasks are assigned; or external meetings with clients – updates, pitches and more. On Zoom, I would say if it's more than two Zoom 'pages' of attendees (say 25), then it's more of a 'webinar' or broadcast. With larger numbers still we are talking 'town hall' or 'all hands'. At that size, it's more about giving presentations. I will deal with that in the chapter on 'Storytelling'.

If you are a meeting attendee

Sometimes, do you think the meeting itself might have gone okay but you feel that *you* could have done better? Give yourself broad objectives for meetings. Essentially you want three things from meetings:

- make yourself heard
- carry your ideas
- collaborate well with others

Prepare yourself

Whether it's your meeting or not, decide what you want from it, then ask what *you* will bring to it. Or are you too busy to allot time to plan? If you are, it's likely that you ended up at a previous meeting with too much on your plate. Learn from that. Many of my coachees observe with a mix of admiration, jealousy and irritation that person who can somehow redirect any 'actions' arising from a meeting to anyone but themselves. Don't be that person. But see how they do it and don't let them do it to you. Be brave if you spot it being done to another. Call it out.

TOOLBOX Pre-meeting hacks

- Look at the agenda – what do you have to say on each item?
- Put in a side-meeting or three: who can you share thoughts with? Create allies. Check out those who may oppose you.
- Prepare a line or two for each topic.
- Have a clear objective in mind.
- What actions/jobs will be up for grabs – which do you want to do or to avoid?

Optimize your impact

Language and communication style are learnt. How we talk is affected by our experience, as is how we listen. Often I coach people to find the small tweaks that mean their ideas will be better received. This could be their pattern of speaking: tone of voice, speed and volume. Too many think their style is a 'given' and that it's 'natural'. They are not even aware they have a go-to style, which may not be creating the impact they want. Does your nervousness come out as under-energized? Does your natural modesty masquerade as aloofness? Does your openness to others' ideas mean you don't contribute your own? Or the opposite – you're so keen to participate you eclipse others? Whether you consider yourself an introvert or an extrovert you can work on improving your impact. It is not a given, so notice what you (and others) do and whether it's effective or not.

DO YOU FALL APART IF YOU HAVE TO SPEAK IN A LARGE MEETING OR IN FRONT OF BIG WIGS?

Don't sabotage yourself. You can and should avoid 'Um, err, y'know, like'. These don't help you sound confident. Your writing will contain none of these disfluencies but your unrehearsed speech may well. Because you will be more nervous in front of certain other people your work may not get the hearing it deserves.

Do you find you can't think of ideas or even cogent responses in the moment? Whereas others seem to do so easily? My answer – cheat! Why not prepare in advance? Use Voice Memo (or Voice Recorder) to rehearse. We all hate the sound of our own voice. Get over it and listen back to the recording of yourself. At least it's not as bad as watching a video of yourself. This process will also help you when preparing a full presentation or pitch. (More at the end of the chapter on 'Storytelling'.)

I told the head of a big consulting firm about Voice Memo. Three years later we worked together again and now she swears by it, to create a presentation – and then to help get comfortable with it once a final version has emerged. You can listen to it in the car, on the train or while in the gym. Your attention will waver, your mind will wander but it's still going in.

EVEN IF YOU'VE REHEARSED SOME THINGS YOU MAY LET YOURSELF DOWN IN THE MOMENT

Avoid apologetic language: 'This may just be me', 'Do you mind if...' are obvious linguistic ways to shoot yourself in the foot, but we often do it with our tone of voice too. Do you fumble for the next phrase? Do you keep saying, 'Well, I may be wrong but...'? Do you fall over, verbally, at the end of your sentence, inviting your contribution to be dismissed? These things are being judged all the time. We are trying to understand others' meaning but also to evaluate each other. Sounds ghastly, doesn't it? Well, it's natural. And you can improve. Listen to yourself on your phone and see if the messenger (you) is letting down your message with an 'um' or waffly self-defeating verbiage. After many years of trying to help people I just say – take a breath instead. In that moment where your mouth could go AWOL, take in some oxygen.

UNDERSTAND YOUR BREATH

Breath supports your voice. Listen back to yourself when you try out a few lines. Do your utterances sound like a deflating balloon or like a bouncing ball? You can hear the difference. Think of your breath carrying your words at least a couple of metres, rather than letting them tumble weedily onto your chin. It's simple. We speak on the out-breath, so consciously pause to breathe in (through your nose) before you commit to words. In that moment (just a second) your brain and body combine to take oxygen, your voice and thoughts sync up, so that what comes out will have more power. Practise seeing if you can take enough air such that it reaches your belly. Your voice will come out stronger so people will listen. Start strong and it will take you all the way to the end of your chosen phrase. And keep noticing your breath. To support your voice, you will need to breathe every three to seven words.

This is something for which so many people have thanked me. We forget that our body is not just a trolley carrying our brain around. It affects the influence we have (or fail to have) on others.

ADAPT YOUR STYLE

Please never say, 'I speak as I find' or 'That's the way I am, take it or leave it.' No. You are different with the news-agent, with your Mum, with your niece, with the doctor, with George Clooney. I read this could be called 'code-switching'.[6] For some, it is how under-represented groups might subsume their own identity so as to fit in, which is problematic. I would rather think of this as being agile, situationally adapt and positively managing the impact you are having on others. Be aware of language, tone of voice, where you sit, the running order, even your hunger levels. These all could affect your impact. Flex your style.

Have you noticed communication differences with men and women, or with different cultures, different nationalities, different job roles? Everything you say communicates an idea but also is negotiating status. We co-create status, in the moment. You can give it to others, without realizing – through your body language, eye contact, tone of voice and what you say, perhaps picking up and reinforcing another's point. As a leader this can be a powerful way of bringing others in and reducing the hierarchy gap, if handled well. On the other hand, I see people undermining their points through subtle, overly deferential, 'non-power plays' (what exactly is the opposite of a power play?).

TOOLBOX Meeting tips: Be aware of the physical, verbal and emotional

- *Eye contact:* Look around the table, not just at the person you know or the one you deem most important. In virtual, keep an eye out for how non-speakers react to what is being said. Look at the camera when speaking.

- *Listen:* Show you are listening with eye contact and body language. Jot notes so you can pick up points made by other people – a great way both to keep people awake by referencing names and to cement alliances.

- *Avoid jargon:* Use words your 11-year-old niece or nephew could understand. Clear language encourages clear thinking.

(One great story a female client told me. This guy was using a lot of jargon, including a particular acronym. Eventually, she asked others if they knew what it meant. No, they didn't. Did the speaker? Gingerly, he said what it stood for. His boss then revealed that he thought it stood for something else.)

- *Accentuate the positive:* Find things that can be celebrated rather than bemoaned. Do you want to be associated with bad news and be seen as a grump? A psychological study showed that if a person gives you a hot drink, you think of them as warm; an iced drink means you feel they are cold.[7] Why not associate yourself with positive vibes?

- *Summarize the points of agreement:* So you look like a team player. Because you will be one.

Sex-based differences?

Researching US children playing together in the nineties, Deborah Tannen found girls tend to focus on rapport in their conversations and boys tend to focus on status.[8] The girls studied tended to spend a lot of time talking, with a single best friend or with a small group. They downplayed ways in which one may be 'better' than others and found ways to show they are all the same. Sounding too sure of yourself could make you unpopular. They might be looking to balance their needs with others.

Boys may have played in larger groups but not everyone was equal. They emphasized rather than downplayed high status. Being 'bossy' was expected of the higher-status boys. Language was a way to negotiate status, a display of abilities and knowledge.

Have things changed since then? I know plenty of men and women who do not conform to these stereotypes. But does your organization or a particular colleague privilege one approach? Whatever your sex, try to be aware of how best to manage your impact. Recently a senior leader at a well-known global tech company told me he was much happier being inclusive, encouraging people, letting them find their own way. But, he admitted, now and again they plead with him, 'please just tell us what to do'. The executives I often coach are men, who may be lovely to work alongside but, for the sake of their team, they need to play a different game when they're at the 'top table'.

CASE STUDY   Boys will be boys? Really?

When I was running a workshop for an international consultancy, we were looking at a client situation. There was a moment when one of the men responded to a question by saying, 'depends how pretty she is'. It may have been classed by some as 'casual' sexism. I say that it should be taken more seriously than that. You won't be surprised to learn that such a moment is not unique. But it is unusual. This man, and the other few men who laughed, were not teenagers. Some were from countries that have – deservedly or not – a reputation for a certain macho attitude. Some were not.

My response is always to immediately satirize the miscreant so I said, 'I don't expect she was as pretty as you. Do you find it hard in business – being so beautiful?' He laughed. The moment passed and the man's demeanour showed that I had made my point. Afterwards all five of the women in the room at the time were gathered in a huddle and called me over. They had not seen misogyny called out in this way. I was surprised. My intent was to stop the behaviour immediately, make the men ashamed but not so ashamed that the 'froideur' in the room would affect the rest of the workshop. Unsurprisingly, they said the dodgy comment was not unprecedented. The senior women could 'take' it, they said, but they were concerned about the women in the lower echelons.

I tell this story not to blow my own New Man Trumpet, but to wonder how much has moved on. Discrimination, like any virus, adapts to new circumstances. It may be much more subtle these days. Or not.

Question: Does it actually have to be a meeting?

Once you've established what need is being addressed, ask if it could be met in other ways. Could it actually be a phone call, a series of emails or even an asynchronous meeting using collaborative software? We use asynchronous communication all the time – you read a text or email or WhatsApp message or listen to a voice mail at some time after I have sent it.

(Asynchronous means we all contribute at different times – of our own choosing. It's the opposite of synchronous, from the Greek sunkhronos *from* sun *(together)* + khronos *(time). See also* Synchronicity – *the fifth and final studio album by The Police. It included the hits 'Every Breath You Take', 'King of Pain' and 'Wrapped Around Your Finger'. Surely each can be taken as an oblique reference to business meetings?)*

If the answer is yes, it DOES have to be a meeting...

You need to ask yourself if it needs to be in person or remote. If it is to be virtual, does it have to be on video throughout? There might be certain sections which are emotionally or mentally draining so need a different kind of focus, maybe with camera off. But this decision doesn't have to be pre-announced. Who needs to be there? It's so easy to CC anyone and everyone. Could it even be two separate, shorter meetings? Don't default to an hour or half an hour unthinkingly. I know of one company in the UK whose calendar automatically plumbs in meetings of 25 or 45 minutes. Why not aim for 15/20 minutes of actual meeting?

When your agenda is ready, be sure others are ready to introduce their item. Send out brief pre-reads. Make it clear what will happen in the meeting and what shape the outcomes are likely to be. Arrive 10 minutes early and welcome people. Allow time for gossip before and after. If it's a client meeting, it's better if people do not introduce themselves but someone else does. Otherwise we mumble and 'throw away' who we are. You can big each other up and the warmth and respect in what you say is contagious.

If you are running the meeting, in person or virtual…

Start and finish on time. You will have to stop loudmouths and chatterboxes hijacking the gig, while bringing in the quieter voices. Encourage everyone to say something early, so it feels less of a big deal when they want to speak later. Spot side issues and tangents – decide which channel to reroute them towards. Lay out the proposition or the 'exam question'.

In virtual, encourage responses in Chat. It can be useful to bring in lots of contributions in a short space of time. David Rock of the Neuroleadership Institute encourages this 'parallel processing'.[9] It's an advantage that video meetings have over face to face. A neuroscientist, he also encourages the use of 'digital body language' like thumbs up or down (not the emoji but where you actually gesture and move your body). Decide if some questions could then be considered in smaller numbers in breakout rooms. This is a good way to keep the momentum should attention waver. That might also be helped by having a different person speaking, a different slide, a different question to address in the Chat or even bringing in a physical prop, which wakes up the viewer's brain as it makes us focus on perspective and depth of field.

With remote teams, make time for looser moments. These can be scheduled – a virtual coffee zone/smokers' corner – or explicitly invite people to voluntarily join a meeting early before the task begins, or stay late once the agenda has been covered. Allow space for informal catch-up and gossip. One organization I worked with found that employees felt, during remote working, that there was too much formal communication and not enough informal.

Organize someone else to take notes (don't assume this should be a junior person) so that you have a very clear follow-up – with action points and key decisions clarified. Distribute soon after. Maybe check in with a trusted person if the notes accord with their recollections and contain no 'hand-grenades'.

Leaders and meetings: makers' and managers' schedules

I came across a brilliant blog from 2009 from Paul Graham about 'makers' and 'managers'. Makers (in which he includes himself, a programmer) have a unit of time which tends to be half a day or more as they focus on a project.[10] A manager will tend to divide their day into one-hour blocks, as they have multiple projects and people to curate. They may not need to 'get their head down' in the same way.

Meetings can really impede the maker's progress. John Cleese suggested that it takes 90 minutes to really get in the zone when writing.[11] Interrupt the flow and you've lost more than the actual time. Paul Graham said, 'I find one meeting can sometimes affect a whole day.' Meetings and making are different modes of working. Having a whole day without meetings lifts the spirits of the maker – and vice-versa. Even the thought of a meeting at the end of a morning might temper what you feel can be achieved beforehand.

This rings so true. The boss's job may consist of little more than meetings – checking up, hearing updates and often telling everyone what happened in other meetings. Just as the hip, Hoxton start-up tech-type gradually might have to trade in their jeans for a suit as their job becomes less software and more soft skills, so 'makers' will feel under pressure to show face rather than show results.

I have met some great leaders who glide by an in-person meeting where I'm explaining my thing, listen to what I say, add two succinct comments which show they've totally 'got' it, apologize for having to leave – unnecessarily, as it happens, because we all know that the business is done, I've got the gig and we can all carry on with our lives. The only regret is that those posh boardroom biscuits remain uneaten.

So leaders really need to be aware of how they can influence meetings – in tone, duration and number. We're all aware – even unconsciously – of status. We adapt our style. I met one leader from a heavy machinery firm who kept asking *not* to be invited to meetings. His people seemed to want him to be there, to give some blessing to proceedings. But they had his blessing already. Another senior executive found it frustrating that any of his loose talk – it might be a suggestion, a comment – would soon crystallize into an ORDER FROM ON HIGH.

Status, of course, is real but dynamic. Job title seems more 'real' but may have little overlap with status. Don't we all know that receptionist or 'back-office' person who is just brilliant and everyone kowtows to them? Or the boss that everyone ignores? That's status in action. You want to elevate your status so that your ideas are heard *and* so you can then encourage others. Huge gaps in status do not lead to productive meetings.

So Status is not just what we take. It's what we give. I find some leaders actually don't feel comfortable wearing the Cloak of Leadership. No matter how much they try to slip it off, it keeps being put on them by others. Part of being a leader is understanding each person's idea of leadership as well as your own, then flexing it. Each moment, each situation may require a different guise – or disguise. You might have to 'fake' it until it becomes unconscious.

So what is your 'linguistic style'? How direct or indirect are you? Do you use jokes, stories, questions (rhetorical or otherwise), metaphor, florid vocabulary? We tend to pay attention to those whose style is similar to our own. If you are in charge, be aware of this. If you are not in charge, also be aware of this. By the way, leaders tend to have a higher opinion of their own meetings than the participants.[12]

Should we ban meetings on certain days?

One tech team I worked with made a policy in lockdown of no video-conferences on Fridays. Another firm in India experimented with a 'no emails on Wednesday' rule. The head of a big practice in a Big Four consultancy in lockdown alternated between an 'introvert' week and an 'extrovert' week. In the latter, he would get out and about, meeting clients outside cafes, in parks or churchyards, as well as fellow partners who lived nearby, even though they may not be working in similar sectors. Such radical, creative reimaginings of meetings are essential.

Can you give yourself an introvert day, at least? Where you spend time reflecting, preparing or putting together proposals? I used to live near John Morton, the brilliant writer–director of BBC TV's *W1A*.[13] I would often bump into him in the park. We'd nod and he'd say, 'I'm writing.' The phrase *solvitur ambulando* roughly translates as 'it is solved by walking', often attributed to St Augustine. I wonder if any mystic ever said 'it is solved by having a three-hour meeting in a stuffy windowless room' or 'only a Friday afternoon of John going through a hundred slides on Teams will unlock deep wisdom'?

The meeting is not going away

'It is the fundamental unit of white collar working life', said Laura Simpson (Global Director at advertising and marketing company, McCann World Group) in a superb BBC Radio programme in August 2022.[14] Though we might no longer be meeting in glassy buildings, in suits, but in a spare bedroom, wearing track pants, we have work to do. Instead of moaning that virtual meetings are heavy-going, let's rise to the challenge and make them more fun and more effective. And whatever innovations we may have learnt from bringing some VaVaVoom to our Zoom in terms of connection, informality and light-heartedness, let's bring them to face-to-face interactions too.

It is very comforting to mutter and complain about them but instead you need to either improve that regular meeting or cancel it. Pre-Covid, one ad agency made meetings take place standing up – at poseur tables (those tall ones where you can put your drink or your finger food) – so that they didn't last too long. How could we flip things so that we actually look forward to meetings? So that they are fun and achieve what they should? Would it be a radical plan to say that certain people don't have to come to the meeting if they would rather not? Is a meeting the best forum for their talents? What about people who actually *enjoy* meetings? Invite them along, to see what they might add. Seek feedback not on the content but the process – how could you be better at the meeting game?

Let's get radical

Do you ever consider that the meeting isn't just about the people in it? It is a forum where certain outside interests are represented (or ignored). Companies may now be investing in hi-tech virtual conference rooms but the gadgets won't win hearts and minds on their own. Yes, it would be better if the remote participants were given parity with those in the room. Yes, it would be better if their view were not of a bunch of silhouettes at the far end of the table, barely audible via one of those ghastly spider mics. But you really need to have the will to make the shared experience not frustrating or humdrum. There are hundreds of articles and books about how to have better meetings, including remotely. One easy win is to spend a moment at the beginning celebrating positives, for example. A recent contract win, a project delivered, or just that Jim managed to get his hair cut at last.

In their *Harvard Business Review* article from 2018,[15] Maya Bernstein and Rae Ringel explore how Design Thinking[16] can help you plan better meetings. Design thinking has much in common with my LASER approach. Another is Cynefin, a Welsh word for an approach which acknowledges that not all problems can be solved in the same way.[17] Rather than 'one-size-fits-all' you adapt to varying circumstances.

Design Thinking and meetings

Design Thinking started, unsurprisingly, with designers who realized that they had to really understand the people for whom they were designing things. It's about explicitly taking into account the *users' perspective*. I first learnt about it through the concept of 'rapid prototyping' – trying it out, maybe before it's quite ready and seeing how it works and adapting. A prototype needn't be high-tech or expensive. It's just something people can experience and offer feedback on. Then you Listen to the feedback, Accept it as an offer, Explore your assumptions and Reincorprate them into the next iteration of the product. Design thinking is often used in terms of solving wicked problems. It's iterative, non-linear, reframing the problem, using conjecture, working without knowing all the information. It uses *abductive reasoning*, which means there is an element of uncertainty or doubt, unlike *deductive reasoning*. So it throws up a conclusion which is plausible but which you can't positively verify, but it's most likely to be effective or the best available under the circumstances... just like improv which is using what is to hand, explicitly acknowledging it is imperfect but recognizing that 'it works'. So in Design Thinking the designer's attention oscillates between the context of problem and ideas for a solution and each evolves together. To me, it means you are constantly trying things out with the customer rather than looking at what worked in the past or in theory. In theatre, you say we are 'putting it on its feet'. Some call it Human-Centred Design. Really it's about finding strategies and solutions that aren't obvious from the understanding you had at the outset.

So how does Design Thinking apply to meetings?

The first step is to *empathize* with the user. Who will be affected by the meeting and how? They might be in the meeting, they might not be, but what are their needs? What are the 'needs' of the broader system? So why not go and ask people?

The second step is *define*. Why not ascertain that if they were to score the meeting 100 per cent, what would that look and feel like? What would they and others do as a result? Why not put their hoped-for outcomes in the agenda? And maybe even a 'stretch goal'? This is very different from merely sending out an invite or accepting it. There is work to be done rather than time to be passed. Why not aim for people to leave with much more of a spring in their step than just the usual, 'oh well, that wasn't too bad'.

The third step is *ideate*. So set about designing the meeting as a user experience (UX). If you know what success looks like, the agenda could be easier to create. How many of your meetings just have a title ('Catch-up') with no agenda? I am a big fan of agenda-less meetings, when it's clear to participants that's the nature of the session, but again you have to know whether you are accountable to Newton or to Darwin. Be clear if this is a moment for the sat-nav or the scenic route. Merely writing the agenda isn't enough. Who 'owns' each item? Will they just screen-share some congested slides which they will talk over? Is there nothing else that can enhance the UX? A video, song, or something to create a different kind of engagement? Perhaps include a prop – something tangible that people can touch or see. As soon as people have an object in their hands, they speak differently, often less self-consciously, creating engagement.

The next step is *prototype*. So go back to your participants, share your draft agenda and some of your design ideas. From this you will gain more *offers,* from which you might have more ideas to refine the design.

Side-meetings are vital. They don't have to be long or with every single participant. But work out who will be your ally – or a blocker. Talk to them ahead of time. Will your approach/idea/suggestion fall flat on its face? Better to find out in advance. Better to incorporate the ideas of others. Better to finesse how you will express your point of view. Or decide to keep it for another forum or a later date. A one-on-one with the blocker could save you time (and 'save face').

Have you ever been subject to a side-meeting? Did it work? Did it mean you supported the idea? Did it mean you saved your colleague from having egg all over their face? Did it save time? A side-meeting can last only five minutes. It could be on the phone or in person. Best to have it spoken rather than written. It might even help you consider if a meeting is actually the best way to move forward or if the invite list includes the right people.

Bernstein and Ringel said that their clients who have adopted this process have found radical changes in the efficacy of meetings and attendees' attitude.[18] It sounds a lot of work but do you want your people to feel heard and leaders to feel connected to their teams? If meetings take up so much of our time, you have to be clearer about goals, you must be willing to experiment. Something as simple as asking for feedback on the agenda increases engagement and accountability. Meetings will only improve if nobody is able to abdicate responsibility for their success.

The future of meetings

For any business, *talking* is its main activity. And so much of that is done in meetings. Every day there are quality control checks on products and customer surveys but is there any audit of meetings? Quality (or quantity) control? If meetings are central to what we do, why not look at how we do them? In global, virtual times, as cultural and cognitive diversity increase, you could be pouring money, energy, goodwill and ideas down the drain with every single meeting you fluff.

If your firm's stated purpose was 'To have as many meetings as possible', would you be close to scoring 100 per cent already? When I hear of people being in back-to-back meetings all day – without even time TO GO TO THE TOILET, let alone have something to eat or go for a walk – I wonder.

Most organizations have evolved to produce the very things they are currently producing – which might be hot air, misery, environmental damage, human connection, paperwork, etc, as well as the thing which they are supposed to be focused on – widgets, services, etc.

As artificial intelligence takes over and humans become ever more redundant, will it just be one algorithm talking to another? Maybe arguing a bit? Perhaps there will be moments when they find their virtual meeting room is double-booked by a robot from Finance. They will have to dawdle in the cyber-corridor as their auto-assistant scurries round to find another space in the cloud where they can swap files, with a stolen glance through the ethernet, perhaps only to be consummated as a hard drive is quietly backed up, late at night. Or maybe a cruel software update will vanquish any memory of moments of connection, any such 'bug' being fixed and dispatched to Trash, probably to disappear automatically after 30 days.

The fact is that meetings are here to stay. So we need to proactively make sure they are not strangling the company, like some flesh-eating autoimmune disease slowly killing its host body.

In meetings, people need to know why they are there and why others are there. Individuals should attend because they can bring their particular skills to it, or because they are materially affected, rather than just be nodding along to something they don't know or care about. It may be that not everyone needs to be there for every item, which is easily achieved in virtual and if the facilitator has worked hard to create a timed agenda and keeps things on track.

Many people I know leave large organizations to set up on their own. Their sigh of relief is almost audible when I catch up with them later. Mostly it's about no longer having to attend the dreaded corporate meetings. How much talent is lost or wasted because of them? Actively monitor how your meetings are being talked about. It might be clear that those 'Monday morning meetings' have a bad reputation or the XYZ [insert acronym] is a forum for antagonism. Remember how we are both acting on and being acted on by a system? Talk to someone about how you might rejuvenate (or cancel) those meetings which are the subject of negative gossip. Spot the patterns that quickly become individual and collective habits. Maybe the boss is always late, Jim has done a spreadsheet, Mike mentions a burning platform or a straw man, Jane has done more prep than anyone else?

Make meetings matter

I wanted to end this chapter with a simple exhortation – just have fewer meetings. To my delight there are some wiser heads (for example, Ben Laker of Henley Business School and three others) who have researched this and come up with the same conclusion. Their piece in the *Harvard Business Review* from March 2022 found that newly promoted leaders hold 29 per cent more meetings than more established managers.[19] Of course they do, because otherwise they must wonder what leadership is: surely, it's that thing you do in meetings? So Laker and co surveyed 76 firms that had reduced the number of meetings over the previous 14 months. Guess what? Employee productivity rose 71 per cent when meetings were reduced by 40 per cent. Laker and his team reported that 'Removing 60 per cent of meetings increased co-operation by 55 per cent.'

We shouldn't be surprised because they found the right communication, often one-on-one that was relevant to the project. Reducing meetings by 80 per cent meant that people's perception of being micromanaged went down 74 per cent. Communication was more effective – judged to be 65 per cent clearer. Using asynchronous tools meant they could check back what had been written, rather than an impression from a verbal conversation. Using a dashboard meant that the state of play was transparent.

Laker and his team guided these firms with some simple rules similar to those I have suggested above:

1 Only have a meeting if it's absolutely necessary.
2 Reduce the invite list.
3 Empower people to cancel or not attend meetings.
4 Make daily 'status updates' or huddles not a meeting but instead ensure everyone sends a message at 9 am about what they are up to (maybe via Slack or some other tool: I suggest using an existing platform, even email or whatever you're all in the habit of using) and even if there are any hurdles they are encountering.

Using these protocols, 47 per cent of the companies they looked at reduced meetings by 40 per cent over a three-month period. Did they manage to have any *no-meeting days*? Yes! A third got to three per week and 11 per cent got to four.

This is radical but everyone needs to buy into it. It's too easy to say 'meetings' are someone else's problem. Whatever your position, it is your responsibility to be part of making them better and empowering others to feel the same. Start today, not tomorrow, in whatever way you can. You can prep your contribution, ensure your listening is more *intentive*, make the meeting shorter, decline the invite, suggest another facilitator, send the agenda ahead of time, bring in a prop or simply make it start with something fun. Just ensuring there is more laughter in your next meeting could bear fruit. That's the subject of the next chapter.

CHAPTER SEVEN

Humour

Humour? You've either got it or you haven't? No!

You can't teach someone how to have a sense of humour, can you? Some people are funny, some aren't, surely? But I am not talking about telling jokes, I am talking about impromptu moments, moments where we share our human frailty or laugh at absurdity or see another perspective. People can be frustrating but they can also be beautiful and kind and selfless and fascinating. And laughing with people is an amazing way to be in the moment with others.

It was, after all, looking into the psychological and physical benefits of humour that propelled me into management training. I wrote an entire chapter called 'Lighten' in my last book about this topic[1] and I have only deepened my conviction since. In 2021 a great book came out, called *Humour*

Seriously, by Jennifer Aaker and Naomi Bagdonas, with robust research on the benefits of humour, a secret weapon that is capable of transforming business, 'a superpower that's completely under-leveraged and underappreciated'.[2] It's not just about guffawing around the photocopier but choosing to be 'on the precipice of a smile'. With the spread of remote working, humour should be taken even more seriously. The lack of it is so often cited as a major shortcoming for virtual interactions, as everyone is in back-to-back meetings, stressed about the task and unable to connect, in more ways than one.

Create more laughter in video calls and the 'problem' of hybrid will go a long way to being solved. When you are physically disconnected, here is a tool available to encourage engagement, psychological safety and well-being. When we laugh together, we are all experiencing dopamine and endorphins. When we share the same state, we trust each other. Even in two dimensions we can find something very human that slices through the screen.

But it's just fun, isn't it? Something to get out of the way before we screen-share a vital spreadsheet? No, it's more than that. Humour is the corollary of self-awareness, a pillar of communication. It's a leader's job (and the whole team's) to cultivate a culture that is productive and connected, so why not prioritize creating joy, especially when it can be lacking in remote interactions? 'Laughter relieves stress and boredom, boosts engagement and well-being, and spurs not only creativity and collaboration but also analytic precision and productivity' wrote Alison Beard in a piece called 'Leading with humour' for the *Harvard Business Review* in 2014.[3]

People talk about blame culture. Nowadays some firms run surveys of well-being but they can tell us only so much. If people are laughing, even if it's a bit subversive, they will be more creative. As I will argue later, we should focus on whether our rituals are actually *stopping* laughter. I am not suggesting strictly enforcing so-called *fun things* like Christmas jumpers or dressing up as a Superman for charity once a year. Mostly, this has to come from the top. The boss should be seen to be sharing, say, a self-deprecating story to lighten the moment or laughing along with a shared memory. Otherwise, people will still laugh, but maybe behind their back.

At the end of a workshop I step back and think that if I have achieved nothing more than providing some shared moments of laughter for the group, then I have achieved something truly worthwhile. Very often leaders whisper to me, 'You know, we so rarely have a chance to laugh together.' This has become even more common since the pandemic. I often work alongside someone, now a good friend, who has been head of leadership for several global outfits and is seriously qualified, including a PhD in All Things Organizational. Yet, we often reflect together that simply bringing top teams together to enjoy each other's company in a light-hearted environment may be all that is needed. Sharing theory and the latest academic thinking and having them 'surface the issues' may actually be secondary. Humour is a 'technology' that costs nothing and has a proven track record in bringing people together.

Psychologists talk about four types of humour:[4]

1 *Affiliative humour* is used in social situations, strengthening relationships and group cohesion, and reducing

tension by telling humorous anecdotes or riffing so as to put others at ease. Those who do it seem to have a high degree of self-acceptance.

2 *Self-enhancing humour* is a way of coping with unpleasant moments, smiling in adversity. You can find humour when something bad has happened. It's a way of coping with stress.

3 *Aggressive humour* involves ridiculing or teasing others. We may or may not always realize it has a negative impact on others.

4 *Self-defeating humour* is overly self-disparaging, perhaps in order to ingratiate oneself or to avoid underlying concerns.

Obviously, I am keen to promote types 1 and 2 but they can stray (or be seen to stray) into 3 and 4. When I teach improv, I often have to calm some participants down, making it clear it's not about 'gags'. I often make two rules: *don't be funny, don't be creative.* Just listen to your partner and add one thing each time. Guess what – funny and creative soon follow.

There is a type in my workshops who tends to veer towards 3 and 4 because he (and it is always a he) thinks that's what funny is. He keeps looking to his small group of male friends for affirmation. Of course, I forgive him because it's just gauche nervousness and by the end of the day, he is listening and letting humour arise collaboratively. I am just as delighted when a very quiet person is the one who does a brilliant scene with me, having lost inhibitions and enjoying it when they are taken by the flow of the moment.

What is a sense of humour?

In 2003, researchers from the University of Western Ontario looked into what it is. They reckoned it was made of six elements:[5]

1 cognitive ability to make, understand and remember jokes
2 appreciation of humour
3 behaviour patterns of laughing and sharing humour
4 a humorous/cheerful temperament
5 a bemused outlook on life
6 a coping strategy, maintaining a humorous perspective in the face of adversity

So it can be both making and appreciating humour. But does it make you happy? A 2010 study for the *Journal of Aging Research* (it's not too early for you to take out a subscription) says yes.[6] One group of senior citizens underwent 'humour therapy' for eight weeks (jokes, laughter exercises, funny stories and more). A 'control' group did not (was it entirely ethical to deprive them of fun? Did they consciously try not to giggle for two months?) Guess what? At the end of the programme the laughers had 'significant decreases in pain and perception of loneliness and significant increases in happiness and life satisfaction', which was quite different from the control group. So here is a highly effective non-pharmacological intervention.

However, just making others laugh doesn't make you happy. In a 2010 study by Ontario University scientists found that 'the ability to create humour is less relevant to mental health than are the ways people use humour in their daily lives.'[7] In my years on the comedy circuit I met plenty of grumpy stand-up comedians. I should say that the 'sad clown' cliché is far from universal though a 2018 study did find that comedians score higher than normal on psychotic traits, most notably 'introverted anhedonia and extroverted impulsiveness'.[8] Anhedonia means you find it harder to experience pleasure. Yes, that sounds feasible. I know some professional comedians who don't laugh almost on principle or who might just grunt 'that's funny' from the corner. But my mission is to make laughter something we all share, like the air we breathe.

Connectedness

I have run many sessions over the years at London Business School. That's how I met Nigel Nicholson, Emeritus Professor of Organisational Behaviour. He told me he was a Darwinian. That all sounded very 'tooth and claw', 'survival of the fittest' to me. But it turns out that it's evolutionary psychology, based on *adaptation,* just as Woodrow Wilson would have it. So I asked him why, in personal ads (in the old days of print media, before Tinder) people wanted to meet someone with a good sense of humour (GSOH was the oft-used shorthand). He explained that, for our ancestral tribes to prosper, to share food and resources, a leader who had good relational skills and who could bring people together would come to the fore. Being able to share humour is powerful for this and is a good indicator of broader skills.

Well-being

Well-being is now considered important in organizations and we have had to take it more seriously since 2020 – but is it just lip service? A karaoke night once a year won't suffice. Laughter is well known to be related to health and to a recent buzz-word – *resilience*. Why isn't humour recognized as vital to an individual's or organization's health?

> *Always laugh when you can; it is*
> *cheap medicine.* LORD BYRON

The Mayo Clinic's report in 2021 was clear that laughter is good for your health both in the short and long term.[9] It relieves stress, stimulating organs, increasing the release of endorphins (natural pain killers) by the brain. Your blood pressure rises when you start to laugh, then dips below normal. Your heart grows stronger. A good belly laugh relieves muscle tension and increases oxygen intake. All this together improves your immune system, relieving pain and improving self-esteem. Margery Hutter Silver from Harvard Medical School co-wrote a book about people living past a hundred and found a common thread – a good sense of humour.[10] She refers to laughing as 'internal jogging'.[11] Mayo Clinic says that a sense of humour can be nurtured by exposing yourself to funny books, videos, podcasts and friends who make you laugh.

I loved the sound of Laughter Yoga when I first read about it in 2002.[12] People just gather and start laughing. They don't need jokes, just the contagion of laughter. It's now in 110 countries. Even forcing a smile is good for you, which can grow to a laugh. If we are busy exercising our pecs, or improving our core stability, or attempting 10,000 steps a day, why not do the same for our laughing gear? A sense of humour lowers mortality rates, especially for women, according to a study reported in *Scientific American* in 2016.[13] The study's Norwegian researchers investigated nearly 54,000 people over 15 years on the link between sense of humour and mortality. The cognitive component of humour might mitigate against conflict and stress, preventing the build-up of cortisol and the like, which suppress immune functions. Sven Sebak, one of the authors said, 'I expect that children who lack adult models for the use of humour as a coping resource in the face of challenges are less likely to activate their sense of humour to cope with everyday life when they grow up.' There's the rub. It's hard to dispel the notion that these things are set in stone, that you cannot 'learn' a sense of humour.

I have seen different, dear reader. LASER has helped people get there. Since my work is often applying improv, a generally comedic form, I know that it can help develop our funny bones. Very often, the breakthrough comes with **R** for **R**eincorporate, when someone realizes that if they bring back something from earlier, that moment of incongruity, creating a narrative linking two unrelated topics, it is a joyous release. Perhaps we have a brief glimpse of the possibility that the universe isn't just an unplanned morass of meaninglessness and instead we do have a nano-moment of control.

The bottom line

Would you believe that when CEOs use humour during the earnings announcements of publicly listed companies, it improves the perception of the results? The stock price increases by more after the call and analysts become more positive about the stock.[14]

A study by Fabio Sala for the Hay Group in 2003, in which he gathered 20 male executives for a few hours and counted their 'humour utterances', found that there was a positive correlation with their bonuses.[15] Then, in a recruiting process, he interviewed 20 men and 20 women, then looked at their performance a year later. Guess what? There was a correlation between their humour and the size of their bonus.

So 'funny is money', right? Sala said that humour is 'intertwined with, and appears to be a marker for, high emotional intelligence'. That might be a reasonable assumption but he coded their utterances above in three ways: negative was putting down a peer, subordinate or boss; positive if used to politely disagree or criticize; neutral if used simply to point out some absurdity. Sala found that outstanding executives used ALL types of humour more than others but did favour positive or neutral. Intriguingly, he found that women consistently used more humour than men, but men did more put-downs. Women tended to use more humour that expresses compliments or warmth, using less negative humour about subordinates and marginally less about superiors.

We know that humour creates power – whether that be 'soft' power or 'hard' power. I reckon we're not always sure of the difference. Certainly, I see people are initially wary or even scared of me at the beginning of a workshop, but can't they see I'm lovely and cuddly and sharing the good news of LASER – diversity, collaboration, vulnerability? But I know that in life, as in improv, status is ever present and is a vital dimension of any scene. It's never *not* there, even if a character with the 'high status' has achieved that by being the most 'needy' at that moment: grabbing all the attention and putting others under their spell. That's why I love doing a scene in my sessions with someone who has never done improv before and she gains high status by wowing her colleagues by simply Listening, Accepting and Sending offers.

Certainly we need more shared laughter at work. I hope I have shown that it is very far from being detrimental so should not be snuffed out when undertaking any 'time and motion' study. Quite the opposite. 'Laughter fast tracks networks in the brain to help you concentrate and focus'[16] said Daniel Sgroi of Warwick University, whose 2015 study[17] found happiness makes people 12 per cent more productive.

Creativity

As I said, some leaders are worried by the idea of my workshops. They tell me who 'to pick on'. They tend to choose extroverts. But I tend not to take their advice because if it looks like I have been told to choose someone, then both the chosen and the not-chosen wonder why. If I am talking about being in the moment and the joys of improv, this detracts from my message. I would much rather choose, transparently, based on what happens in the moments during the workshop, even if those whom I ask say no. My criteria are fairly simple: do they have a sense of being open and do others seem to cherish them? Also, do they look like they will hit me? Almost without fail, I am complimented on the people I choose, but it is mostly intuitive. More likely, however, it is simply that the spirit of improv takes care of them once they are invited.

We do need to tread carefully where laughter is concerned. Genuine affiliative humour is not what some Brits call 'banter', which easily descends into bullying. I assumed this included sarcasm, until I found an article by the Harvard professor, Francesca Gino, called 'The surprising benefits of sarcasm'.[18] Sarcasm can be seen negatively, a sign of contempt. With the caveat that there must be a base level of trust, Gino found that though there might be some interpersonal conflict in a group who were exposed to sarcasm, they actually did better on creativity tasks: 'The processes involved in initiating and delivering a sarcastic comment improved the creativity and cognitive functioning of both the commenter and the recipient.' We have to tread carefully here, but I am convinced that where there is a spirit of embracing irony in a team, which discourages a static 'mono' view of the world, that allows different perspectives to emerge on any problem or opportunity.

Your brain is thinking more creatively when it has to understand the difference between the literal and the intended meaning. Isn't it true that we seem to assume those who make us laugh are more intelligent? Not in an academic sense, of course, as I know some brilliant comic minds who've not had as much formal education as others who somehow missed the module on 'Irony and its Applications in Everyday Life' at university. Observational stand-up comedy is often telling us what we already knew unconsciously but had not rationalized or it's showing us meaning where we had previously assigned none. But isn't that, after all, also what the best data scientists do?

In our interconnected world, I have found that laughter knows no boundaries, not across borders nor across functions. I am in the business of making people laugh in person and virtually. I never start with jokes. I start with what participants give me. In fact I never do 'jokes' which I define as the prepared 'did you hear the one about' type of utterance.

Why do we laugh?

Psychology, philosophy and neuroscience have all tried to give answers as to why we laugh, but none is complete, I feel. Various reasons were collated in a *Scientific American* article from 2019:[19]

- *We feel superior:* either to others or to earlier versions of ourselves.
- *Relief of tension:* Freud said that pent-up 'nervous energy' is released when we broach a taboo or dangerous topic. The 'punchline' makes us feel safe again.
- *Incongruity:* a juxtaposition of incompatible concepts or a double meaning becomes clear, highlighting a discrepancy between what we expect and reality.
- *Benign violation:* humour is tragedy plus time. A bad thing turned out okay in the end.
- *Evolutionary advantage:* Group cohesion, smoothing social interactions or conflict.

But we still don't know all the different reasons. Like physics, laughter refuses to be subsumed into one General Theory. Of course, I'm glad it does. Laughter may be the only competitive advantage we have over robots so let's keep it mysterious. But actually, humour doesn't always bring laughter. And laughter isn't always because of humour. Bagdonas and Aaker suggest that getting an actual laugh is less important than being *appropriate*.[20] A humorous sign-off in an email won't have us rolling around on the floor but engages the reader. An internal smile will do.

There are two types of laughter. I first discovered this from Professor Sophie Scott, a neuroscientist from University College London and sometime stand-up comedian. There is *spontaneous laughter*, which has many features in common with animal vocalizations, including kea parrots, cows and weasels. Primates laugh and so do rats. It turns out they like being tickled.[21] She led a team who published a study in 2022, which showed that we can tell the difference between spontaneous and *communicative laughter*, which I have also seen described as controlled laughter.[22] I have read various stats but it seems only 10–20 per cent of laughter is in response to an actual comic trigger. The rest of the time we are making others feel at ease, showing that we like them and that we want to connect with communicative laughter. Most of the time, we are probably mixing both. Humans seem to have adapted to control laughter for conversation (or to deride others). We can tell how close two people are by the sound of their laughter. We can tell people apart by their communicative laughter but not by the spontaneous sort, suggesting the latter is more universal.

I know that laughter is contagious. A big audience laughs more than a small one. It's not a linear correlation. A crowd of four hundred laughs more than double one of two hundred. An audience in a theatre, sitting side by side, facing the stage, laughs more than one seated dispersed around tables.

(Note to conference organizers: you call it 'cabaret' seating, I call it 'catering' seating. Vital laugh waves and other social connections are broken up by the space and furniture between people.)

When I first started doing improv workshops on Zoom in March 2020, people were unmuted. I heard one person laugh at a time, who was then muted as another laughed. Or more likely, I heard them drop their pencil. It was weird, and stand-up comics told me they had to change their rhythms. Since then, virtual comedy producers have found ways for collective laughter to be heard but I generally rely on seeing laughing faces and smiles and nice comments in Chat, which is still enough for the moment to be shared.

Social context plays a big part in how much we laugh[23] so how do we make our remote meetings more fun? How do we deal with the loneliness that some may feel with hybrid working? How could I bring the energy and fun of an improv workshop or show to the Badlands of Remote? There was plenty of advice from people who had been working with remote teams for years, including Caryn Vanstone, who had taught me so much when she was at Ashridge Consulting and had been exploring how dispersed teams work since 2003: 'All the research over the last 20 years has shown that virtual and remote working is a NEW CRAFT with entirely new competencies and techniques, tools and ways of working.'[24]

Rereading this now, I realize how much it inspired me. Simply doing what you did before but through a laptop would be like trying to use a quill pen on a Smart board. I have run some corporate Zoom events where people can bring family members. It's wonderful to see two or three people on one camera. I came across a phrase, 'Zoom Fatigue, Netflix Intrigue'. Television doesn't linger on a shot of a single person, it cuts to a wide view, a shot of two people, an aerial shot, a close-up of the gun and so on. The most exciting thing in your video call might be when someone stops their 45-minute screen-share and you spot a living creature flitting across the back of the screen. It might even be the presenter, now showing a few vital signs after draining any semblance of life from the entire internet.

With these sessions we even had young people – under 10s sometimes. Why not 'bring them to work?' Also, as soon as a pet appears, there is energy in Teams which it so often lacks. Why not have more than one employee on screen for business meetings? People could get together at one another's houses if they live close. Too often people in the same office block have to separate themselves. Why? People are *30* times more likely to laugh if they are with other people, says Sophie Scott.[25]

It was when I went to see the psychologist Frank Farrelly demonstrate Provocative Therapy in the late nineties in the Netherlands that I discovered there were people called 'executive coaches' and it led me to becoming involved in leadership development (and daring to create a satirical character called The Gangsta Motivator).[26] Phil Jeremiah, a former senior mental health social worker, now working with all sorts of people in personal development and beyond, uses Frank's humorous methods and continues to develop them. He talks about a 'Bubble of Possibility'. Humour can help break old patterns and establish new ones. Too often we are 'stuck' with a problem. Humour can help us shift perspective. I have seen this many times with Provocative Therapy, demonstrated by Frank and Phil and the man who introduced it to me, Dr Brian Kaplan (check out *Almost Happy,* the book he wrote with his wonderful wife, Hephzibah, which shows how to use these methods),[27] as well as in my own practice. Frank would say he was teasing people back to mental health by satirizing their self-limiting beliefs. Phil says he shifts clients 'from problem states to resource states'. That's the Bubble of Possibility and it's directly related to laughing.

So we need to make that bubble cover more of our lives. Making video calls more sociable is one thing, but how much of your time do you spend on email or some other messaging platform? It's so often the cause of disconnection – a badly phrased sentence which is unclear or, worse, tetchy.

Instead of making hackles rise, why not make spirits rise?

Aaker and Bagdonas have some simple suggestions to make emails a tiny parcel of goodwill. Many of us use them already:

- **Reincorporate** (**R** from LASER). It's known as a 'call-back' in North American sitcoms (like my favourites

Frasier and *Seinfeld*), when something or someone pops up early in an episode and then reappears later. With particularly ornate plotting it pops up near the end and is the very thing that saves (or ruins) the day. In a subsequent email mention something you had discussed – a domestic situation, a meal, a mistake, even Rick Astley. You shared a moment before and you bring it back in order to create another moment of connection. It is simple, ethical and authentic. And you're unlikely to offend since you will be using something they shared with you first. It shows you listened. Maybe you discussed buying a coat, so you could mention you are now wearing it or scouring the internet to buy it. With remote working, there are more opportunities for this, as we see deeper into people's home-lives; something in their background (or foreground), another member of their household, an unexpected delivery and more.

- **A sign-off or PS** that's like a wink. It could be a **Reincor**porate as above, or something that popped into your head (*Yours, looking out the window, eagerly awaiting my holiday*); or a cheeky reference to the content of the email which sits above it. It's a compliment, a moment of vulnerability, showing you trust them enough to be playful, inviting them to respond in kind. Maybe you drank some coffee in the shared video call (*Yours, in caffeine*). Or a throwaway line with a tinge of irony (*PS: Nothing makes me happier than making spreadsheets*).

Many years ago, I asked a group of management consultants to share some tricky moments they had had with clients. We then used these as the basis for an exercise. Bear in mind, these were very clever people. Then this younger woman said that on the phone, a client, talking about a forthcoming one-on-one they would be having, asked, 'Will you be wearing a mini-skirt?'

How do you answer that, when you know your firm's job is to 'serve' the client? You are coming up with an 'answer' to their problem. You want the client to engage your firm again on future projects. This was during a session when I was introducing them to ethos of *Yes And*. Hard to do with this 'offer'. But it's about using what the other person said in your response. So I suggested she could have said, 'The question is, will *you* be wearing a mini-skirt?' A humorous, yet assertive way of saying, 'that's inappropriate'. I know I could say that easily in the calm of the rehearsal room, as a man (an older man, a comedian, an outsider), with no need to worry about ramifications. In reality, she told us that she paused and moved on to the subject at hand. And didn't wear a mini-skirt to the meeting and took someone else with her.

Summary

1. Funny doesn't equal Frivolous

I am serious, so I laugh a lot. You need to laugh. You don't laugh enough. I don't trust anyone who doesn't laugh. MAYA ANGELOU

Life is serious, business is serious, many organizations are doing powerful, life-enhancing things. That's no reason to reject something that is essential to our humanity – humour and the ability (the necessity?) to look at life from different angles. Being empathetic means sometimes being solemn and sometimes being light-hearted. Every funeral I have attended has had moments of laughter alongside tears. At the very least take advice from THE body language expert, Mark Bowden.[28] He teaches Zoom employees, among many others, how to have a better impact on video calls. He has a Post-it note above his webcam – on which he has drawn a simple smiley face. You can't help but smile when you look at it – and it keeps your head up, rather than down.

Robert Provine is a leading laughter scientist. He said that 'laugher existed before humour' and that the key ingredient to laughter is another person, not a joke.[29] Bear that in mind.

2. You don't have to be a brilliant joke-teller

In fact, maybe it's better you're not. Just be a great laugher. Enjoy giggling, getting it wrong and putting on a silly hat once in a while. Give permission to others to laugh with you. Find the funny in the ordinary. Make time for sharing small moments of humour on video calls. It might just be the mug you're drinking from or the socks you're not wearing. Remember Listen and Accept offers? So be open when someone else may happen upon or create a moment of levity.

But do try the occasional Reincorporate.

3. Be appropriate

Sometimes jokey isn't the right response. Even if (as we comedians say) 'it's crying out for it' where the punchline seems to write itself. We don't always know what will offend others, even one in a hundred. And one is too many.

4. Are your processes and rituals actively mitigating against humour?

When I run a virtual session, people tell me that they have never experienced Zoom used like it. But I'm just a needy improv comedian – I want responses, I thrive on interaction, I look for the laughs. But I work my socks off (*disclaimer: I don't normally wear them for video calls*) to create the mood, the feeling that people can speak freely and they would be foolish to miss a word. Can you build something like that into your gatherings? Explicitly allowing humour, an investment in group cohesion for the next moment when the 'task' is undertaken. Don't just hope for the best, think of it as something just as important as your team's 'five a day' or 10,000 steps. Why are we afraid to laugh at work? Happier workers are more productive.[30]

CHAPTER EIGHT

Serendipity

This is a chapter I have been looking forward to writing for months, if not years. The idea came to me when I heard the boss of a famous management consultancy use the word 'serendipity' as he explained that he was paid to network: 'Your network generates luck. You want to maximize your share of the lucky market.' The lucky market. It's not the whole market but it is part of it.

Sport, science and the arts embrace happenstance. Improv theatre actively sets out to find it. Why not business? Somehow it seems wrong to admit that things happened that we didn't plan. In the chapter on leadership I talked about complexity. Did it feel that, without control, it's not clear how much a leader can do? You cannot control much of the outside world, so focus on nurturing the myriad relationships that keep your business afloat – internally and externally. We would like to think in terms of cause and effect, where everything is linear, like a machine. But we are part of an ecosystem.

Serendipity is different from *luck* and from *fate*. The Merriam–Webster online dictionary says it is 'the faculty or phenomenon of finding valuable or agreeable things not sought for'.[1] Fate is 'something that happens to a person'. Luck is similar to fate but both can be good or bad. Serendipity is positive, it isn't just about what happens to you. It is how you view events and data. Are you ready to be a *serendipitist*? How do you find (and capitalize on) 'valuable or agreeable things not sought for'?

This is not fatalism, 'whatever will be, will be'; it's about how you use what's there and what you make of it. In business school or leadership training you may hear about the notion of 'sense-making'. For me that means both discovery *and* invention. Don Sull, speaking to McKinsey about his book (*The Upside of Turbulence: Seizing opportunity in an uncertain world*) was clear.[2] In uncertain times, the temptation is to do more of what you were doing: 'Step on the gas, spin the wheels harder, and hope to get out of the rut. Usually you end up digging yourself deeper.' He calls that 'active inertia'. Or you might think that you can predict the future. 'The record of people's predictions in business, or in any domain, is very, very poor.' The upside Sull refers to is when new opportunities, consumer demands and resources are emerging. Unless there is a little slack in your system you cannot adapt.

You can be operationally agile – which means making the most of opportunities within an existing industry or business model. Or switch your portfolios, cutting back resources from one area to give to growing areas. Sull's third category is 'strategic agility... seizing golden opportunities that arise every so often'.

We know how awful the pandemic was for countless families and organizations. So many loved ones were lost and so many are still suffering greatly. But plenty of people have said that the changes that were forced on us in three days or three weeks would have taken years otherwise. At one internal briefing I attended in mid-2020, before the depth and duration of what was unfolding was fully understood, someone very senior remarked that we might in future talk about something being *corona'd* – that is, a necessary, radical change happening in a much shorter space of time than previously thought possible.

As you may have surmised, I have been collecting newspaper and magazine articles for a quarter of a century and I have one from the *Sunday Telegraph* from 27 September 1998 which reports on a survey conducted by WFD Consulting and *Management Today*. In the top 10 List of Wishes are the following:

3 work flexible hours
4 reduce commuting – or avoid it
5 work from home

These have now become an immutable reality. Why did it take a pandemic for this to happen? But look at what's above them in the 1998 chart:

1 being able to work fewer hours
2 a change in the company culture

How's that going then?

Embrace anomalies and outliers

I find my mind fascinating. It's full of nonsense. It doesn't do what's best for it (e.g. persuading me that the next glass of wine is not a necessity) but it can remember all sorts of things, yet forgets others. A long time ago, it helped me pass all sorts of exams, which I couldn't pass now. Who was that young student? Why can I do many of the things he could do but can't quite remember some formulae from high school physics? A Cambridge University study (quoted in *Neuroscience News*, March 2022) found that some parts of the brain are plastic, changing rapidly, while other parts have long-term stability.[3] This representational drift means that neural circuits are able to 'talk to each other without continuously having to relearn the things that they have already learnt'. Robots can't do that yet. Humans are able to learn continually. AI not so much. The problem is 'how to build algorithms that can learn continually without corrupting previously learnt information', said Dr O'Leary, Associate Professor in the Department of Engineering.

The test of a first-rate intelligence is the ability to hold two opposed ideas in the mind at the same time, and still retain the ability to function. F SCOTT FITZGERALD

Our brain is always looking for cause and effect but is often wrong. Doing a two-hour show without a script is impossible, according to a waiter near the Comedy Store when we tried to explain it to him, but we do it every week. Doing all your shopping online would have seemed absurd 20 years ago (and still does to my Mum) but, for many, it is the default. It is this plasticity which is, at the moment, giving us an advantage over robots. But do our busy schedules and org structures allow for serendipity? Black swan events come along now and then but what about allowing more latitude for everyday lateral thinking?[4] This involves spotting surprising patterns, seeing coincidences, asking better questions. This ethos can create breakthroughs, taking advantage of accidents, mistakes, misalignments and limited information. Improv actively sets out to embrace and use the unexpected. It's not 'luck', it's an attuned mind. Some organizations adapted quickly to remote working and learning while others just turned on the laptop camera and carried on as before – with no thought for well-being, inclusion, engagement or innovation. It was haphazard but, it seems to me, too many have simply carried on in that way.

We ignore outliers at our peril. In a brilliant blog for the *MIT Sloan Management Review* in June 2022, Dr Ayanna Howard, Dean of the College of Engineering at The Ohio State University, warned against 'standardization'.[5] For example, until 2003, most crash-test dummies were male. When assessing car safety design, you'd think using a female dummy was hardly an 'out-there' choice but a study by the University of Virginia in 2019 showed that women had a 73 per cent greater chance of being seriously injured in a frontal car crash than a man. How could this not have been noticed? Because people were looking at the wrong thing – or were not looking at things in the round. We need to constantly give space and time to see what has been overlooked. People talk about a 'gap in the market' but what about a 'market in the gap'?

Curiosity is the yin to serendipity's yang. Dr Howard says anomalies should not be discarded but 'treated as royalty'. She's not just talking about data but people too. Give them a voice, otherwise divergent ideas may remain unarticulated.

In fact, one scientist, Ellen Brennan, wrote about how improv had made her a better scientist, because you have to 'avoid second-guessing ourselves. Sometimes scenes go in unexpected directions. The best improv happens when performers stay open to different possibilities.'[6] Faced with some confusing data in her research, she Listened to it, Accepted and kept Exploring and ended up identifying a new type of cell. Improv had silenced her inner critic, opening her up to looking at the edge.

Imagination is more important than knowledge. For knowledge is limited, whereas imagination embraces the entire world, stimulating progress, giving birth to evolution. It is, strictly speaking, a real factor in scientific research. ALBERT EINSTEIN

I repeat this is not about fate. It's an attuned mind, attentive to possibilities and to different views. I am keen to show that this is not luck but conscious, focused effort. For me, it's really well summed up in author Greg Satell's blog from 2018, which he called 'four skills great innovators share'.[7] They are: applied curiosity; effective networking; comfort with confusion; and, finally, rigour. Be interested in things, as well as people, in sharing ideas and observations, even if they don't seem to mean much yet but then you follow through. To me this is improv 'listening' writ large. 'Intentive' listening without an agenda other than to use what you notice. The rigour may surprise you. It's not just luck that you spotted something. You then made the idea a reality.

Networking

I often ask my workshop participants if they love networking. Very few hands go up. It sounds superficial and like hard work. But remember the 'lucky market'? A networking event does indeed sound ghastly but if you reframed it as an *offer* – a moment you are given to host others getting to know each other – you might feel differently. Give yourself a target after which you have permission to leave (say, after an hour or after you have met three people) and it will feel easier. So often leaders tell me that they sponsor (at some cost) an event only for their people to just chat to one another. One senior lawyer told me that he doesn't find it easy but just decided to 'jump in' and get on with it. Often people tell me they don't know how to disengage. Easy – introduce the person you are with to someone else. Even better if you can bring them to someone you know, then you can deftly offer a starting point for their conversation as you head elsewhere. 'Janet just got back from a skiing holiday/loves cheese/has Barack Obama's autograph.'

Networking should be on your weekly agenda, and it should be happening internally too. Think of it as giving others the opportunity to learn who you are and how you might help them. And it's a great chance to practise your

LASER skills. We are happy to talk about IT 'networking' whereby computer systems and devices share data and resources, so why not human beings?

TOOLBOX   Networking

- Is just about being open to people.
- You can cross-pollinate your network – and offer even your 'weak ties' to others.
- Talk to people outside your team.
- Talk to people outside your firm.
- Talk to people outside your industry.
- You can learn from everybody.

Weak ties

What are 'weak ties'? These are with people you sort of know; good for psychological well-being and, apparently, for business. Tim Leberecht (*The Business Romantic*) said, 'I miss the friends of my friends.'[8] We missed them a lot during lockdowns, didn't we? The cheery chat at the corner shop; the nod to the other commuter; the smile at the sandwich bar. Weak ties are surprisingly important for mental well-being, but not to be overlooked when thinking about creativity. They could be snatched conversations or deep interactions with those with whom we may not be in daily contact. Your network isn't just your contacts. It also includes your contacts' contacts, so embrace their possibilities.

Serendipity: Spotting where the energy is emerging

Are you open to serendipity?

Are you open to unexpected opportunities?

It's all about noticing. We do it all the time in the arts. There is not an area in business where you cannot be 'creative'. However, it seems such a silly word to use when applied to kind of, y'know, ordinary stuff. But don't we love it when someone makes it easier for us to find the paperclips, submit expenses or make coffee? Or shows us how to hide self-view on Zoom?

Is there enough slack in your system?

Too many organizations are focused on efficiency rather than efficacy. Everyone's got their head down to get things done, rather than looking around once in a while to see if maybe they should be doing something else. I was very taken with the idea of impact players, as described by Liz Wiseman in her book of that name.[9] I know from soccer that this is applied to a player perhaps who comes on mid-game as a 'super-sub' and can turn it around with their particular skills, in a particular moment. In American football coaches know these players can engineer a transformative play or crucial turnover to switch the momentum of the game. What a great idea for business! As Wiseman and her fellow researcher Lauren Hancock note, firms face Messy Problems, Unclear Roles, Unforeseen Obstacles, Moving Targets and Unrelenting Demands. We all know those people who are able to step up, though not officially the leader, bring others with them and step back when the moment is over and revert to following others. This fluid leadership is similar to flocking birds, who take it in turns to be at the front of the V. This reduces drag so that they can actually go 70 per cent further than a bird flying solo. Being at the front all the time is tiring.

When my wife, who is not from showbiz, came to visit me when I was filming on the set of *Austin Powers: Goldmember* she couldn't believe how many people were involved: or, more precisely, *not* involved. There seemed to be about a hundred people milling around but only a handful actually near the camera working at any given moment. That's because lots of the work had been done much, much earlier (e.g. building and dressing the set, erecting the lighting) but that many people needed to be there for brief but vital moments – for hair, costume and make-up checks, to adjust lights, to bring in a prop 'just in case', sound, continuity, video playback, or to be background artistes, or to be 1st, 2nd or 3rd assistant directors (making sure all is ready, bringing in actors, or shouting 'quiet please' and 'action') and so much else besides. Then there's catering.

Perhaps a good way to think of it is, would you hire a spare generator for a movie shoot? It seems an extravagance but imagine how much you would have to pay to bring back all those people and hire the studio for another day if you lost power? People who do 'stand-by props' have a truck-load of objects that might suit that day's set or sets. The vast majority won't be used but if you need, say, a bedside light from the 1930s in a hurry, you want to have an array of different sizes and colours because you don't want all those people waiting around (and going into overtime) while you pop down to the antique shop several miles away.

Can we possibly think of our organizations in this way? More work is project-based and lots of professional service firms don't want their people 'on the bench'; they want maximum 'utilization'. In the public sector, this could be harder to justify but imagine if a reward structure could be found to make this feasible: with remote, project-based work and job-sharing.

How much other talent out there has been lost because it doesn't fit into how things are currently organized? But what if your organization were a little more... disorganized?

Let's get disorganized!

I was once interviewed for a book published by the think tank Demos, called *Disorganization*.[10] This was in 2005 and it addressed the fact that people wanted looser working lives, maybe with smaller organizations. It looked at individualism and identity, flexibility and human scale, leadership and participation. Some of the benefits they foresaw were 'informality, flexible working, devolving autonomy to the frontline, inclusive decision-making, open membership, integration through shared technology, asserting the primacy of values'. Prescient, much?

We see how this has developed since but 'disorganization' may look very different depending on where you are. For some, it might feel like job insecurity. The Demos report cited Henry Chesbrough's idea of 'Open Innovation' where ideas are shared.[11] Think of Linux. *Innovation cannot be subject to control: may a thousand flowers bloom.* Companies realize that they don't have a monopoly on bright people so they tap into innovative talent outside. That's easier now that anyone can start a business with a good idea, a laptop and a kitchen table. Maybe not even a kitchen table. Or laptop. Or good idea – maybe just someone else's good idea but with snazzier tech.

The reality is that big players swallow little players and sometimes squeeze out (or organize out?) what made the culture different and innovative. Many small organizations are working flat out so they can be bought out. In the end it may all come to EBITDA, whatever that means.

The Demos book concludes that:

> organizations that succeed will create more opportunities
> than they close down... they may only be able to disorganize
> successfully in some areas if they can organize more
> effectively in others.

The areas where they need to organize better are in 'mapping knowledge and skills'. This is exactly what I exhort so many of my clients to do. Share your stories with colleagues, listen to theirs. So many organizations have 'data' – hard or soft – but it doesn't flow. That's what the *serendipist* does – they are on the lookout for connections. Alongside that, I have worked with a tech firm who look at the data that firms collect and see how it can be used better. It's amazing how it's not lack of data that matters, but where it flows or doesn't.

Life is a balance between holding on and letting go. RUMI

I once saw Jules Goddard of London Business School talk about 'Uncommon Sense' which became a book.[12] Many organizations share certain practices which are useful ('common sense') and some which are not ('common nonsense'). There may be some dumb stuff which is peculiar to your outfit ('uncommon nonsense') but what you want to maximize is your 'uncommon sense' – clever things unique to your company. One of my favourite management writers is Simon Caulkin, formerly of *The Observer* newspaper. In a piece from 2009, headlined 'Inside every chief exec, there's a Soviet planner', he wrote that 'most companies are zombie-like in their structural and strategic similarity. This is why, too, they are unable to learn.'[13]

What has amazed me over the years is how much nonsense is common to so many teams. Just because you are a big organization (public or private) it seems that people have to follow unhelpful protocols or not enough power is devolved to those talking to customers or where the decisions need to be made. This is the opposite of 'mission command' which I mentioned in the chapter on 'Leadership Mindset'.

Has 'order' become an end in itself?

Have you considered the possibility that 'order' could actually be a *risk* if it stifles creativity, collaboration and well-being? In his book *Weird Ideas That Work* Stanford Professor Bob Sutton suggests you should hire people who are *slow* to learn the 'organizational code'.[14] Let them bring their outside perspective rather than slot quickly into your team's routines. (This is the E of LASER: Explore assumptions that established practices are actually useful.) People naturally want to fit in but I remember Don Sull being very excited when I told him that, when the Comedy Store Players have guest performers, we try to let them play their natural game and we work around them.

The opposite of serendipity is blinkered-ness. (Spellcheck is allowing me that word, albeit with a hyphen.) I am not against routine for certain things (like brushing your teeth) but I have seen too many executives tell me that the way they or their firm do things is the only way. Except they don't realize that is what they are saying.

For example, doing some Forum Theatre on a leadership course, I was trying to help one person 'sell' his idea to the (highly connected) chairman. But his whole demeanour was of shrugging diffidence. It didn't make one inclined to listen to him. So I asked him to show me how he would tell his daughter to get to bed. One of the observing participants was horrified that I might expect him to use that voice on the big boss. But I didn't. We had exhausted the rational possibilities as he muttered all the good reasons why his project was the one to go with. I just wanted to shake him out of the fixed mindset (and 'bodyset') that he had. So he tried that voice and, just like any good rehearsal, it helped him to find a better, more suitable and effective tone. Coming at things obliquely is often the only way I can disrupt people's habits as they have plenty of reasons why they need not or cannot change.

The cost of order

I was intrigued to find that that there could be a *cost* to order, because I'm sure we all feel guilty that we don't follow all the protocols of Marie Kondo, the Queen of

Declutter.[15] But what if there were a downside to being *too* organized?

In 2007 Eric Abrahamson and David Freedman wrote a book called *A Perfect Mess*.[16] In an entertaining video of a talk he gave at Google, Abrahamson tells us that he is personally messy even though he is a professor of *organization*.[17] Freedman is a journalist who was investigating randomness. (I wonder how they met?)

They claimed that 'ever since Einstein's study of Brownian Motion, scientists have understood that a little disorder can actually make systems more effective'. But most people still shun disorder – or suffer guilt over the mess they can't really avoid. It's extensively quoted that 70 per cent of organizational transformations fail. (I tried to find the source of this number but failed. Even McKinsey use it without citation.[18]) That costs a lot, both in the doing and what has been lost by losing what was there already.

Abrahamson says that 'mess engenders creativity because it juxtaposes things that would have otherwise been separate by order'. He even ran a computer simulation, comparing two processes:

1 do some work – stop to tidy – carry on with work *versus*
2 do some work – carry on working in mess – stop to tidy at the end

How he did this I don't know, but the 'computer said' the latter was better and that 'moderate messiness' is the sweet spot. He even found that filing things away one at a time was less efficient than a temporary mess (which meant waiting till a build-up of 10 things, then filing). His rough-and-ready web poll found that people with an orderly desk spent 60 per cent more time finding things than people with a disorderly desk.

If a cluttered desk is a sign of a cluttered mind, of what, then, is an empty desk a sign? ALBERT EINSTEIN

I remember the global head of a massive division of a very large company telling senior leaders how hard he was working to cut bureaucracy and wondering how even he, with his elevated position, was struggling to make it happen. Then a few years later, I went to his executive assistant's leaving do. Taking her with him to his new major CEO role would not have been an easy negotiation, given her years of service at the old firm, but he relied on her completely. Apparently, he liked to keep lots of data, memos and more *on paper*. She had turned the boot of her car into a filing system for him. He just had to give her a vague idea of the topic and date before she would go to her car and retrieve the relevant document within moments.

So is there enough of a balance in your week, in your team? How much of what you are doing is just servicing organizational needs with no intrinsic value? Do you put yourself in the right environment for the right moment? A study by the University of Minnesota found that a tidy desk may lead to conventionality, even healthy eating and generosity.[19] However, a messy desk may promote creativity, stimulating new ideas. How many organizations offer different environments for different types of activity? Is your organization like many I visit, where the 'working space' for employees is rather grey, cramped and unloved? The 'client areas' are more friendly and open, with natural light, plants and glossy magazines on the coffee table wait-ing rooms. Perhaps with WFH we can give ourselves a space for moments of serendipity and a space for moments when you 'get your head down and get on with it'.

Many years ago, I was invited to a huge global firm's Creativity Centre. It was a train journey outside London. The building had been divided up into different environ-ments to stimulate different ways of thinking and feeling. One was a teenage bedroom, another a family living room and the most fun was one in the shape of a brain – with a curved ceiling and different parts labelled accordingly. There was also a boardroom set-up. Which do you think most of their meetings defaulted to? Yes, the boardroom. Even if they did go to the brain room, they took in those chairs like you see in school with a little wooden desk-y attachment for writing. When I was in the brain room I wanted to lie on the floor, something we often do in theatre rehearsals to access other parts of our mind and body. Are you surprised to hear that the Centre closed down within a couple of years? 'Cost-cutting' apparently.

This got me thinking. How much guilt do we have with not being organized enough personally? There are many re-organizations of companies every year at huge cost, with perhaps no benefit, but what are the real *costs* of making an end in itself of being organized in a particular way that looks good on paper (or in a pukka pdf)?

Yet the German biophysicist and 1969 Nobel Laureate Max Delbrück (who discovered that bacteria become resistant to viruses as a result of genetic mutations) coined *The Principle of Limited Sloppiness*.[20] 'If you're too sloppy, then you never get reproducible results, and then you never can draw any conclusions; but if you are just a little sloppy, then when you see something startling... you nail it down.' Bob Sutton said that 'long-term plans act like blinders to new opportunities'.

How do you structure serendipity (and budget for it)?

Can intuitive and analytic thinking sit alongside each other? Bumping into people and having spontaneous chats is vital – face to face and virtually. That needs to be a priority. How do we plan time in the office to allow for conversations and agenda-less meetings? How will work-spaces need to be redesigned? Deloitte unveiled their new 'future of work' office in Newcastle in March 2022, radically redesigned for the new ways of working, a blueprint for them and their clients. They took out traditional desks, with spaces for less formal collaboration, connection and networking (that word again) and used recycled material where possible.[21] Of course, hybrid was an essential element, so they have high-quality video and audio, with 360-degree cameras aiming to make remote participants feel included. The space is flexible, adaptable so that small rooms can be opened up for bigger events. 'Building relationships' was explicitly mentioned as a priority.

I like Bob Sutton's idea of 'slow learners' who can bring different perspectives but they need a guide, someone who makes sure that their ideas do indeed receive a hearing. Does your organization assign someone to each new recruit, who can diplomatically help them bring their novel suggestions to the right table? I expect it's assumed that their boss will do that but that doesn't always happen and it shouldn't necessarily be the default position.

Sutton also thinks you should hire people 'who make you uncomfortable, even those you dislike' (though I note he later wrote *The No Asshole Rule*).[22] I prefer to say that, alongside the daily doing of your team, 'pilots' can be run, which may or may not succeed. I shall revisit this idea of 'studio time' later but the dual aims of keeping performance up while forging new ideas should be central to your and your team's outlook.

Is 'strategy' a straight line?

I once saw Henry Mintzberg speak at a conference for management consultants. He's a Canadian business school professor who's strongly critical of business school orthodoxy. He's dubious of all the literature written about apparently deliberate strategies followed by leaders when the reality is much more about 'emergent' strategy, which arises informally and at any level, not just the top table. I would call that improv, of course. He called management 'conversations, interrupted' and once described his journey whereby, when he was a graduate student at business school, nobody talked about management – surely the very thing that people needed to learn. In his first book in 1973, he observed that managers are interrupted a lot, that it's very action-oriented.[23] The literature had been all about planning, controlling, co-ordinating and, yes, organizing, yet that didn't accord with his observations of what actually went on with leadership teams.

He drew a very simple diagram (Figure 8.1) to illustrate his point on strategy. It's too easy to portray it as starting at Point A and then drawing a straight line to Point B. But the reality isn't like that; it's more like a funnel, with lots of little arrows, in different directions, which in aggregate lead you to somewhere like Point B. He saw that this was the case in formulating the strategy, then tidying it up, post-rationalizing it and presenting it to the board. But I would say that it's the same in execution. Just sort out the rough direction of travel and start.

Inventing Point B?

Then I came across Amy Whitaker and her approach and book *Inventing Point B*.[24] I talked about Design Thinking before. This is Art Thinking. *Not* how do we find creative ways to travel from A to B but finding, creating, discovering what B is on the journey. This is improv. We are finding where we are going as we go there. I saw Amy Whitaker at the Meaning Conference in Brighton which I hosted in 2018.[25] She went to study painting after having done an MBA; what an odd choice you might think. She even calls the 10 years after that as her 'wilderness years of narrative incoherence'. Business and art, don't mix, do they? Business

FIGURE 8.1   Strategy: Straight line or funnel?

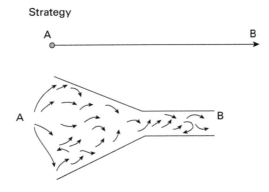

is all about efficiency, isn't it? While art is the very opposite, some might think, as the louche artist awaits inspiration and cares little for how their creations are received by the world. This stereotype has never been true. Van Gogh may have had little recognition in his lifetime but the Medicis sponsored art, while Charles Dickens wrote what he knew would sell.

Whitaker used the example of Roger Bannister. He came fourth in the Olympics in 1952. Less than two years later, he had broken the four-minute mile barrier. He had given himself a deadline, after which he had to go full-time as a doctor. Whitaker calls that a 'grace period' and the running that he did in his lunch break, 'studio time'. What if we were to think of our work like that, as we ponder what Whitaker calls a 'lighthouse question'? Could this be a way of making sure the job gets done *and* we have time to, um, think outside the box? Ambidexterity? But do you even have space for 'studio moments'? What is that costing you?

In her book, Whitaker talks about two kinds of creativity – writing the letter and designing the envelope. The former is product design and the latter is the business model. Think of Airbnb: it's a great envelope. They didn't build a single room yet are, arguably, now the world's biggest 'hotel chain'.

She made the point on that day that Point B thinking is happening anyway. We may well be creating an endpoint, but unconsciously, yet it may not be one we want. As I keep saying, not enough effort has gone into how we do remote working. We just turn on our laptop camera and carry on. Couldn't this be the way that we can have studio time, to think outside the to-do list, the email inbox and the Outlook calendar?

Are we taking the robots' jobs?

Do you and your organization have the presence of mind to spot opportunities and use them? Is your team set up for this or just following a script? Or worse – pretending to be alert but just keeping their head down?

What actually concerns me most is not that the robots are taking our jobs but that we are becoming the robots. Higher education has become so expensive that people think about whether they are getting their money's worth. That calculus shuts down many forms of open-ended exploration and risk-taking. Instead of going to college and forming your own Point B as a person, you get adept at solving perfectly for what's in front of you. To borrow a term used by Bill Deresiewicz in 2008, we become 'excellent sheep' – people who can answer questions perfectly but not ask them.[26] I want people to ask questions where there is no answer or where there are multiple answers and being able to live with that as they forge the future.

It's about spotting unexpected patterns, seeing coincidences, asking better questions. This ethos can create breakthroughs. Improv takes advantage of accidents, mistakes, misalignments, limited information. Improv sets out to embrace and use the unexpected. Mistakes and happy accidents are actively sought. It's not 'luck', it's an attuned mind which will mean you are making connections and spotting opportunities which may not otherwise have existed.

And it can be fun.

CHAPTER NINE

Storytelling

*There have been great societies that did not use the
wheel, but there have been no societies that did not
tell stories.* URSULA K LEGUIN

Why stories?

Daniel Kahneman (who was awarded the 2002 Nobel
Memorial Prize in Economic Sciences) talked of the difference between the 'experiencing self' and the 'remembering
self'.[1] The experiencing self lives in the moment (about
three seconds) and the remembering self is the one that
tells you stories after the events, giving them meaning.

Retelling the story is how we come to terms with the past and make decisions about the future. Beginnings and endings loom large, while our brain lets go of what it considers minor details. The story we tell ourselves means we know who we are, what we want and what we can and cannot do. But we may not be right and stories can be rewritten because hindsight can be dynamic.

More and more I am asked to run workshops on storytelling. However, it's not always clear what people understand this to mean. Is it just better presenting skills? Or tidying up the flow of your PowerPoint deck? Or a better way of selling that's less 'sell-y'? Or something that's a bit like purpose or brand? Or something fundamental about what makes a narrative qualitatively different from merely recounting a sequence of events or from bullet points on a slide? *(Spoiler: it can be all of those but I'm most interested in the last one and from that flow all the others. I will give my presenting tips in the Toolbox at the end of the chapter.)*

CASE STUDY   CEO no-no

I was shocked when a professional services firm had spent over half a million pounds flying in their people and putting on an expensive conference, yet the CEO hadn't prepped a speech. He did have a scruffy piece of paper – a little bigger than two cigarette packets – on which he had written a few notes in the tea break. I met lots of consultants in the following years who had left that firm. Presentation skills – which means preparing – are not a 'nice-to-have'. They are vital. If the CEO can't be bothered to put in the time (and they should), then at least organize a Number Two who can.

What lies beneath

I am convinced that *story* is what underpins all my work – the story of your team, your organization, your customer, your colleagues and being able to co-create stories with others, as well as letting your own story unfold, embracing moments of the past, the present and the future. Part of that is being able to stand up and tell that story. The medium and the message are not separate. I was struck by this when running a workshop near São Paolo. Three young thirty-somethings, from Argentina, Brazil and Uruguay, came to me afterwards for advice about overcoming nerves before a presentation, just as people of all ages have from London to Leeds, from Milan to Manhattan, from Oxford to Oslo, from Southampton to Singapore, from Dublin to Durban, from Shanghai to Shoreditch. Of course, the superficial answer is 'rehearse' but the deeper answer is: tell stories you believe in.

I worked with the innovative marketing consultancy, Contagious, who would hold events called 'Now Next Why': what's happening now, what's happening next and why?[2] A great structure: just one of many with three 'acts' which are memorable for teller and for audience alike. When I suggest storytelling as an essential business skill (and definitely for leaders and would-be leaders) people tell me they are no good at it. So I ask them to tell a non-business story or even one of a failure at work. They reveal not only that they do possess this skill but I also learn much more about who they really are. 'Purpose' is hard to nail as a concept but tell me a couple of stories and I begin to understand you.

Then I came across Marshall Ganz and his formulation of 'Public Narrative':[3]

- *A story of now*: What's your current challenge or vision, for which action is required at this moment?
- *A story of us*: What are the values or aspirations that will lead others to action?
- *A story of self*: What brought you to this moment and where did those values come from?

These are very powerful, especially when you hear the moving stories of those who have chosen to lead in the public sector, where the destinies of many families, many people, young and old, could be very fragile.

Story is the original human software. It existed (apparently!) even before spreadsheets, even before language. The earliest cave drawings are more like stories than bullet points on a slide.[4] Story identifies causal linkages, connecting events from our past or to our present, daring us to predict the future. Keith Oatley (novelist and Professor Emeritus of Cognitive Psychology at Toronto University) says that stories are more than entertainment, they are a kind of mental 'flight simulator' for social situations.[5] Every time I ask people to share stories (and we always start with personal not business tales), something profound happens. I am not saying that each story is deep and meaningful. Sometimes they are just funny or sweet, revealing human foibles which are common to us all.

(Full disclosure: once in a while the stories people bring are dull or not even a story but an event where nothing was at stake which may give nothing away about the storyteller. That in itself is instructive. The person might be young or is

just not ready yet to share vulnerability. I watch them listen-
ing to the stories that others bring or even better when they
tell someone else's story and the seed in their imagination
has been planted of how this powerful and accessible tool
could enhance their communication prowess.)

More and more, I see that an audience at an improv show, whether they know it or not, is looking for story beyond laughter. Short sketch stories, perhaps (though there are plenty of brilliant theatre troupes that do 'long-form' where they tell more involved stories), but also the story of that night's show – how we six work with each other, Reincorporate themes from earlier moments and even how audience members become a micro-story as they grow in confidence to give suggestions.

Story theory

So I have looked at the theory of story structure, about which much has been written. Joseph Campbell wrote *The Hero With a Thousand Faces* based on his study of mythology and religion influenced by the work of Freud and Jung and other 20th-century thinkers.[6] It tells of the stages of the archetypal hero's journey, which has many common elements across many different traditions. It is the basis of many screenwriting workshops, with the 12 steps used as the go-to story structure for Hollywood and beyond.[7]

I once went through these elements (including The Call to Adventure, The Mentor, Crossing the Threshold, Seizing the Sword, The Ordeal, Resurrection, The Return with the Elixir and others) with a business school audience. Big

Mistake! There was too much highfalutin detail, leaving my audience of middle-ranking managers puzzled. They just wanted a spreadsheet.

That's why I like the three-act structures I mentioned above (from Ganz and Contagious). Others might have four and sometimes five (Shakespeare, for one). Even with three acts, people might struggle, it feels a bit of a stretch. But it is worth it if I can help them see beyond just 'I was told what to do, I did it.'

Even asking them to think of what the situation was *before* (what was wrong or lacking) and what it was *after* (things were better, we saved money, energy or lives) helps them begin to create a narrative, since those could be Acts One and Three of a story.

Simple story structures

Story involves ups and downs, learning lessons, changes, intention, purpose, surprises, heroes, side-kicks, enemies and love. Many stories fit into the classic three-act structure:

Act One: Put a man up a tree
Act Two: Keep him there
Act Three: Bring him down

Does Act Two feel a little light? Surely he's busy trying to get down? Or learning what it's like to live up a tree? Many of the organizations I work with are stuck up a tree. A half-day workshop will make them understand the leaves and branches and each other a little better but won't answer the question of why they shouldn't be up that tree – or another tree – or on the ground or even that some are eating more fruit than others. (I may have extended this metaphor too far. Sorry.)

Then I read about the wonderful Brene Brown giving a talk at Pixar Animation Studios.[8] President Ed Catmull said that the middle of the creative process is hardest. In Act Two, for example, the protagonist must endure a difficult journey to learn a lesson. Brown picked up on this. Don't skip the second act. Company reports don't tend to mention that difficult bit. It is airbrushed out of the picture as they reduce it to 'We faced a situation, then we overcame it': thank you very much shareholders, no need to worry. The reality is more complex. There are false turns, blind alleys, panic, boredom, fallings out, betrayals. We omit what Brown calls that 'potential for shame'. But that's what make mere events into a story. What was at stake? What obstacles were overcome? What new strengths and skills were forged in the moment?

The power of story

'Stories bring together the external, observable, objective world and our internal experience of our minds,'[9] says Dr Dan Siegel, author of *The Developing Mind: How relationships and the brain interact to shape who we are.*[10] The stories we tell children of our own childhood affect them deeply. 'The best predictor of a child's security of attachment is not what happened to his parents as children, but rather how his parents made sense of those childhood experiences.'[11] Making sense is about creating a 'life narrative', which acknowledges both positive and negative moments but which made them who they are. This applies to leaders too. The stories leaders tell their teams create (or fail to create) the necessary psychological safety.

Why is this so? When we tell and listen to stories, neurons are firing in our brains. 'Neurons that fire together wire together' said Donald Hebb, a Canadian neuropsychologist in 1949. In 2010 some Princeton researchers found that the engaged listener's brain actually syncs up with that of the storyteller.[12] They also found 'areas that exhibit predictive anticipatory responses' but that this spatial and temporal coupling 'vanishes when participants fail to communicate'.

This makes intuitive sense. A story isn't just what is happening; it's the anticipation created in the listener's mind for what could happen next and where it may lead. I see this in my workshops all the time: the audience invests – whether it be a simple story of a holiday mishap, a surprise romantic moment or a seemingly mundane set-up that leads to extraordinary life changes.

Isn't it a bit like when a stand-up pauses because the audience is ahead of them? Or 'dramatic irony' in a play or movie when the audience 'gets' something before the characters? It's delicious. No wonder scientists talk about 'narrative transportation', where you are so involved you feel you really are 'there' rather than in the real world.[13] And that is where there are so many possibilities for storytelling – for connection about a story told but also one foretold about what the future may hold, especially in leadership and business development.

With something this powerful is it any wonder more and more organizations are asking for help with their storytelling skills? Here, again, is a 'technology' accessible to all, which can enhance motivation, inclusion and well-being. It costs nothing except time and energy, which are in short supply but it pays great dividends.

So you should begin to make this part of your toolbox. Every day, you will see others tell a story. It may even be as short as a sentence but take note of what they are trying to achieve in telling it. In your notebook, jot down stories of your own life and work which could come in handy: tales of success, failure, insight learnt through experience. Carl Jung once asked himself 'what is the myth you are living?', but I think that this myth can change and develop, sometimes becoming understandable in hindsight, sometimes changed by a conscious decision about the future.[14]

What elements make a story?

These include protagonist, obstacles and setbacks, jeopardy, choice, not ducking the challenge, insight formed through action, mentor, dilemma, a gripping start, a clear ending, not just action but 'colour' and detail, agency and purpose. In the telling, some details may be left out and others enhanced and the order matters.

Stories affect our brains and bodies

They bring ideas to life, inspiring emotions of fear or amazement. They actually affect us mentally and physically. If improv could be said to be a left-brain approach to right-brain creativity, then story surely involves both logic and emotion, both big picture and details. So both parts of your brain are working and that increased neural activity means that connections are being made between what you are seeing and hearing afresh and what you already knew. You don't have to dump the old data but it's integrating with the new. You might even call this wisdom. Stories help us define who we are as individuals and as collectives. Buzzwords like brand and purpose are really just story in a tuxedo.

Stories began when we were wearing animal skins. They were told around the campfire. How else to share the best hunting zones or the danger spots? Stories smoothed the wheels (even before they were invented) of collaboration, which meant we could seize opportunities, avoid pitfalls but also nurture a sense of belonging. When we forget the stories of our predecessors, we are liable to repeat their mistakes.

Professor Nicholson of London Business School told me that, presented with three facts, we may remember them. But string a story together connecting the three facts and we not only remember them but believe the story. That's why I always encourage my presentation coachees to use stories, preferably their own. There's no need for lengthy scripting or bullet points because you know the material: it's yours. Just tell the story to make a point. It's easier to recall for both speaker and audience.

Oxytocin is the bonding hormone, enhancing empathy for others, and storytelling helps increase it.[15] We feel connected to the characters but more open to varying perspectives. This is why I encourage you to have as many stories at your fingertips as possible. Use the one or two that fit the people and the situation in front of you. It's not just about happy endings. We all love a story of a billionaire failing. A cautionary tale warning against a certain course of action is very persuasive. Have some in your armoury ('Well, of course, you could go with Jim's management consultancy but so did another of our clients... and six months later they called us in to clear up the mess.')

Dopamine is released when you learn something new or your interest is piqued or you feel inspired and it helps you remember. Endorphins are released when, among other things, we laugh or our emotions are aroused. Endorphins improve cognitive function and promote memory formation. What role does dopamine play in memory and why? Psychologists Daphna Shohamy and R Alison Adcock investigated this in 2010 saying that 'Memory is essential to adaptive behaviour because it allows past experience to guide choices.'[16] Dopamine helps your 'adaptive memory' because it files moments that are relevant, keeping them accessible and useful for informing future actions: 'Dopamine release before, during, and after an event supports hippocampal plasticity and episodic memory formation... enabling memory for past experience to support future adaptive behaviour.'

So now we know. Robots aren't there yet. By the way, 'adaptive forgetting' can be useful too, can't it? Both for our emotional well-being and for streamlining the story and for simple data retrieval. 'A memory system that retained the ability to reconstruct all knowledge and experiences might become unwieldy, so a system that forgets is likely efficient', found two researchers from Purdue University in the United States.[17] Robots should be jealous of our efficacious systems. If only they could feel any emotions, the heartless rotters. But storytelling isn't just about recounting facts. It's about including what matters (in the right order) as well as excluding what doesn't matter.

Mirror neurons

I wrote about mirror neurons in my last book which was about people skills.[18] When you observe someone do something or express an emotion, you mentally mirror them, possibly unconsciously. You feel tearful when the protagonist in the movie cries. There's a read-across from what we observe to what happens within our own neural wiring in the motor and sensory regions. There is some controversy about mirror neurons, because not all scientists are on the same page.

In 2000, the famous neuroscientist VS Ramachandran wrote an article speculating that 'mirror neurons would do for psychology what DNA did for biology'.[19] It was thought that they might help us understand autism (the 'broken mirror' hypothesis) but that has not been the case. Nevertheless, the notion of mirror neurons is accepted and even a prominent sceptic thinks that 'they probably play a role in enabling imitation, given that there must be *some* mechanism in the brain that converts an observed action to a series of muscle commands.'[20]

Actually, Dr Uri Hasson of the Princeton Neuroscience Institute, using magnetic resonance imaging (fMRI), found that brains become aligned when listening to the same story.[21] Our brains show similar activity. Thrillingly, when Russian and English speakers listened to the same story (in their own language) there was still alignment. It doesn't stop there. When one person described a scene from the

BBC TV show *Sherlock* to another who had not seen it, there was alignment between the two people. For the first person, even the brain activity when retelling was similar to that when they watched it themselves. This is powerful and has, obviously, been used for good and ill. A story doesn't have to be true to create this impact. Demagogues know this. Remember that story is unavoidable because narrative emerges regardless of facts.

Story combines logic and emotion

Stories are memory aids, instruction manuals and moral compasses. ALEKS KROTOSKI[22]

Because emotions are at play, we are better able to remember. The improved processing means we are able to retrieve the 'data' later. People recall moments that made them cry or laugh much more readily. Why? It seems that emotions are a flag to the brain that what you are experiencing is important.

(Have you ever flagged an email? Because I am a twerp, I once flagged my entire inbox. I then had to un-flag each message by hand. I can tell you, there was some emotional language muttered that day.)

Emotion is crucial to survival. According to research from the University of Basel, published in October 2022, 'Both positive and negative emotional experiences are stored particularly well in memory.'[23] The cerebellum becomes involved, which is a big deal, leading to better recall. 'The cerebellum is an integral component of a network that is responsible for the improved storage of emotional information', said Professor

Dominique de Quervain. This isn't always a positive thing. I do notice some friends are frustratingly good at recalling mostly bad stories. My intention is that this book creates a new narrative – encouraging you to explore what you are capable of already and how you might apply it plus what might be possible, as well as making you think about the moments you can prepare and those in which you can face uncertainty with a creative mindset.

Story is pervasive

You don't have a choice – people will make up their own story about events and about people: right or wrong. They will assign meaning, agency and motivation to others and to incidents – whether you like it or not. Think about gossip. This is nothing more than sense-making through story – assigning motive and intention whether it's true or not. In a famous 1949 experiment Fritz Heider and Mary-Ann Simmel found that people made up a story to fit the movements of animated geometric shapes, attributing agency and motivation.[24] Stories are viral. So unless you get your story out there and it is relatable and shareable, then the 'fake news' story could win out. So storytelling isn't just a nice-to-have, it's more than that.

I love the notion of Positive Gossip which I learnt from studying the Solutions Focus.[25] Positive gossip is about articulating when someone has done something of value. Not only do people then begin to notice more but also we tend to live up to those raised expectations. Gossip is really just sharing stories. It need not be antithetical to team-building or productivity.

A friend of mine, Martin Shovel, writes speeches and says 'story is a great invention because it means you don't have to say everything.'[26] In fact, 'if you do try to say everything, you end up saying nothing.' So often, when working on presentations, I find that a story fits the bill. There's no need for slides or even writing a script, because my client knows the story, having lived it. Story is easier to recall for teller and audience as I have said and which I see every day. So in your bullet-point script you can just put such and such story and there's several minutes of your presentation that you know will land.

Stories have psychic tension

Why do stories keep us hooked? This is partially due to the Zeigarnik Effect. Bluma Zeigarnik was a Lithuanian–Soviet psychologist, writing in 1927, studying the phenomenon whereby waiters failed to remember orders once they had been paid but could recall as yet unpaid orders.[27] Her hypothesis was that people were more likely to remember incomplete tasks because they spurred 'psychic tension'. Once someone completes a task, this relieves psychic tension, thus they can release it from their memory, no longer using cognitive effort to remember the task.

Your brain might over-focus on that single unresolved thing, rather than the many issues that have been resolved. I know if someone doesn't reply in good time, I can imagine all sorts of bad scenarios why not (I said the wrong thing, they don't want to give me the gig, they don't know how to tell me I'm charging too much). Each of these can be true, but more often it is that they have been busy/away/checking-with-the-boss or their reply got 'stuck in Drafts'. This is why stories keep us hooked. We know a negative outcome is possible, likely even, so we need to keep watching/reading/listening because our brain's 'cause-and-effect' buttons have been pressed. We can't help but become involved.

> *The confidence that individuals have in their beliefs depends mostly on the quality of the story they can tell about what they see, even if they see little.* DANIEL KAHNEMAN[28]

Story is what really engages an audience. It makes sense of the past, gives context to the present and inspiration for the future. A story can make a strategy come to life. Story is the original 'human software'. It is still the way we 'make meaning'.

Underpowered by PowerPoint, dazzled by data

PowerPoint lacks psychic tension unless it is used very skilfully. Very often, ineffective presenters talk *to* a slide instead of talking to their audience. They've laid it out, then they read it out: no surprises, no dots for the audience to connect. There is plenty of data out there but good data scientists must become storytellers too, to give real insight which can lead to action. I work with tech firms, eager to tell their stories. You see the numbers don't always 'speak for themselves'. They need careful interpretation. I heard the country head of a big management consultancy say that CEOs don't like PowerPoint. One even assumed you were lying if you resorted to it.

I don't go that far but I always ask, 'what if you had to do this in candle-light?' What if there were a power outage?

The bottom line is that the written word can convey detail, while inspiration is mostly about the spoken word. Using PowerPoint means you fall between two stools. Can you remember an amazing PowerPoint presentation? One? Two? Two stick out in my mind. Both of them were just a series of pictures. No text. One was the head of a media company. Each photo was a striking image – mostly nothing to do with the sector, often funny. Each was a metaphor to explain how she saw the past, present and future. She spoke for 15 minutes. Looking around the room, I could see everyone leaning in, looking at the picture when it came up, fully concentrating on her as she spoke. In my head I thought, 'This is buying 18 months to two years of strong commitment from the audience.' She was full of energy and looked at home onstage.

The other person I recall was not as ebullient as her. He was the head of IT of a supermarket talking to a British Telecom audience about a recent transformation they had done together. His presentation was basically like a 'holiday album' of the process – just photos of people involved, from both companies. We saw the first day of the project and various moments along the way. We saw the day it was scheduled to finish but inevitably it hadn't, so people looked rather frazzled. Then he showed an elated bunch on the actual last day. He didn't hold back. He had been annoyed with BT at times, as they fussed over rebranding of the division and forgot about their customer, but this meant the story stuck as he shared lessons learnt.

Much of my work these days is working with leaders who have lost the art (or is it science?) of story. Since PowerPoint came along, computer slide decks have become the common language of business presentations (or the Tower of Babel?) They are often created by a stressed junior who wants to be seen to have done a good job by putting in as much stuff as possible. So a 50-slide deck is deemed 10 times 'better' than five slides. But the real work is not in putting slides together but in grappling with what message or story needs to be conveyed.

The leader is too busy (or too nervous about the whole idea of presenting) to sift through and choose what the actual message is, so is left to stand alone at the conference intoning some semi-articulated opinions, clicking through interminable, over-crafted unfiltered images and text. I usually find that, when pressed, the leader can articulate their case well. It needs only a few slides or none. Often, perhaps about two-thirds the way through, there is a single slide that says it all. It's usually a picture, a simple image or possibly a graph.

However, beware the graph. Graphs are a summary. Always look at the scales. Do they start at zero? Are they logarithmic? Ask the journalist, do you mean exponential? Or do you actually mean quadratic? Numbers are not in short supply: justified analysis is.

Patient pathway versus surface survey

My first inkling that story should be an organizational tool was when working with the NHS. I coached two leaders on their presentations. One walked me through her slides. We reached one that was so stuffed full of explanatory notes that it would have taken me 10 minutes simply to read the words. She carried on with her talk. It bore no relation to what I was looking at. 'Hang on', I said, 'Should I be listening to you or looking at this slide?'

'Oh. I'd never thought of that', came her beautifully candid answer.

She (and so many others like her) had not considered the audience. It was like handing in an essay. She was to talk and show her slides and that was her duty done. What the audience took from it (or not) was up to them. Interestingly, the other leader was talking about the 'patient journey'. Yes, she had some slides but the fascinating insight was that patients might often tick the 5 (out of 5) box in their feedback but include something in the 'Any Other Comments' section that showed that parts of their experience had been way below par. None of the 'tick-box' questions had detected this. So there was now a new way of understanding the 'patient pathway'. Ask them. Let them tell their story. This 'data' was much richer.

Since then, technology has been developed which can quantify this 'qualitative' information even from telephone conversations. If you tick 3 out of 5, I learn hardly anything. Every questionnaire will leave something out. Donald Rumsfeld might call it the unknown knowns or the unknown unknowns. Asking people (customers, suppliers, interviewees, vendors and more) to tell their story is often a great way to unearth this profound data.

Applying storytelling to business

Politics is the art of competitive storytelling. JOE KLEIN[29]

Business is no different. Stories are so useful in business because they bring clarity and engagement while helping us aspire to the heights or assuage the lows. They are especially useful as a leadership or sales tool.

Leader as storyteller

After over 20 years of doing this management training malarkey, I have found that one thing looms larger than others – the notion of leader as storyteller. I've talked about humour, but you don't have to be a joke-teller though you do have to be comfortable with *story* to persuade and engage. This is not just about how to improve presentation skills, but how to make sense of what is going on. A story can handle ambiguity, uncertainty, the past, the future and a complex present.

I saw Tom Peters speak at the London Business Forum in the early 2000s and he said that 'leaders don't make decisions, they create meaning'. So it is the responsibility of the leader to articulate the story of what brought us here and where we are heading. That may be enough. Everything else may be detail or even micromanaging. It takes courage to step back and not be the lead character in every scene.

The idea of leader as storyteller may leave you cold or raising your eyes to heaven. Isn't it just another fad, overemphasizing the 'soft' over the, hard' skills? Isn't leadership about getting on with the job, knowing the numbers, managing bad performance, recruiting the right people, speaking up at board meetings, answering emails and, you know, wearing a suit and turning up at the team-build ten-pin bowling night and buying the drinks and making sure the new young chap behaves himself and gets home safely?

Yes, it can be all those. None of that precludes the notion that your job as leader is to give some sense of direction, purpose and hope as your team struggles with head office edicts, personality clashes and new car parking arrangements. Early in my meanderings into management training, I was lucky enough to meet the late Iain Mangham of Bath University Business School.[30] It was he, I can now reveal, who put me off taking an MBA. 'Oh no, you don't want to do that', he said, though he himself had taught on such courses. 'You'll talk like *them*.' For him, management was, 'Have a plan. Communicate it.'

That is deceptively simple. What is a plan? Does it look like a spreadsheet? Numbers and stuff? And how do you communicate it? Send out an email? The answer to both – having a plan and communicating it – is STORY. It is about shaping a narrative that admits flaws but sees them as steps along the way, not episodes to be forgotten or dismissed.

Case studies are stories

I always tell clients that they should have a tapas menu of stories in mind. Small dishes, some of which may not excite your client and some of which they will love and re-order. Do you like tapas? Some people might have multiple iterations of *gamberoni* or *patatas bravas*, but you should have a wider array of stories available to fit the moment. As well as successful case studies, include personal tales, maybe where you've failed or been helped, but for which you are grateful. Have about 10 stories that reflect the breadth of what your team have achieved in the past, which illustrate what you could do for others in the future.

I work with a lot of management consultants and many of them, younger mostly but not exclusively, cannot easily articulate what it is they do (even if they can recite the company 'purpose'). Or if they try, they slip into business jargon nonsense, LinkedIn lingo. So we do an exercise: describe the project in two ways. First, with as many buzzwords as possible (leverage, alignment, KPI, digitization, blue-sky thinking, scalable solutions, deliverables, outcomes, medium-term goals and many more). Second, describe it to your eight-year-old niece or nephew in everyday terms. Some struggle with the second part. So I often suggest using metaphor – we tidied up their data cupboard, we uncrossed some wires, we installed a clever widget that helped reduce waste.

A story structure: SCQA

Many people struggle when I ask them to think of their work in terms of story. So I am going to give you some simple structures that can help. For those who would like a bit of left-brain type structure, there are plenty on offer. Barbara Minto, an ex-McKinsey consultant, came up with Situation, Complication, Question, Answer.[31]

Here is a quick summary:

Situation: What is the context? How did the problem emerge?

Complication: Something has changed. Why is it important to solve this now?

Question: What actually is the nub? What are we trying to solve?

Answer: What are the next steps which lead to the solution?

I know some clients who find this so useful that they use it when composing emails. Others can't separate Situation and Complication because they seem as one. That's fine. We go with a three-act structure.

A story structure: Set-up, conflict, resolution

This is the three-act structure that many Hollywood movies use. I referred above to sorting out Acts One and Three, then filling Act Two, but here are some more pointers.

Start strong. Grab your audience; clearly something relatable is in play. Not 'thanks for your time, I won't take long, here's the first slide' type of start. Andrew Stanton of Pixar says, 'Make me care.'[32] Show me that something is at stake, that a surprise, a laugh, a twist or an insight are on the way. You do that with the words and your manner. Stories can inspire or excite or reassure or frighten. They tend to be great at selling, when the customer identifies with the unfolding narrative.

Another three-act story structure: Overview, approach, outcome

Executive coach Joel Garfinkle talks about individuals telling their story but I think it works for teams and organizations too.[33] He calls Act One the *overview*. What was wrong or missing? Give a number (say, money spent or time taken or customers lost). He calls Act Two the *approach* – what did you do? What skills or expertise did you draw upon? Make Act Two more compelling by mentioning some difficulties or blind alleys, perhaps. Your audience should be rooting for you. Then Act Three describes the *outcome*, the new state of affairs, with a number directly comparable to the one mentioned earlier in the overview. This really helps crystallize thoughts for some of my clients – especially if I make them write Acts One and Three first, simply and succinctly, just a sentence before filling in Act Two.

Different genres of business story

Depending on the type of business, I have found it useful for people to think of a variety of narratives to have at their fingertips. So think of the following categories:

1. THE STORY OF THE PAST

- How did the business start (could be rags to riches or someone with a twinkle)?
- How did our team evolve?
- How did the client get where they are?
- How did the market come to be as it is?

2. THE STORY OF NOW

- What are the facts on the ground? The state of the market.
- On what 'pitch' is the client actually playing? What are the 'elephants in the room'?

- What are we up to right now? Sexy projects that 'I shouldn't really be telling you about'?

3. THE STORY OF THE FUTURE

- What are our next steps?
- How do we envision the story ending – for the client or the end user?

Two handy story genres

1 *Defeating the Dragon:* how we overcame the odds (we conquered the downside).
2 *The Quest for the Treasure:* how we gained something of value (we secured the upside).

There tends to be a baddie in most stories. The other day I was running a workshop for the financial services division of a management consultancy. One cheeky chappy asked if the regulator could be cast as the baddie. Structurally, yes of course. 'Defeating the dragon' could simply mean obeying the rules, in a timely and cost-efficient manner.

Sales and storytelling

Stories are a great device in business development. They engage people without seeming sell-y. You ask for nothing more than attention. But you need different stories for different moments:

- When the client has no real idea who you are. Do you have a defining story?
- The client knows a little about you and has given you a brief. How can you offer a unique insight?

- You are already working with the client but they don't know the breadth and depth of what you do. Listen to what might be keeping them awake at night.

Who is your protagonist (the hero or heroine of your story)?

- you
- your team or organization
- your boss
- your client
- your client's customer, the end user
- the product/device/software you made
- the project itself

Try out your stories on colleagues

Why not ask a colleague if you can try out your story on them, ahead of a meeting? Offer to do the same in return. Tell them what you are going to say. Then have them repeat it back to you – as close to the actual words you said as possible. It's a great exercise, since you can be surprised because what you *think* you said is *not* what they heard. But it could be that they say it better than you. So steal that. Plus it means they have a little bit more investment in your story. That could be handy for a future project.

Can you co-create story in the moment?

So arm yourself with stories from the past, but it's even more effective if you can listen to a client or colleague and then, in the moment, reframe their story – of where they are or where they want to be. Story has such power, so bring it to emerging, as-yet-unwritten situations.

You will create real engagement if you are able to listen to someone, then reframe the events and aspirations as a story, showing you have insight into where they are and where they could be or what could be done to solve the problem or take advantage of the opportunity. Story is not just how we see our past. We can be simultaneously 'discovering' and inventing the narrative.

Can you tell your own personal story?

Can you make sense of your mistakes and the good fortune that has fallen your way? I saw Amy Cuddy speak at the London Business Forum about *presence*. Luckily for her, it's also the title of her book. She describes 'presence' as being able to tell your own story, with relaxed confidence so that afterwards you feel that you showed the best of yourself.

I find in virtual sessions that people are more willing to share something of themselves, because they are in their home. I ask them in advance to bring an object that illustrates something or means a lot to them, maybe how they managed through lockdown or what they aspire to. I had seen similar things tried before 2020 but it's so much easier to bring an object to your laptop camera than to have to pack it in hand luggage. I have heard some amazing stories. I do a more instantaneous version too. During the workshop, I ask them to go and find a hat; or something made of wood; or something yellow; or something that makes them smile. The energy lifts – in their face and body and voice – which is so often lacking in business presentations.

It's okay to be personal. It needn't be self-indulgent or vain but be judicious. I was once scheduled to speak in five minutes' time when a particular leader (from the food and beverage sector) stood up. He shared a charming personal story. I was impressed by his candour and his audience were really 'there'. Not for long. Eighty minutes and two marriages later I'd had more than enough. So had his team.

However, if you don't know your story, it's hard for you to make sense of the world and perhaps hard for us to make sense of you. If we know a little more about you we will comprehend why you are doing what you do and why you might want us to do something. We want to understand people through their stories.

Every moment is a story or is contributing to a story. Our narrative brain is always making story, whether we ask it to or not. We are defined by and are defining that story, in the moment, whether it be three seconds or three decades. So, before reading my Toolbox on presenting, make yourself scribble some notes – half a dozen stories that would help others understand you. Don't go into detail yet, just the title will do. Mix in personal and work moments.

TOOLBOX   Presenting

You can learn the skills but I often find that the anxiety has to be managed as well, so I adopt a twin approach – working on the skills while seeking to uncover what may be blocking people from trying them out.

There are three elements to any presentation – content, delivery and structure. Too often people just think about content. Think about telling stories. They are easier for you to remember and to engage the audience.

Prepping a presentation

1 Record yourself speaking a few rough ideas on your smartphone. You can be free and easy, no pressure. And you are using the spoken word, not the written word.

2 Listen back to yourself a few times. Write down what you like and add some bullet points.

3 Using your early draft script, record a version, even though you don't feel ready.

4 Listen back. You will be surprised that you are probably over 50 per cent of the way there. Decide what you need to add: extra thoughts, precise data.

5 Now write a new running order. Then rehearse with that by your side.

Microstructures

To stop your presentation being boring, introduce some microstructures, maybe after your first draft. Make sure you have a strong start. This may actually be the last thing you write. Have an equally clear close; even better if it back-references your opening. This 'bookending' is very satisfying.

Here are some other microstructures I suggest speakers use:

- *Metaphor/analogy* (try to find ones that aren't over-used such as, 'we're on a journey', 'on the front foot', 'leaning in'…).

- *Rule of three* (A, B, C; red, white and blue; beginning, middle and end. The Greeks called this the tricolon. It's rhythmically satisfying and easy to recall for speaker and listener).

- *Rhetorical question:* more engaging than merely stating the facts as it makes the listener do some work as they conjure an image ('What would it feel like to work with us?', 'Could you do without your mobile phone for a day?').
- *Killer facts:* a number that says it all (we saved $20 million). I say 'killer' not filler. Mention too many numbers and they lose their power.

Conserve your energy

Have a post-presentation ritual. So that you are not thinking, 'I've got another meeting after this'; deliberately put in something calm after the event, otherwise you won't give the presentation full energy (which is particularly tempting for virtual presentations). It could be a walk, a cup of tea (or something stronger) or a meet-up with a friend. My own go-to rites are to tidy up the room where the workshop took place, to put back the chairs, take the paper off the flip-chart, then have a walk or sit down without talking to anyone before I begin the journey home. This is harder with virtual, but I 'de-rig' my set-up whereby my laptop, mic and webcam are balanced on boxes and books so I can stand and deliver. Ideally, I change all my clothes too, since they are all drenched in sweat (too much information?). But I give as much in a workshop as I do for a one-man show. I don't know any other way.

VECTOR

I have prepared plenty of presentation handouts over the last 20 years – to ad agencies, global corporates, students and beyond. I mulled over each one but none quite captured what I wanted to share with a particular audience recently – clever people, accomplished in their chosen career, probably good at giving technically robust yet dry presentations but now having to extend themselves into both inspiring their teams and selling to outsiders. (Oh, all right, I'll spill the beans: they were lawyers.)

A handy new acronym didn't come to me. Sometimes, once I have a few letters and a word is emerging, I work backwards to see what the remaining letters might suggest. Some would call this 'backing into' a solution. Cynics would call it 'crowbarring'. I call it creative inspiration. When I came across the quote, 'How do I know what I think until I see what I say?', by EM Forster, I was delighted. We acknowledge that the unconscious guides us, so how about being a bit conscious and allowing a letter to inspire you to nail the answer?

I came up with VECTOR:

Voice
Eye contact
Conversational
Transition
Own the space
Rehearsal

A great word, that I mentioned in Chapter 1 on the discussion about momentum. Speed tells us how fast something is going. A vector tells us that PLUS its direction. It is helpful in determining the position of one point in space relative to another. I liked it in connection to presenting – because it's not just about expending energy waywardly but harnessing it in the direction that will create the best impact.

Voice

Your voice is very important – even more so in virtual, where it may be the only 'signal' being received. In an instant the hearer will decide if you are sure of yourself or not. This is not a 'given'. You can have the impact you want but work on your voice. Make yourself take a breath in before speaking on the out breath. Avoid monotone, that 'reading out my essay' vibe. Slow down. Speak loudly enough – even if you have a mic. Avoid disfluencies ('y'know', 'um', 'like') and obvious repetitions where you haven't bothered to vary your wording (usually repeating superlatives like 'brilliant' or 'amazing' or nervous tics like 'basically'). You are allowed only one such word per presentation, okay? This will be helped by rehearsal and listening back to yourself on a voice note app.

Eye contact

Look at your audience. All of them, not just the nice ones or the important ones. Spread it around. Connect with one person at a time. That momentary energy will transfer to everyone in the room. Don't look down at your notes for more than a glance. DO NOT KEEP LOOKING BEHIND YOU AT YOUR SLIDES ON THE SCREEN. This will be helped by rehearsal.

Conversational

Be conversational in tone. Speak in real, human terms, not jargon. Your audience may be technically qualified so you can use relevant vocabulary but if EVEN ONE person is baffled by your fancy words make sure you explain them. This will be helped by rehearsal.

Transition

Transitions between speakers can be so messy. I always make teams rehearse these so that they flow and add credibility to the individuals and to the team. 'Passing the ball' cleanly is vital. You need to know who is coming next, where they are sitting and exactly how to introduce them.

Messy transitions between speakers include:

- 'Do you want the clicker?'
- 'Um, who's next?
- 'Here's Phil. He's going to talk about boring stuff.'

It also looks bad when the person picking up the ball says 'I've got to hurry now because we're over-running'. Don't draw attention to the fact the team are under-rehearsed; much easier to do if you are, um, properly rehearsed.

Also, look at transitions in your presentation. Do you have a flow, building to a memorable call to action or conclusion, or do you just have a sequence of slides spliced together because you didn't have time to marshal your argument? And how are your transitions from one slide to another? Ever heard someone say the following?

- 'This isn't really relevant but I forgot to take it out from the last presentation I did or from the pack that someone has ordered me to inflict on you.'
- 'We think this is a good slide but don't know where to put it so bunged it in here. Please let me gloss over it.'

No? But you know that's what the subtext was. You wouldn't turn up to a presentation without having checked your trousers, so check your slides too – ahead of the day, and on the day, in situ.

This will be helped by, you guessed it, rehearsal.

Own the space

Confident body language. You are the centre of attention. Keep it that way. Don't fidget. Don't keep adjusting yourself. Use gestures to bring in the audience and add emphasis. You can move but only with intention. Don't saunter aimlessly. Make sure you have moments of stillness, especially for the important points.

This will be helped by rehearsal.

Rehearsal

Rehearse before you're ready – standing up – with some bullet points you haven't spent too long agonizing over. Doing a 'bare bones' run-through often shows that you are more prepared than you thought. But record it on your smartphone. Listen back – make notes based on what you said. You probably came up with some great phrases that would not have come from sitting at a computer. Embrace the cycle of rehearsing and rewriting. Only prepare slides once you have nailed your thread, your flow, the point you are actually trying to make. Maybe aim for the number of slides to end up being one or zero.

Rehearsal is vital. It means you are comfortable with what you are saying, and you are not fumbling about thinking what comes next, and you KNOW HOW LONG IT LASTS. DO NOT LEAVE IT TO THE LAST MINUTE TO SAY THE WORDS OUT LOUD. Your slides may be great but if you are ill-prepared to deliver the presentation which they are supposed to accompany, your discomfort is *all* that your audience will remember.

People don't like rehearsing

What they don't like is what they think rehearsal is – having to memorize it – or doing it a few times, maybe just enough times to make you feel uneasy about the content or the structure. So rewrite, rejig, cut and paste. Proper rehearsal means running it enough times that it doesn't sound rehearsed. That's a lot of times. Double figures, easily.

> *The whole thing about rehearsal is discovery.* ROBERT DE NIRO

You can still have notes in front of you; preferably bullet points, handwritten in your own fair hand, with which you have rehearsed. You will have put something together which fills you with confidence and RUNS TO TIME. But if you don't like rehearsing new material, have a bunch of stories you are comfortable with and don't mind telling on different occasions. You CAN use LASER skills to create (or co-create) the content and then use them if there is a Q&A session.

Virtual presenting

When the Comedy Store closed on 15 March 2020 and all my workshops and speaker engagements were cancelled or postponed, I had to 'pivot' quickly. I soon realized that my background in theatre, but especially in television, radio and commercials would be of great use. I spent years doing 'pieces to camera' and voice-overs. You have to animate your words. While you may not always make love to the camera, you must at least treat it to a success-ful first date.

TOOLBOX   Tips for virtual presentations

Prepare the sound

- Avoid the kitchen or other echoey places with tiles, wood and metal.

- Soft furnishings help warm up the sound (bed, sofa, cushions).

- Speak more slowly than in normal life but not in a monotone.

- Speak loudly, as if in a large room. Mics and speakers on laptops are not great.

- If you have a headset, check with a friend that it's not rubbish; you know, that tinny World War Two pilot sound? The laptop mic could actually be better.

Prepare yourself

- Stand up: you can bring more energy, you can gesture.

- Rehearse.

- Do not have your script on a screen, most definitely not on the screen of the laptop whose camera you are using. You will come across as very dull.

- Have your script in bullet points (handwritten by you) pinned on the wall near and at the same height as the camera.

- If you do use something type-written, have it in a **HUGE FONT, BOLD AND DOUBLE-SPACED.** Otherwise you will be looking at it a split-second too long to decipher it so will lose momentum and engagement.

- Rehearse with your notes. Maybe even with a friendly colleague at the other end.

- Smile.

CHAPTER TEN

Where next?

I know from many individuals and teams over the years that LASER works. I know that preparing yourself and your presentation works too. We can give both Newton and Darwin their due. I have waited a long time to write this book. I can convey only so much in the written word. Reader, it's up to you to take my suggestions and stories and make them your own. But the good news is that you can start immediately. I hope you have already.

Please go and see an improv show. Take an improv course. This is so much easier now that we are used to doing them online. There are many improv books out there, suggesting improv games, but I suggest that you find a class. You can join from anywhere in the world. I know lots of people who have done these in their spare time and not a single one of them didn't find it of use in so many ways, for their creative, communication and collaborative skills, and much more in ways they didn't expect. And it's fun.

Paul Z Jackson, inspirational trainer, author and co-founder (in 2002) of the Applied Improv Network,[1] suggested to me that one day we would no longer have to go under the banner of 'Creativity' or 'Teambuilding' or whatever, but that we could proudly be titled 'Improv' because its power and applicability would be understood. We are not quite there yet but are so much closer than when I nervously started this adventure in 1999.

In August 2022 an MIT Sloan Fellow, Loredana Padurean, listed the '10 smart, not soft skills' you need.[2] Guess what: every single one of them (adaptability, cognitive readiness, emotional maturity, followership, humility, listening, managing up, multiple perspectives, productive inclusion and validation) will be enhanced by the LASER mindset and by practising the skills associated with improv theatre. That list is extracted from her book by *The Job Is Easy, The People Are Not!*[3] What a great title – but that only tells part of the story. People can be great. Get that bit right and your job will be highly fulfilling.

However, it is in this area that careers do falter. A couple of researchers from the consultancy ghSMART in 2018 found that 'often careers of talented executives stall or even derail because of seemingly trivial issues, many of which are utterly fixable.'[4] What were the top four issues? Executive presence, communication style, peer-level relationships and, in a small number of cases, excessive optimism or perfectionism. They give a typical case – the candidate whose resumé checked all of the boxes (and then some), but his Achilles heel was a long-winded, almost philosophical communication style. That is exactly who I am often brought in to help.

These things are not set in stone. If you have the will, you can learn the skill. I see this, week in, week out. Fear does impede people and this sometimes looks like lack of motivation but, with one-on-one attention, from someone who believes you can do it, going at the right pace and finding your particular buttons, it is possible.

For example, for each person I have found one thing that anchors their confidence when presenting. For one, it was just saying 'Good morning, Vietnam', channelling Robin Williams before going on. For another, she just had to say 'ham' to herself, as in 'ham it up', which means to over-express.[5] With that exaggerated picture in her head, she was able to bring energy and confidence, never again to freeze in mid-sentence and having to be led away in a vital presentation, which was the reason she had been brought to me.

We always find a process or stimulus that puts them in the right zone. We have to embrace Woodrow Wilson's Newton/Darwin dichotomy. You can treat yourself as a machine, tuned up, rehearsed and prepared with your routine... so that you are confident in the moment to be fully adaptable.

I wonder if remote working has made things harder for you or easier? Surrounded by familiar items, perhaps in your slippers, do you feel more able to give a polished performance or seize the moment and jump in to conversations? There is a whole new set of parameters to play with in the virtual dance but you should ensure that you are even better prepared, with bullet points tacked to the wall, great sound and vision...

I started this book mentioning the twin shadows of Remote and Robots. I wanted to show that there are so many opportunities to be grasped and that we still have the edge over robots because humans can be creative and truly engage with other humans. But with artificial intelligence, we cannot be haphazard either. Investment of time, energy and money will be necessary. Some jobs will be lost but others created and people will need training:

> Although there is a net-benefit to the labour market and to wages of these technology implementations, it does not immediately translate to benefits to individual workers. Yes, more jobs are created than are lost to technology, but those jobs are likely to demand a different set of skills...

says the researcher Dr Angelos Theodorakopoulos from Oxford's Martin School.[6] This book is about those very skills, some of which I have laid out here, some of which will be found and honed using the LASER mindset.

Reading this book has been a fairly passive act for you. I hope you have enjoyed it but I'm looking for more from you, frankly. The change expert, Allister Frost (Microsoft's first ever Head of Digital Marketing Strategy) talks about a 'Future Ready Mindset'.[7] We don't really know what jobs will become redundant in the coming years, what doors technology will open, nor what our human-affected earth will demand. So he suggests choosing a 'thing' to follow and explore, with an open mind, asking unexpected questions about the difference it could make to your job or our world. Amy Whitaker talked of studio time to work

towards a Point B that you create as you go. I hope in reading this book, your Point B has become clearer – but now
go find it. I thought I wanted to be a comedy writer–
performer, then along came improv. The next offer was
bringing improv to business and it's taken me to so many
places, physical and metaphorical.

I thought it was great that some firms famously allocate
side-project time so that employees can go off piste to play
with new ideas. Then I met someone who worked at one
such company, which, it turns out, have let this slide so it
doesn't happen any more.

So why not make improv your 'thing'? Allister did and
now he's addicted. Or could your thing be coding? Maybe
that's the way to stay ahead of the robots? But I read an
article from Harvard Business School by Professor Linda
Hill, entitled 'Curiosity, not coding: Six skills leaders need
in the digital age'.[8] Oh.

Professor Hill and her team surveyed 1,500 executives
in more than 90 countries. They said that 'adaptability was
the most important leadership quality' followed by 'creativity, curiosity and comfort with ambiguity'. The chairman of a major African retailer was clear: 'It's the soft
skills that I argue are not soft any more.' You have to be a
storyteller, to be present, to be a catalyst, to explore, to be
courageous – all of which you can learn from improv but
not necessarily from a business school or other training
course and certainly not just from reading a book.

So get thee to an improv class. Bring it to your organization, for building these skills, but maybe go one step
further. I've gathered lots of teams who then do a show for

the rest of their colleagues, titled, 'Whose Firm Is It Anyway?'… a nod to the improv television show.

So has Darwin won out over Newton? No, as I have argued, you need to be organized and prepared for meetings (especially virtual ones), certainly for presentations (for which scripting and rehearsing are essential) and collaboration won't be productive in a haphazard environment – it needs choreographing and the right rhythm. Different moments demand different moods. I do improv but I love watching my children play in their music groups – highly orchestrated, tightly rehearsed – so we share a moment of giving and receiving beautiful music.

I started this journey over two decades ago because I felt that people might enjoy their work a bit more and maybe even be a little more effective if they could borrow the skills of improv theatre. That early inkling has become a firm belief. Only recently, a highly experienced director of children's services (a terrifyingly responsible post in UK local government covering education and social care) introduced me to a group who were training to step up to this demanding role. She said that she'd attended my workshop 10 years ago. The LAGER beermat had sat on her desk ever since, a constant reminder of the mindset she would need as she faced people, problems and opportunities and that it had helped immensely in so many moments every single day of her subsequent career. Hurrah.

Just reframing what others say as an *offer* or series of offers will make a difference. Simply being aware of what might be your assumptions will lead you to understand others better. And reincorporating an earlier offer in a new context will bring a smile or a creative breakthrough. At the end of 2022 I read a blog where the writer (by the name of Gurwinder) talked about what he had learnt in the year.[9] He said that there's 'nothing constant about a person. The self is a work-in-progress being constantly rewritten. And yet we're all judged as if we're final.' Including by ourselves, I would add. He mentioned the Buddhist concept of *anatta*, which is (to over-simplify) the idea that there is no such thing as the unchanging self, just a series of experiences. I am not sure I would go that far, but perhaps, just as an organization is simply an aggregation of conversations, you are a series of moments.

So treat this book as an offer. Say *Yes And* to it. You could just say, 'Yes and... I did nothing.' I hope you don't. Now you own the *And*. The next steps are yours. Let me know how it goes.

Notes

Chapter 1: Improv and me

1   Quoted in *What is Progress?* by Woodrow Wilson (1856–1924)
    Reprinted from *The US Constitution, A Reader*, published by Hillsdale
    College. This speech, delivered during his successful campaign for
    president in 1912 and included in a collection of speeches called *The
    New Freedom*, puts forward the idea of an evolving, or 'living'
    constitution, constitutingamerica.org/what-is-progress-by-woodrow-
    wilson-1856-1924-reprinted-from-the-u-s-constitution-a-reader-
    published-by-hillsdale-college/ (archived at https://perma.cc/C75A-
    65TZ)
2   School21. www.school21.org.uk (archived at https://perma.cc/
    D6WR-NZN5)
3   P Hyman. Enough of the lost generation: Instead let's reimagine school
    for our children, *The Guardian*, 2021, www.theguardian.com/
    commentisfree/2021/mar/07/enough-of-the-lost-generation-instead-lets-
    reimagine-school-for-our-children (archived at https://perma.cc/8XE3-
    FP9H)
4   G McSherry. Scrap GCSEs and A-levels says Tony Blair Institute, in call
    for radical reform, *The Guardian*, 2022, www.theguardian.com/
    education/2022/aug/23/replace-gcses-and-a-levels-with-regular-
    assessments-says-tony-blair-institute (archived at https://perma.cc/
    T4TC-KSJS)
5   C Rovelli (2018) *The Order of Time*, Riverhead Books, New York
6   Dr Brian Kaplan. drkaplan.co.uk/ (archived at https://perma.cc/72MH-
    JKGC)
7   R Poynton (2008) *Everything's an Offer*, On Your Feet
8   S Chapman (nd) *Can Scorpions Smoke*, www.canscorpionssmoke.com/
    (archived at https://perma.cc/XB2B-7WTS)
9   M Csikszentmihalyi. Flow: The secret to happiness, TED Talks, 2004,
    www.ted.com/talks/mihaly_csikszentmihalyi_flow_the_secret_to_
    happiness?language=en (archived at https://perma.cc/833W-23L4)

Chapter 2: Human connection

1   J Kaatz Marketing Rule of 7s, 2022, www.marketingillumination.com/
    single-post/marketing-rule-of-7s (archived at https://perma.cc/
    B7YM-DAPR)
2   Grammarly/Harris Poll (nd) The state of business communication,
    www.grammarly.com/business/business-communication-report
    (archived at https://perma.cc/2GJP-LRBN)
3   performanceofalifetime.com/member/cathy-salit/ (archived at https://
    perma.cc/8M76-EHR6)
4   T Fey (2012) *Bossypants*, Little, Brown and Co, New York
5   D Kahneman (2011) *Thinking, Fast and Slow*, Farrar, Straus and
    Giroux, New York
6   www.resiliencedynamic.com/ (archived at https://perma.cc/9XL2-SUJJ)
7   R Kovach. Covid killed the commute for many of us... and that might
    not be a good thing, The Psychology of Work, *Psychology Today*, 2022,
    www.psychologytoday.com/us/blog/the-psychology-work/202202/
    covid-killed-the-commute-many-us (archived at https://perma.
    cc/8XQW-VQC8)
8   J Hobsbawm It's the commute, stupid, 2022, juliahobsbawm.substack.
    com/p/its-the-commute-stupid?sd=fs (archived at https://perma.cc/
    N5H5-XM2U)
9   K Makortoff. Apple workers launch petition over firm's return-to-office
    stance, *The Guardian*, 2022, www.theguardian.com/technology/2022/
    aug/22/apple-workers-launch-petition-over-return-to-office-stance
    (archived at https://perma.cc/ZM8S-9JG3)
10 G Nicholas. JP Morgan CEO Jamie Dimon rips remote work and
    Zoom as 'management by Hollywood Squares' and says returning to
    the office will aid diversity, *Fortune*, 2022, fortune.com/2022/08/15/
    jpmorgan-ceo-jamie-dimon-remote-work-from-home-hollywood-
    squares-diversity-return-to-office/ (archived at https://perma.cc/
    P5EX-86XK)
11 R Partington. Working from home 'damaging Britain's creative
    potential and economic wellbeing', *The Guardian*, 2020, www.
    theguardian.com/business/2020/oct/26/working-from-home-damaging-
    britains-creative-potential-and-economic-wellbeing (archived at https://
    perma.cc/ZK5Z-9QLE)

12 K Naughton. Ford to let 30,000 employees remain at home post-pandemic, Bloomberg, 2021, www.bloomberg.com/news/articles/2021-03-17/ford-to-let-30-000-employees-remain-home-workers-post-pandemic (archived at https://perma.cc/5PQP-CXNH)

13 Zoom (2022) The hybrid advantage: How and why the UK can strive to become the world leader in hybrid work, explore.zoom.us/media/uk_leader_hybrid_work_report.pdf (archived at https://perma.cc/HZ4H-DFHP)

14 N Bloom (2022) *The Great Resistance: Getting employees back to the office,* Stanford Institute for Economic Policy Research (SIEPR), siepr.stanford.edu/publications/work/great-resistance-getting-employees-back-office (archived at https://perma.cc/74JA-VXHL)

15 D Bayntun-Lees and A Cross (2022) *Rethinking Leadership for the Hybrid World of Work,* Hult/EF Corporate Education, www.hultef.com/en/insights/research-thought-leadership/rethinking-leadership-hyrid-work/ (archived at https://perma.cc/4YPZ-ASEL)

Chapter 3: Collaboration

1 Said by Professor Andy Cross in webinar on 11 August 2022 to launch the report he co-wrote, *Rethinking Leadership for The Hybrid World of Work,* D Bayntun-Lees and A Cross (2022), Hult/EF Corporate Education, www.hultef.com/en/insights/research-thought-leadership/rethinking-leadership-hyrid-work/ (archived at https://perma.cc/4YPZ-ASEL), and andy@andycrossconsulting.co.uk

2 C Ingraham. People who seek solitude are more creative, study finds, *Washington Post,* 2017, www.washingtonpost.com/news/wonk/wp/2017/11/22/people-who-seek-solitude-are-more-creative-study-finds/ (archived at https://perma.cc/572S-XC8N)

3 Why do most transformations fail? A conversation with Harry Robinson, 2019, www.mckinsey.com/capabilities/transformation/our-insights/why-do-most-transformations-fail-a-conversation-with-harry-robinson (archived at https://perma.cc/VV2H-2YGD)

4 A Snook. Do 70% of transformations fail? Learning Accelerators [blog], 2019, www.learningaccelerators.com/do-70-of-transformations-fail/ (archived at https://perma.cc/AZE3-4CML)

5 D Fortson. The rise of WFH staff secretly working for more than one firm, *The Times*, 2022, www.thetimes.co.uk/article/the-rise-of-wfh-staff-secretly-working-for-more-than-one-firm-6gpj08ls2 (archived at https://perma.cc/7P9D-CNLY)

6 Sent in a private LinkedIn message to me on 29/11/22. But he said I could use it.

7 Morris Minor's Marvellous Motors. This is the theme, www.youtube.com/watch?v=ojyX_Nko_-I (archived at https://perma.cc/CN8L-TH5X)

8 Do check out Tony Hawks giving hilariously useless advice to skateboarders, www.tony-hawks.com/skateboarding/ (archived at https://perma.cc/HB4Q-UEVH)

9 Hegel's Dialectics. *Stanford Encyclopedia of Philosophy*, plato.stanford.edu/entries/hegel-dialectics/ (archived at https://perma.cc/J7QK-HZ4G)

10 MT Hansen. When internal collaboration is bad for your company, *Harvard Business Review*, 2009, hbr.org/2009/04/when-internal-collaboration-is-bad-for-your-company (archived at https://perma.cc/EB8P-CEGX)

11 *Financial Times*. What top employers want from MBA graduates, 2018, www.ft.com/content/64b19e8e-aaa5-11e8-89a1-e5de165fa619 (archived at https://perma.cc/VN7W-54ZG)

12 E Bernstein, J Shore and D Lazer. How intermittent breaks in interaction improve collective intelligence, *Proceedings of the National Academy of Sciences*, 2018, 115 (35), 8734–8739, doi.org/10.1073/pnas.1802407115 (archived at https://perma.cc/FCA4-YKAJ)

13 N Cummings. A brief history of the travelling salesman problem, The Operational Research Society, 2000, www.theorsociety.com/about-or/or-methods/heuristics/a-brief-history-of-the-travelling-salesman-problem/ (archived at https://perma.cc/HB68-96GN)

14 A Williams Woolley, CF Chabris, A Pentland, N Hashmi and TW Malone. What makes teams smart, *MIT Sloan Management Review*, 2010, sloanreview.mit.edu/article/what-makes-teams-smart/ (archived at https://perma.cc/2EBX-YCZ4)

15 R Cross, R Rebele and A Grant. Collaborative overload: Too much teamwork exhausts employees and saps productivity. Here's how to avoid it, *Harvard Business Review*, 2016, hbr.org/2016/01/collaborative-overload (archived at https://perma.cc/5EP7-PZ62)

16 R Hinds and B Sutton. Dropbox's secret for saving time in meetings, Inc.com, 2015, www.inc.com/rebecca-hinds-and-bob-sutton/dropbox-secret-for-saving-time-in-meetings.html (archived at https://perma.cc/WC5R-LWU3)

17 R Cross. Are you suffering from collaboration overload? 9 beliefs and fears that help drive it, TED.com, 2021, ideas.ted.com/are-you-suffering-from-collaboration-overload-9-beliefs-and-fears-that-help-drive-it/ (archived at https://perma.cc/G3AY-ASY4)

18 R Cross, R Rebele and A Grant. Collaborative overload: Too much teamwork exhausts employees and saps productivity. Here's how to avoid it, *Harvard Business Review*, 2016, hbr.org/2016/01/collaborative-overload (archived at https://perma.cc/5EP7-PZ62)

19 C Gregoire. The giving habits of Americans may surprise you, *Huffington Post*, 2017, www.huffingtonpost.co.uk/entry/are-you-a-giver-huffpost_n_3785215 (archived at https://perma.cc/8GFK-NJZD)

20 M Hellman and C Chen. Same behavior, different consequences: Reactions to men's and women's altruistic citizenship behavior, *The Journal of Applied Psychology*, 2005, www.academia.edu/27193222/ (archived at https://perma.cc/6RGD-38K5)

21 L Yang, D Holtz, S Jaffe, S Suri, S Sinha, J Weston, C Joyce, N Shah, K Sherman, B Hecht and J Teevan. The effects of remote work on collaboration among information workers, 2022, *Nature Human Behaviour*, 6, 43–54, doi.org/10.1038/s41562-021-01196-4 (archived at https://perma.cc/Q3SA-TJQD)

22 E Bernstein, J Shore and D Lazer. Improving the rhythm of your collaboration, *MIT Sloan Review*, 2019, sloanreview.mit.edu/article/ improving-the-rhythm-of-your-collaboration/ (archived at https:// perma.cc/P39A-BHWG)

Chapter 4: Creativity

1 A Peshin. The 4-hour workday: Why you should only work 4 hours instead of 8, 2022, www.scienceabc.com/humans/the-4-hour-workday-why-you-should-only-work-4-hours-instead-of-8.html (archived at https://perma.cc/458R-GNWN)

2 K Johnstone (1987) *Impro: Improvisation in the Theatre*, Routledge

3 T Chamorro-Premuzic. Why group brainstorming is a waste of time, *Harvard Business Review*, 2015, hbr.org/2015/03/why-group-brainstorming-is-a-waste-of-time (archived at https://perma.cc/ Q2Y8-29SE)

4 P Taylor. Remote work is always efficient but efficient isn't always effective, 2021, Paul Taylor [blog] paulitaylor.com/2021/07/02/ remote-work-is-always-efficient-but-efficient-isnt-always-effective/ (archived at https://perma.cc/A9LF-4JD5)

5 Signature Consultants (nd) Kind leadership is pivotal to a great revival, HumanKindex, www.humankindex.com (archived at https://perma. cc/33HR-KQA9)

6 AC Edmondson and P Hugander. 4 steps to boost psychological safety at your workplace, *Harvard Business Review*, 2021, hbr.org/2021/06/4-steps-to-boost-psychological-safety-at-your-workplace (archived at https://perma.cc/PL9T-NSTR)

7 P Vlaskovits. Henry Ford, innovation, and that 'Faster Horse' quote, 2011, hbr.org/2011/08/henry-ford-never-said-the-fast (archived at https://perma.cc/4Q2M-C3E3)

8 Technical Innovations Centre 40 Principles, triz.org/principles/ (archived at https://perma.cc/VGG7-CCCM)

9   S Blank. Why companies do 'Innovation Theater' instead of actual
    innovation, *Harvard Business Review,* 2019, hbr.org/2019/10/
    why-companies-do-innovation-theater-instead-of-actual-innovation
    (archived at https://perma.cc/YRC2-XL7W)

10 Don Sull, former Professor of Strategy at London Business School.
    donsull.com/ (archived at https://perma.cc/BG8N-4XDN)

11 D Sull (2009) *The Upside of Turbulence: Seizing opportunity in an
    uncertain world,* HarperBusiness

12 S Liu, HM Chow, Y Xu, MG Erkkinen, KE Swett, MW Eagle, DA
    Rizik-Baer and AR Braun. Neural correlates of lyrical improvisation:
    An fMRI study of freestyle rap, 2012, *Scientific Reports,* 2 (834), www.
    nature.com/articles/srep00834 (archived at https://perma.cc/4X57-
    68JX)

13 W Goldman (1985) *Adventures in the Screen Trade,* Warner Books

14 T Viki. Innovation is management, *Forbes,* 2017, www.forbes.com/sites/
    tendayiviki/2017/01/08/innovation-is-management/?sh=307e21703e65
    (archived at https://perma.cc/4Q7E-AMS2)

15 W Stroebe and M Diehl (1994) Why groups are less effective than their
    members: On productivity losses in idea-generating groups, *European
    Review of Social Psychology,* 5 (1), 271–303, www.semanticscholar.
    org/paper/Why-Groups-are-less-Effective-than-their-Members%3A-
    Stroebe-Diehl/0b14aec509495207a330e8a5def81ec75289a1b7
    (archived at https://perma.cc/K37H-G4TR)

16 L Thompson. Virtual collaboration won't be the death of creativity,
    MIT Sloan Management Review, 2020, sloanreview.mit.edu/article/
    virtual-collaboration-wont-be-the-death-of-creativity/ (archived at
    https://perma.cc/34GN-RXDV)

17 W Stroebe and M Dieh. Why groups are less effective than their
    members: On productivity losses in idea-generating groups, *European
    Review of Social Psychology,* 1994, 5 (1), 271–303, www.
    semanticscholar.org/paper/Why-Groups-are-less-Effective-than-their-
    Members%3A-Stroebe-Diehl/0b14aec509495207a330e8a5def81ec752
    89a1b7 (archived at https://perma.cc/K37H-G4TR)

18 M Barden and A Morgan (2015) *A Beautiful Constraint,* Wiley,
    New York

19   D Hajek. The man who saved Southwest Airlines with a '10-minute'
     idea, NPR, 28 June 2015, www.npr.org/2015/06/28/418147961/
     the-man-who-saved-southwest-airlines-with-a-10-minute-idea
     (archived at https://perma.cc/48DN-8KLC)
20   W Stroebe and M Dieh. Why groups are less effective than their
     members: On productivity losses in idea-generating groups, *European
     Review of Social Psychology*, 1994, 5 (1), 271–303, www.
     semanticscholar.org/paper/Why-Groups-are-less-Effective-than-their-
     Members%3A-Stroebe-Diehl/0b14aec509495207a330e8a5def81ec752
     89a1b7 (archived at https://perma.cc/K37H-G4TR)
21   King's College, London. Do we have your attention? How people focus
     and live in the modern information environment, 2022, www.kcl.ac.
     uk/policy-institute/assets/how-people-focus-and-live-in-the-modern-
     information-environment.pdf (archived at https://perma.cc/533Q-
     YGQL)
22   M Barden and A Morgan (2015) *A Beautiful Constraint*, Wiley,
     New York

Chapter 5: Leadership mindset

1   Paula Mackenzie quoted by D Hipwell. KFC chief has learnt some
     nuggets from chicken crisis, *The Times*, 2018, www.thetimes.co.uk/
     article/kfc-chief-has-learnt-some-nuggets-from-chicken-crisis-
     bcfchx25w (archived at https://perma.cc/QDX7-BQSJ)
2   FJ Barrett (2012) *Yes to the Mess: Surprising leadership lessons from
     jazz,* Harvard Business Review Press, Boston, MA
3   MP Follett (1924) *The Creative Experience,* Longmans, New York
4   RD Stacey (1996) *Complexity and Creativity in Organizations,*
     Berrett-Koehler, Oakland, CA
5   R Heifetz and M Linsky. A survival guide for leaders, *Harvard Business
     Review,* 2002, hbr.org/2002/06/a-survival-guide-for-leaders (archived at
     https://perma.cc/Z45X-8HVD)
6   K Grint (2007) *Leadership, Management and Command: Rethinking
     D-Day*, Palgrave Macmillan, Basingstoke

7 H Rittel and M Webber. Dilemmas in a general theory of planning, *Policy Sciences*, 1973, 4 (2), 155, urbanpolicy.net/wp-content/uploads/2012/11/Rittel+Webber_1973_PolicySciences4-2.pdf (archived at https://perma.cc/698J-44BW)

8 I Turbitt. A good crisis and how not to waste it, leadershipforchange. org.uk/wp-content/uploads/A-Good-Crisis-pre-reading-and-questions. pdf (archived at https://perma.cc/CU8X-VAPF)

9 D Marquet (2017) *Turn the Ship Around!: A true story of turning followers into leaders*, Portfolio Penguin

10 David Marquet. Twitter.com/ldavidmarquet (archived at https://perma. cc/YR9K-HHG7)

11 Quoted in *The Times*, 21 September 2006

12 M Gladwell (2000) *The Tipping Point*, Little, Brown, New York

13 D Seidl. Luhmann's theory of autopoietic social systems, Munich School of Management, 2004, www.zog.bwl.uni-muenchen.de/files/mitarbeiter/paper2004_2.pdf (archived at https://perma.cc/XN7K-ZWXT)

14 CA O'Reilly and ML Tushman. The ambidextrous organization, *Harvard Business Review*, 2004, hbr.org/2004/04/the-ambidextrous-organization (archived at https://perma.cc/ZG8M-KM55)

15 T Kinni. When it comes to changing culture, think small, Strategy & Business, 2022, www.strategy-business.com/blog/When-it-comes-to-changing-culture-think-small (archived at https://perma.cc/75UX-SURJ)

16 CR Lide and FJ Flynn. Communication miscalibration: The price leaders pay for not sharing enough, *Academy of Management Journal*, 2022, www.gsb.stanford.edu/faculty-research/publications/communication-miscalibration-price-leaders-pay-not-sharing-enough (archived at https://perma.cc/Z2AF-DXTQ)

17 E Seppälä and K Cameron. The best leaders have a contagious positive energy, *Harvard Business Review*, 2022, hbr.org/2022/04/the-best-leaders-have-a-contagious-positive-energy (archived at https://perma. cc/4L88-56SU)

18 E Sloan. Is it more important to surround yourself with positive energy or be the origin of it?, Well and Good, 2022, www.wellandgood.com/positive-relational-energy/ (archived at https://perma.cc/HP67-XGQT)

19 APA Dictionary of Psychology. 'Surgency', dictionary.apa.org/surgency (archived at https://perma.cc/583U-6F8G)

20 SJ Martin and J Marks (2019) *Messengers*, Random House Business, New York

21 R Sadun, J Fuller, S Hansen and PJ Neal. The C-suite skills that matter most, *Harvard Business Review,* 2022, hbr.org/2022/07/the-c-suite-skills-that-matter-most (archived at https://perma.cc/74DZ-8R3P)

22 The Center for Servant Leadership, www.greenleaf.org/what-is-servant-leadership (archived at https://perma.cc/3SR4-QHMZ)

23 KM Sutcliffe and K Weber. The high cost of accurate knowledge, *Harvard Business Review*, 2003, hbr.org/2003/05/the-high-cost-of-accurate-knowledge (archived at https://perma.cc/ZM3B-A7BB)

24 Korn Ferry. A new blueprint for performance management, 2021, www.kornferry.com/insights/featured-topics/workforce-management/blueprint-for-performance-management (archived at https://perma.cc/W6QR-GQ6U)

Chapter 6: Meetings

1 Kate @Katiohead. Three stages of career development are: I want to be in the meeting, I want to run the meeting, I want to avoid meetings. [Twitter] 17 August 2022, twitter.com/Katiohead/status/1559950094534815746 (archived at https://perma.cc/NTC7-UU42)

2 C Chen. Shocking meeting statistics in 2021 that will take you by surprise, 2020, Otter.ai, otter.ai/blog/meeting-statistics (archived at https://perma.cc/T26H-PAN9)

3 S Zauderer. Time wasted in meetings: 59+ meeting statistics, CrossRiverTherapy, 2022, www.crossrivertherapy.com/meeting-statistics#money-that-is-lost-&-wasted-because-of-meetings (archived at https://perma.cc/QUQ4-96W4)

4 S Rogelberg. The cost of unnecessary meeting attendance, 2022, public. otter.ai/reports/The_Cost_of_Unnecessary_Meeting_Attendance.pdf (archived at https://perma.cc/J4YK-TEXW)

5 V Low. Quiet please! Amazon meetings begin in silence, *The Times,* 2018, www.thetimes.co.uk/article/quiet-please-amazon-meetings-begin-in-silence-wd0zmhzc0 (archived at https://perma.cc/83QT-JY65)

6   M Thompson. Five reasons why people code-switch, NPR, 2013, www.
    npr.org/sections/codeswitch/2013/04/13/177126294/five-reasons-why-
    people-code-switch (archived at https://perma.cc/BMA7-SJ24)

7   LE Williams and JA Bargh. Experiencing physical warmth promotes
    interpersonal warmth, *Science*, 2008, www.science.org/doi/10.1126/
    science.1162548 (archived at https://perma.cc/Q2F4-9DKR)

8   D Tannen. The power of talk: Who gets heard and why, *Harvard
    Business Review*, 1995, hbr.org/1995/09/the-power-of-talk-who-gets-
    heard-and-why (archived at https://perma.cc/25ZZ-XUC2)

9   D Rock. Five ways science shows us how to work better virtually,
    2020, davidrock101.medium.com/5-ways-science-shows-us-how-to-
    work-better-virtually-3f74aea8dd7a (archived at https://perma.cc/
    BD5D-9R6R)

10 P Graham. Maker's schedule, manager's schedule, 2009, www.
    paulgraham.com/makersschedule.html (archived at https://perma.
    cc/9JGT-VVWT)

11 J Cleese. Lecture on *Creativity In Management*, 23 January 1991,
    Grosvenor House Hotel, Video Arts, 2017, www.youtube.com/
    watch?v= Pb5oIIPO62g (archived at https://perma.cc/BS9B-UZ4R)

12 D Leach, S Rogelberg, P Warr and J Burnfield. Perceived meeting
    effectiveness: The role of design characteristics, *Journal of Business and
    Psychology*, 2009, 24, 65–76, link.springer.com/article/10.1007/
    s10869-009-9092-6 (archived at https://perma.cc/5JB4-TFCC)

13 John Morton. www.imdb.com/name/nm0608017/ (archived at https://
    perma.cc/M6ZC-WKES)

14 BBC Sounds. Meeting up, Four Thought, 2022, www.bbc.co.uk/
    programmes/m0019r41 (archived at https://perma.cc/4KB4-FSXC)

15 M Bernstein and R Ringel. Plan a better meeting with Design Thinking,
    Harvard Business Review, 2018, hbr.org/2018/02/plan-a-better-meeting-
    with-design-thinking (archived at https://perma.cc/8ZTG-BZ2R)

16 RF Dam and TY Siang. What is Design Thinking and why is it so
    popular? Interaction Design Foundation, 2022, www.interaction-
    design.org/literature/article/what-is-design-thinking-and-why-is-it-so-
    popular (archived at https://perma.cc/TK72-7BN6)

17 DJ Snowden and ME Boone. A leader's framework for decision making, *Harvard Business Review*, 2007, hbr.org/2007/11/a-leaders-framework-for-decision-making (archived at https://perma.cc/R34W-2LFS)

18 M Bernstein and R Ringel. Plan a better meeting with Design Thinking, *Harvard Business Review*, 2018, hbr.org/2018/02/plan-a-better-meeting-with-design-thinking (archived at https://perma.cc/8ZTG-BZ2R)

19 B Laker, V Pereira, A Malik and L Soga. Dear manager, you're holding too many meetings, *Harvard Business Review*, 2022, hbr.org/2022/03/dear-manager-youre-holding-too-many-meetings (archived at https://perma.cc/THX4-UFSB)

Chapter 7: Humour

1 N Mullarkey (2017) *Seven Steps to Improve Your People Skills*, London Business Forum, London

2 J Aaker and N Bagdonas (2021) *Humour, Seriously: Why humour is a secret weapon in business and life (And how anyone can harness it. Even you.)*, Currency

3 A Beard. Leading with humor, *Harvard Business Review*, 2014, hbr.org/2014/05/leading-with-humor (archived at https://perma.cc/3K36-PHM9)

4 V Zeigler-Hill, GA McCabe and JK Vrabel. The dark side of humour: DSM-5 pathological personality traits and humor styles, *Europe's Journal of Psychology*, 19 August 2016, 12 (3), ejop.psychopen.eu/index.php/ejop/article/view/1109 (archived at https://perma.cc/M8YT-NVZ3)

5 RA Martin, P Puhlik-Doris, G Larsen, J Gray and K Weir. Individual differences in uses of humor and their relation to psychological well-being, *Journal of Research in Personality*, 2003, 37 (1), www.sciencedirect.com/science/article/abs/pii/S0092656602005342 (archived at https://perma.cc/PR7B-83C8)

6   MMY Tse, APK Lo, TLY Cheng, EKK Chan, AHY Chan and HSW
    Chung. Humor therapy: Relieving chronic pain and enhancing happiness
    for older adults, *Journal of Aging Research,* 2010, pubmed.ncbi.nlm.nih.
    gov/21151506/ (archived at https://perma.cc/3VM5-EDUS)

7   KR Edwards and RA Martin. Humour creation ability and mental
    health: Are funny people more psychologically healthy?, *Europe's
    Journal of Psychology,* 2010, 6 (3), 196–212, ejop.psychopen.eu/index.
    php/ejop/article/view/213 (archived at https://perma.cc/AX5U-EDRJ)

8   V Ando, G Claridge and K Clark. Psychotic traits in comedians, *British
    Journal of Psychiatry*, 2014, 204 (5), 341–345, pubmed.ncbi.nlm.nih.
    gov/24434072/ (archived at https://perma.cc/8TEU-C7BU)

9   Mayo Clinic Staff (2021) Stress relief from laughter? It's no joke, Mayo
    Clinic, www.mayoclinic.org/healthy-lifestyle/stress-management/
    in-depth/stress-relief/art-20044456 (archived at https://perma.cc/
    P6RZ-PVK7)

10 TT Perls and M Hutter Silver (1999) *Living to 100: Lessons in living
    to your maximum potential at any age,* Basic Books, New York

11 Quoted in *Daily Telegraph*: Raj Persaud. Why you laugh your head off,
    30 August 2000, www.telegraph.co.uk/ (archived at https://perma.cc/
    TRY9-B7KB)

12 Laughter Yoga International, www.laughteryoga.org (archived at
    https://perma.cc/CES9-U8AL)

13 T Rodriguez. Laugh lots, live longer, *Scientific American,* 2016, www.
    scientificamerican.com/article/laugh-lots-live-longer/ (archived at
    https://perma.cc/Z4L9-TXFL)

14 J Faurschou. Further reading: Humour in earnings conference calls,
    Investors Chronicle, 2019, www.investorschronicle.co.uk/shares/
    2019/10/24/further-reading-humour-in-earnings-conference-calls/
    (archived at https://perma.cc/C8GP-7UYE)

15 F Sala. Laughing all the way to the bank, *Harvard Business Review*,
    2003, hbr.org/2003/09/laughing-all-the-way-to-the-bank (archived at
    https://perma.cc/2PTC-63LL)

16 Quoted in V Mckeever. Why laughter can make you more productive
    at work, CNBC, 2021, www.cnbc.com/2021/07/08/why-laughter-can-
    make-you-more-productive-at-work.html (archived at https://perma.cc/
    Y6J4-3N3D)

17 AJ Oswald, E Proto and D Sgroi. Happiness and productivity, *Journal of Labor Economics*, 2015, 33 (4), 789–822, wrap.warwick.ac.uk/63228/ (archived at https://perma.cc/L4VD-BYSF)

18 F Gino. The surprising benefits of sarcasm, *Scientific American*, 2015, www.scientificamerican.com/article/the-surprising-benefits-of-sarcasm/ (archived at https://perma.cc/53UP-UWDJ)

19 G Sabato. What's so funny? The science of why we laugh, *Scientific American*, 2019, www.scientificamerican.com/article/whats-so-funny-the-science-of-why-we-laugh/ (archived at https://perma.cc/RXJ8-TMMZ)

20 J Aaker and N Bagdonas (2021) *Humour, Seriously: Why humour is a secret weapon in business and life (And how anyone can harness it. Even you.)*, Currency

21 E Underwood. Watch these ticklish rats laugh and jump for joy, *Science*, 2016, www.science.org/content/article/watch-these-ticklish-rats-laugh-and-jump-joy (archived at https://perma.cc/2MYN-D6W9)

22 SK Scott, C Quing Cai and A Billing (2022) *Robert Provine: The critical human importance of laughter, connections and contagion*, Royal Society Publishing, London

23 SK Scott, C Quing Cai and A Billing. *Robert Provine: The critical human importance of laughter, connections and contagion*, Royal Society Publishing, London

24 C Vanstone. Working from home, time to get it right, Lacerta Consulting, 2020, www.lacertaconsulting.co.uk/news_blogs/24/working_from_home_time_to_get_it_right (archived at https://perma.cc/86F4-ZW32)

25 S Scott. Why do humans laugh?, BBC Ideas, 2021, www.bbc.co.uk/ideas/videos/why-do-humans-laugh/p09df6l6 (archived at https://perma.cc/EB3E-F39B)

26 www.succeedy.com (archived at https://perma.cc/R3JE-HQSC)

27 B Kaplan and H Kaplan (2022) *Almost Happy: Pushing your buttons with reverse psychology*, Loba Publishing, almosthappy.com/ (archived at https://perma.cc/WN84-YRTL)

28 Mark Bowden, Truthplane, truthplane.com (archived at https://perma.cc/TR44-SZK4)

29 Quoted in Oliver Burkeman's article: This column will change your life, *The Guardian Weekend,* 11 August 2007

30 E Proto. Are happy workers more productive?, IZA World of Labor, 2016, wol.iza.org/articles/are-happy-workers-more-productive/long (archived at https://perma.cc/S7ZD-26LE)

Chapter 8: Serendipity

1 www.merriam-webster.com/dictionary/serendipity (archived at https://perma.cc/RYK5-HLNJ)

2 McKinsey Quarterly. Strategy through turbulence: An interview with Don Sull, 2009, www.mckinsey.com/capabilities/strategy-and-corporate-finance/our-insights/strategy-through-turbulence-an-interview-with-don-sull (archived at https://perma.cc/JS28-QP9G)

3 How changes in the neural code unlock the brain's inner learning. *Neuroscience News,* March 2022, neurosciencenews.com/plastic-stable-neurons-20169/ (archived at https://perma.cc/B3BL-3QPM)

4 Nassim Nicholas Taleb (2007) *The Black Swan,* Allen Lane, London

5 A Howard. Unleash the superpowers of your 'one and onlys', *MIT Sloan Management Review*, 2022, sloanreview.mit.edu/article/unleash-the-superpowers-of-your-one-and-only-employees/ (archived at https://perma.cc/E3CD-E4BZ)

6 EKW Brennan. Why improv training made me a better scientist, 2020, www.science.org/content/article/why-improv-training-made-me-better-scientist (archived at https://perma.cc/CQD9-QG2R)

7 G Satell. 4 skills that all great innovators share [blog] 2018, greg-satell.medium.com/4-skills-that-all-great-innovators-share-67c12108e64f (archived at https://perma.cc/2RLF-G542)

8 T Leberecht (2015) *The Business Romantic: Give everything, quantify nothing, and create something greater than yourself*, Harper Collins, timleberecht.com/books/ (archived at https://perma.cc/WGT7-CLTJ)

9 L Wiseman (2021) *Impact Players: How to take the lead, play bigger, and multiply your impact,* Harper Business, New York

10 P Miller and P Skidmore (2005) *Disorganization: Why future organizations must 'loosen up'*, Demos, London

11 H Chesbrough (2003) *Open Innovation: The new imperative for creating and profiting from technology,* Harvard Business Review Press, Boston, MA

12 J Goddard (2012) *Uncommon Sense, Common Nonsense: Why some organizations consistently outperform others,* Profile Books, London

13 S Caulkin. Inside every chief exec, there's a Soviet planner, *The Observer,* 2009, www.theguardian.com/business/2009/feb/15/banking-managment-capitalism (archived at https://perma.cc/7S5Q-SV9J)

14 RI Sutton (2002) *Weird Ideas That Work: 11 and 1/2 practices for promoting, managing, and sustaining innovation,* The Free Press, New York

15 M Kondo (2014) *The Life-Changing Magic of Tidying: A simple, effective way to banish clutter forever,* Vermilion, London

16 E Abrahamson and DH Freedman (2007) *A Perfect Mess: The hidden benefits of disorder – how crammed closets, cluttered offices, and on-the-fly planning make the world a better place,* Little, Brown, New York

17 E Abrahamson. Perfect mess: The hidden benefits of disorder, Talks at Google, 2008, www.youtube.com/watch?v=fy4xm3n2iXE (archived at https://perma.cc/CW32-NNKY)

18 M Bucy, A Finlayson, G Kelly and C Moye. The 'how' of transformation, McKinsey and Co, 2016, www.mckinsey.com/industries/retail/our-insights/the-how-of-transformation (archived at https://perma.cc/4FZE-HE66)

19 K Vohs. Tidy desk or messy desk? Each has its benefits, Association for Psychological Science, 2013, www.psychologicalscience.org/news/releases/tidy-desk-or-messy-desk-each-has-its-benefits.html (archived at https://perma.cc/A5Q9-KSER)

20 Biography of Max Delbrück, Nobel Prize website, www.nobelprize.org/prizes/medicine/1969/delbruck/biographical/ (archived at https://perma.cc/U29K-EF9F)

21 Deloitte. Deloitte opens first 'future of work' designed office in Newcastle, press release, 2022, www2.deloitte.com/uk/en/pages/press-releases/articles/deloitte-opens-first-future-of-work-designed-office-in-newcastle.html (archived at https://perma.cc/F7PZ-FHZL)

22 B Sutton (2010) *The No Asshole Rule: Building a civilized workplace and surviving one that isn't*, Piatkus, London

23 H Mintzberg (1973)*The Nature of Managerial Work*, Harper & Row, New York

24 A Whitaker (2016) *Art Thinking: How to carve out creative space in a world of schedules, budgets, and bosses*, Harper Business, New York

25 A Whitaker. Inventing Point B [video] World Meaning Conference 2018, held in Brighton, England, meaningconference.co.uk/videos/amy-whitaker (archived at https://perma.cc/B8LW-BLWL)

26 W Deresiewicz (2015) *Excellent Sheep: The miseducation of the American elite and the way to a meaningful life*, Free Press, New York

Chapter 9: Storytelling

1 Dr Claudia Aguirre. Remembering vs experiencing, Headspace, www.headspace.com/articles/remembering-vs-experiencing (archived at https://perma.cc/W6ZF-AX22)

2 Contagious. www.contagious.com/ (archived at https://perma.cc/9948-J89L)

3 ML Ganz. What is public narrative: Self, us & now, Harvard Library, 2009, nrs.harvard.edu/urn-3:HUL.InstRepos:30760283 (archived at https://perma.cc/42Q9-76TY)

4 Reuters Staff. Indonesian cave art is earliest known record of 'story telling', 12 December 2019, www.reuters.com/article/us-indonesia-art-idUSKBN1YG0Y0 (archived at https://perma.cc/3ANH-RF9U)

5 K Oatley. The mind's flight simulator, British Psychological Society, 10 December 2008, www.bps.org.uk/psychologist/minds-flight-simulator (archived at https://perma.cc/7S8M-N8Q5)

6 The book was originally published in 1949 by the Bollingen Foundation through Pantheon Press as the 17th title in the Bollingen Series. This series was taken over by Princeton University Press, who published the book through 2006

7 B Flynn. The hero's journey stages and structure, Skillshare [blog] 30 June 2021, www.skillshare.com/en/blog/the-heros-journey-stages-and-structure (archived at https://perma.cc/UWA2-UT42)

8   KR Naasel. Brené Brown wants you to wallow in your failure, Fast
    Company, 2015, www.fastcompany.com/3048648/wallow-in-your-
    failure (archived at https://perma.cc/Q6NZ-6A9M)

9   JudeTrederWolff. The therapeutic benefits of telling your stories, 2015,
    judetrederwolff.medium.com/the-therapeutic-benefits-of-telling-your-
    stories-3244a07af60d (archived at https://perma.cc/SGV2-ERDX)

10 D Siegel (2002) *The Developing Mind: How relationships and the
    brain interact to shape who we are*, Guilford Press, New York

11 D Siegel. Making sense of your past, Psych Alive, 2010, www.
    psychalive.org/the-importance-of-making-sense-of-our-pasts-by-daniel-
    siegel-m-d/ (archived at https://perma.cc/ADJ8-S9XN)

12 GJ Stephens, LJ Silbert and U Hasson. Speaker–listener neural coupling
    underlies successful communication, *Proceedings of the National
    Academy of Sciences*, 26 July 2010, 107 (32), 14425–14430, doi.
    org/10.1073/pnas.1008662107 (archived at https://perma.cc/MJZ2-
    VZLR)

13 MC Green. Transportation into Narrative Worlds, in *Entertainment-
    Education Behind the Scenes*, eds LB Frank and P Falzone (2021)
    Palgrave Macmillan, Cham, doi.org/10.1007/978-3-030-63614-2_6
    (archived at https://perma.cc/6D86-T78Z)

14 C Jung (2012) *The Red Book: A reader's edition*, WW Norton, New York

15 G Brockington, APG Moreira, MS Buso, SG da Silva, E Altszyler, R
    Fischer and J Moll. Storytelling increases oxytocin and positive
    emotions and decreases cortisol and pain in hospitalized children,
    Proceedings of the National Academy of Sciences, 24 May 2021, 118
    (22), doi:10.1073/pnas.2018409118 (archived at https://perma.cc/
    P3MQ-TWHE)

16 D Shohamy and RA Adcock. Dopamine and adaptive memory, *Trends
    in Cognitive Sciences*, October 2010, 14 (10) 464–472, doi: 10.1016/j.
    tics.2010.08.002 (archived at https://perma.cc/BU5Q-J9KQ). Epub
    2010 Sep 9. PMID: 20829095

17 J Karpicke and M Coverdale. The adaptive value of forgetting: A
    direction for future research, *Journal of Applied Research in Memory
    and Cognition,* January 2020, learninglab.psych.purdue.edu/
    downloads/2020/2020_Karpicke_Coverdale_JARMAC.pdf (archived
    at https://perma.cc/F9YQ-USUR)

18 N Mullarkey (2017) *Seven Steps to Improve your People Skills*, neilmullarkey.com/sevensteps (archived at https://perma.cc/DD4V-C5UC)

19 V Ramachandran. Mirror neurons and imitation learning as the driving force behind the great leap forward in human evolution, Edge, 31 May 2000, www.edge.org/conversation/mirror-neurons-and-imitation-learning-as-the-driving-force-behind-the-great-leap-forward-in-human-evolution (archived at https://perma.cc/S82U-TCRF)

20 J Taylor. Mirror neurons after a quarter century: New light, new cracks, *Science in The News*, 2016, sitn.hms.harvard.edu/flash/2016/mirror-neurons-quarter-century-new-light-new-cracks/ (archived at https://perma.cc/D936-ME9C)

21 Thu-Huong Ha. What happens in the brain when we hear stories?: Uri Hassan at TED 2016, [blog] TED Talks, 2016, blog.ted.com/what-happens-in-the-brain-when-we-hear-stories-uri-hasson-at-ted2016/ (archived at https://perma.cc/RGT2-CS3L)

22 A Krotoski. Digital stories as memory aids, instruction manuals and moral compasses. Relay from openmythsource.com, 2011, openmythsource.wordpress.com/2011/08/22/digital-stories-as-memory-aids-instruction-manuals-and-moral-compasses-by-aleks-krotoski-relay-from-openmythsource-com/ (archived at https://perma.cc/24GL-9F34)

23 M Fastenrath, L Spalek, D Coynel, E Loos, A Milnik, T Egli, N Schicktanz, L Geissmann, B Roozendaal, A Papassotiropoulos and D de Quervain. Researchers discover a new function of the cerebellum, 2022, www.pnas.org/doi/full/10.1073/pnas.2204900119 (archived at https://perma.cc/8ZMX-HHZ8)

24 F Heider and M Simmel. An experimental study of apparent behavior, *The American Journal of Psychology*, 1944, 57 (2), 243–259, doi. org/10.2307/1416950 (archived at https://perma.cc/3Y7F-3ZRA)

25 The Solutions Focus, www.thesolutionsfocus.com/ (archived at https://perma.cc/CZ6C-R6MZ)

26 Creativity Works, creativityworks.net/ (archived at https://perma.cc/E22V-JMJM)

27 B Zeigarnik. Das Behalten erledigter und unerledigter Handlungen [Remembering completed and uncompleted actions], *Psychologische Forschung*, 1927, 300–314

28 Quote from D Kahneman, 10 May 2010, *Thinking, Fast and Slow*, Penguin, London

29 Quoted by Andrew Rawnsley in November 2022 in *The Observer*. What Keir Starmer needs to do if Labour is to successfully challenge Rishi Sunak, www.theguardian.com/commentisfree/2022/oct/30/what-keir-starmer-needs-to-do-if-labour-is-to-succefully-challenge-rishi-sunak (archived at https://perma.cc/8HYM-YR37)

30 It was Iain who told me that jesters, far from being the ones to tell the truth to the king (as I had thought previously), were there to keep it from him, to keep him entertained and happy. I often wonder about the modern parallels. Are some comedians questioning the status quo or actually reinforcing it? Iain wrote a lot about organizations as theatre, explicitly so in *Organizations at Theatre: A social psychology of dramatic appearances* (1987) Wiley Blackwell, New York

31 Barbara Minto. The Minto Pyramid Principle, www.barbaraminto.com/ (archived at https://perma.cc/UUA6-Y44N)

32 A Stanton. The clues to a great story, Ted.com, 2012, www.ted.com/talks/andrew_stanton_the_clues_to_a_great_story?language=en (archived at https://perma.cc/U28V-4WDE)

33 J Garfinkle. Learn to write accomplishment statements as success stories, Smart Brief, 20 December 2021, corp.smartbrief.com/original/2021/12/learn-write-accomplishment-statements-success-stories (archived at https://perma.cc/87LK-SAUC)

Chapter 10: Where next?

1 Applied Improvisation Network, 2022, www.appliedimprovisationnetwork.org/history-of-ain (archived at https://perma.cc/58TH-2NWW)

2 M Somers. 10 smart – not soft – skills for leaders, MIT Sloan School, 2022, mitsloan.mit.edu/ideas-made-to-matter/10-smart-not-soft-skills-leaders (archived at https://perma.cc/W6YL-AF98)

3 L Padurean (2022) *The Job Is Easy, The People Are Not! 10 smart skills to become better people*, START Disrupt (M) Sdn Bhd, Malaysia

4   E Botehlo and K Creagh. What to do if your career is stalled and you don't know why, *Harvard Business Review*, 2018, hbr.org/2018/11/what-to-do-if-your-career-is-stalled-and-you-dont-know-why (archived at https://perma.cc/8YWS-X86L)

5   Cambridge Dictionary. dictionary.cambridge.org/dictionary/english/ham-it-up (archived at https://perma.cc/3F3L-KX48)

6   A Theodorakopoulos. Don't fear the robots: your tech anxiety is misplaced, *Management Today*, 2022, www.managementtoday.co.uk/dont-fear-robots-tech-anxiety-misplaced/opinion/article/1796410 (archived at https://perma.cc/6ZAP-EEFL)

7   A Frost. Is your mindset future-ready? Allister Frost, futurereadymindset.com (archived at https://perma.cc/3ZHK-UUUZ)

8   LA Hill, A Le Cam, S Menon and E Tedards. Curiosity, not coding: Six skills leaders need in the digital age, 2022, Harvard Business School Working Knowledge, hbswk.hbs.edu/item/six-unexpected-traits-leaders-need-in-the-digital-era (archived at https://perma.cc/N83Y-K6E8)

9   Gurwinder. The 10 best ideas I learned in 2022, gurwinder.substack.com/p/the-10-best-ideas-i-learned-in-2022 (archived at https://perma.cc/JK5K-JE2U)

Index

CPSIA information can be obtained
at www.ICGtesting.com
Printed in the USA
BVHW091042020623
665279BV00018B/312